A Dictionary of the Booksellers and Printers who Were at Work in England, Scotland and Ireland from 1641 to 1667

Henry Robert Plomer

BIBLIOLIFE

A DICTIONARY OF THE BOOKSELLERS AND PRINTERS WHO WERE AT WORK IN ENGLAND, SCOTLAND AND IRELAND FROM 1641 TO 1667.

BY

HENRY R. PLOMER.

‾LONDON:

PRINTED FOR THE BIBLIOGRAPHICAL SOCIETY,

By BLADES, EAST & BLADES.

———

1907.

List of the Society's Publications.

THE BOOKS printed by the Bibliographical Society can only be supplied to its own members, but new members may purchase the publications of previous years, and members who have lost or damaged any of their books can obtain a second copy at the prices named. But where an asterisk is prefixed, the books can only be supplied in sets, and in no case can more than one duplicate copy of any book be supplied to the same member. Subject to this condition purchase for presentation is also allowed, but the Council retains the right of refusing any application, without necessarily assigning a reason.

NOTE.—The Society's *News-Sheet*, issued, instead of a post-card notice of meetings, in the five months, November–March of each Session, is not reckoned as necessary to a complete set of the Society's Publications, everything of interest in it being reprinted in the *Transactions*.

FIRST SERIES.

[Sm. 4to. Grey wrappers. Printed by Blades, East & Blades.]

Transactions of the Bibliographical Society. Vols. I–VIII. *London: Printed for the Society, etc.* 1893–1907.

With the exception of Volume IV, each volume was issued in two sections. The first section of Vol. I was called "Parts 1 and 2," the second section, "Part 3." In other volumes the sections were called Part I, Part II, respectively on the wrapper, and Part I had also a temporary title-page, while that to Part II covered the whole volume. In Volume VI the title-page to Part II was inadvertently made to refer to that Part only instead of to the whole volume, and an additional title-page was afterwards sent out. Volumes I and II are sold only in complete sets. Prices:—Volume I, Part III, 3*s.* 6*d.*; Volume III, Part I, 7*s.*; Part II, 3*s.* 6*d.*; Volume IV, 10*s.* 6*d.*; Volume V, Part I, 6*s.*, Part II, 4*s.* 6*d.*; Volume VI, Part I, 5*s.* 6*d.*, Part II, 5*s.*; Vol. VII, 10*s.* 6*d.*; Vol. VIII, 10*s.* 6*d.*

[Temporary title.] Hand-Lists of English Printers, 1501–1556. Parts I–III, 1895–1905. [4*s.* each.]

Robert Wyer, Printer and Bookseller. A paper read before the Bibliographical

A Classified Index to the Serapeum. By R. Proctor. *London: Printed, etc.*, November, 1897. [5*s.*]

An Index to Dibdin's Edition of the Typographical Antiquities first compiled by Joseph Ames, with some references to the intermediate edition by William Herbert. Printed from a copy in the Library of Sion College. *London: Printed, etc.*, December, 1899. [3*s.* 6*d.*]

A List of English Plays, written before 1643, and printed before 1700. By W. W. Greg. *London: Printed, etc.*, March, 1900, for 1899. [5*s.*]

A List of Masques, Pageants, etc. Supplementary to a List of English Plays. By Walter Wilson Greg. *London: Printed, etc.*, February, 1902 for 1901. [5*s.*]

Abstracts from the Wills of English Printers and Stationers, from 1492 to 1650. By Henry R. Plomer. *London: Printed, etc.*, February, 1903. [3*s.*]

A Century of the English Book-trade. Short notices of all printers, stationers, bookbinders and others connected with it, 1457-1557. By E. Gordon Duff. *London: Printed, etc.*, 1905. [7*s.* 6*d.*]

A Short Catalogue of English Books in Archbishop Marsh's Library, Dublin, printed before 1641. By Newport J. D.

PREFACE.

THE object of this work is to bring together the information available respecting the men and women who printed and sold books during the twenty-seven years from 1641 to 1667. It is an attempt to fill the gap between the Stationers' Registers and the Term Catalogues so ably edited by Mr. Edward Arber. The information consists of imprints showing the various places in which such booksellers and printers carried on their business, such biographical details as could be gleaned from various printed and manuscript sources, and an indication of the character of the trade carried on by each bookseller. As a further help to the bibliographer, I have included a notice of all publishers' lists that I have met with. It was my original intention to have given an indication of the work of each printing house, but I soon found that this was impossible. Such printing houses as those of the Fletchers, Roycroft, or Warren are in themselves a study, and any attempt to generalize was worse than useless.

The chief sources of information have been: (1) The Thomason Tracts; (2) the Bagford and Ames Collections of Title-pages; (3) Hazlitt's Collections and Notes through the medium of Mr. G. J. Gray's invaluable Index; (4) the Registers and Apprenticeship Books of the Company of Stationers; (5) the State Papers and other documents at the Public Record Office; (6) the Reports of the Historical Manuscripts Commission; (7) Wills in the Prerogative Court of Canterbury at Somerset House.

I have made no attempt to distinguish between booksellers and publishers. There is no evidence to show that any of the men mentioned in this dictionary, with the single exception of John Ogilby—who has been included for the excellence of his work—were publishers in the sense in which we understand the term now. Every publisher is a bookseller in so far that he sells the books he publishes, but some publishers, Longmans and Methuen for example, are not booksellers in the sense of selling all kinds of books. On the other hand, Hatchards, of Piccadilly, and others that could be named, are not only retail booksellers in a large way of business, but they are also publishers. Such I conceive Herringman and Moseley are to be considered. Others again, such as Cornelius Bee and Samuel Thompson, visited the chief marts abroad, and bought largely on commission, and though they held shares in all the most important literary ventures of their day, and their names appear in the imprints, they are to be considered rather as retail booksellers than publishers.

I have not inserted any initials in this book. In the first place it must be remembered that during this period, when the censorship of the press was severe, printers and booksellers often contented themselves with placing their initials in the imprints, and almost every name that figures in this volume might have been duplicated amongst the initials, thus swelling the volume to an inordinate size, without any corresponding advantage to the student. Identification of such initials as, say, "T. B.," which may apply to half a dozen different men, must be largely guesswork, unless based on a special study of the work in which they occur.

There are no doubt many shortcomings in this book. Names may have been omitted that ought to be here, and the information is in many cases meagre. But I trust the reader will accept it as "spade" work in a field which has hitherto been almost totally neglected, and as a foundation upon which in time to come another builder will erect a more lasting edifice.

In conclusion, my thanks are tendered to a host of friends for kindly help : to Mr. A. W. Pollard for bringing the work under the notice of the Bibliographical Society, and to the Council of the Society for undertaking its publication; to Mr. G. K. Fortescue, Keeper of the Printed Books in the British Museum, for permission to see the proofs of the catalogue of the Thomason Tracts; to Mr. F. C. Rivington for allowing me access to the Registers of the Stationers' Company ; to Mr. G. J. Gray, of Cambridge, Mr. F. Madan, of Oxford, Mr. Robert Steele and Mr. R. A. Peddie, for many notes and suggestions ; and lastly, to Mr. E. R. McC. Dix, of Dublin, for much valuable information respecting the booksellers and printers of Ireland. For those of Scotland, I am wholly indebted to Mr. H. G. Aldis's notes, published in his *List of Books printed in Scotland*, issued by the Edinburgh Bibliographical Society in 1905.

H. R. PLOMER.

44, CROWNHILL ROAD,
    WILLESDEN, N.W.

INTRODUCTION.

WHEN, on the 3rd November, 1640, the Long Parliament met, it found the book-trade suffering from an acute attack of censorship. Ever since the days of Elizabeth there had been two great impediments to the expansion of that trade. One of these was the Government, which objected to criticism and sought safety by bribing the press and strangling the free circulation of books. The other was the Company of Stationers, which desired to keep the trade in the hands of its privileged members and objected to any increase in the number of presses, or of booksellers, because the greater the number the smaller the profits of the monopolists. The duty of meeting a legitimate demand weighed little with men who cared for nothing save their own interests, and naturally, the Company seeking its privileges from the Government, was at all times the willing instrument of that Government. The result was that the book-trade was cramped, printing was bad—there being no encouragement to the printer to produce artistic work—and the most saleable books, such as school books, bibles, and service books, were printed at secret presses.

All these evils had, during the previous ten years, been intensified by Archbishop Laud and his brother bishops, who attempted to stem the growing onset of Puritanism, with the pillory, branding iron, and prison cell. Sir John Lambe had carefully winnowed the London printing houses, and Laud and his friends hoped that by the Star Chamber Decree of 1637, which gave to the Stationers' Company increased powers of search, they had effectually muzzled the press. As vainly did Mrs. Partington with her mop try to keep out the sea. Had the state of England been normal, there would have been no need for the decree of 1637, and conversely, the public mind being in a highly excitable state, the decree of 1637 was overwhelmed and swept aside by the events which immediately succeeded it. Almost the very first act of the Long Parliament was to appoint a Committee for Religion, which called before it booksellers and printers who had been interfered with by "my lord of Canterbury," thrown into prison, and otherwise grievously maltreated, and great was the punishment they exacted in return. So too there were Committees of printing, which listened to the woes of Michael Sparke and recommended that he should be repaid the sum wrung from him by the Star Chamber. Meanwhile, with religion at fever heat, and public events moving with a rapidity hitherto unknown, the cry was for "News!" and "More News!" Thus the Star Chamber decree that there were to be no more than twenty printers was speedily disregarded.

So for the next three years printers and booksellers alike were left unmolested, and grew and multiplied prodigiously. News-sheets poured from the press in ever increasing numbers, and were hawked broadcast through the city and suburbs of London, and pens of all kinds "walked," to use the quaint expression of the period, fast and furiously in the political and religious controversies that were rending the country, to the entire exclusion of all other forms of literature.

Then came a change. The Parliament began to find itself criticised, as even the most popular of Parliaments is bound to make some enemies, and it liked the process as little as the King and the bishops had done. It looked about for weapons to defend itself and found two, the old rusty censorship and the pen. Half ashamed to go back to the methods it had so vigorously denounced, the Long Parliament adopted the censorship very mildly at first, while freely engaging writers such as Milton to meet the onslaught of its foes with the pen. The first

Ordinance against the book-trade was that of the 9th March, 164⅔, which gave the Committee of Examinations power to appoint searchers for presses employed in printing scandalous and lying pamphlets. They were instructed to demolish and take away such presses, their materials and the printers' nuts and spindles, and to bring the printers, or their workmen, before the committee. They were also given power to commit to prison alike the printers, the vendors, and any persons who should refuse to allow their premises to be searched, and anyone so committed was not to be released until all the charges incurred in the seizure had been paid. The following stationers were appointed to act as searchers under the foregoing order, Felix Kyngston, Samuel Man, George Miller, John Bellamy, William Lee, junior, John Partridge, Christopher Meredith, Robert Dawlman, Matthew Walbancke, Richard Cotes, Joseph Hunscott, and John Raworth. Felix Kyngston was one of the oldest members of the Company, having taken up his freedom as far back as 1597. Samuel Man was warden of the Company, and the remainder were probably chosen for their known Presbyterian tendencies. At the same time, the Common Council of the City of London passed an act for the apprehending of all vagrant persons, men, women and children, who should be found hawking or crying pamphlets or books about the streets of the City.

Barely three months later, on the 14th June, Parliament sets out another Ordinance against the book trade. This begins with a preamble in which it is admitted that the previous Order had had little or no effect, and that in spite of it, *very many, as well stationers and printers, as others of sundry other professions not free of the Stationers' Company, have taken upon them to set up sundry private Printing Presses in corners, and to print, vend, publish, and disperse Books, Pamphlets, and Papers, in such multitudes, that no industry could be sufficient to discover or bring to punishment, all the several abounding delinquents*, and then proceeds to try and perform the feat which it has just declared impossible. The sundry other professions here alluded to were chiefly drapers and haberdashers, but no doubt Parliament had in its mind at that moment, Henry Walker (*q.v.*), who from being an ironmonger, had turned tub-thumper, pamphleteer, and bookseller. This Ordinance further stated that several persons, stationers themselves and members of the Company, out of revenge against those appointed to carry out the orders of Parliament, had taken the liberty to print the most profitable vendible copies of books, belonging to those privileged members. It then proceeded to enact (1) That no order of either House of Parliament, should be printed by anyone, except by order of one or both Houses; (2) That no book, pamphlet, or paper, should be printed, bound, stitched, or put to sale, without the licence of the person appointed by Parliament to licence it and without being entered in the Registers of the Company; (3) That no book which was the property of the Company should be printed without their consent, or that of the owner of the copyright; (4) Nor should any such books formerly printed in England, be imported from abroad. The Company, the Serjeant of the House of Commons, Justices of the Peace, and Constables were given the right of search.

Incidentally, this ordinance affords an insight into the condition of the Company, which is amply borne out by the Registers of that period. The Company was at war within itself, and the men who entered in the Registers were those who, for the time being, were uppermost in its councils, and these took care that their opponents should not have the right of registration. Neutral men, such as Humphrey Moseley, who appears to have entered whatever and whenever he wished, were not meddled with; but the small number of men whose names are found in these Registers between 1641–1650, is the strongest possible evidence that they were not open to all impartially. Indeed, the fact is further emphasized by the action which Roger Norton brought against the Company, for striking out of the Register certain grammatical books, which were his copyright. Roger Norton was a Royalist, and the prevailing party in the Company at that time were Roundheads. Thus the entries in the Registers for those years, interesting and valuable as they must always be, represent only a fractional part of the output of the press.

Another Ordinance of the year 1643 must not be passed over, as it shows that amongst the much despised Roundheads, there were some in authority who sympathized with the book lover. It was the outcome of the wholesale sequestration of Royalist property that was then taking place, and let us hope that it had the effect of preventing the dispersal of many a valued library of books. This Ordinance, which was dated the 18th November, 1643, directed that books, evidences, records, and writings, sequestered or taken by distress, were not to be sold, but that an account of such books, etc., was to be rendered to Algernon, Earl of Northumberland, Theophilus, Earl of Lincoln, William, Lord Viscount Say and Seale, John Selden, Francis Rous, Sir Simonds D'Ewes, Samuel Browne, Edward Prideaux, Gilbert Millington, Roger Hill, and Walter Young, or any two of them. Nor is there wanting other evidence that Milton and his literary friends were exerting themselves to preserve what was worth preserving, as witness the order made in 1645 for printing the *Codex Alexandrinus,* a project that unfortunately came to nothing, and also Milton's own pamphlet on the Liberty of the Press. But in this the great thinker was at least two centuries ahead of his time. The din of battle was too loud and his voice was drowned. Yet for the next four years there was a lull in the persecution of the book-trade, and it was not until the 28th September, 1647, that any further attempt was made to regulate "the press." The Ordinance then issued by Parliament closely resembled those that had preceded it, but it went a step further, by fixing the penalties that were to be inflicted upon offenders. The author of the offending pamphlet or book was to be fined forty shillings, or imprisoned for a term not exceeding forty days, the printer was to be fined twenty shillings or twenty days, besides having his press and implements destroyed, the bookseller or stationer issuing the offending publication was liable to a fine of ten shillings or ten days' imprisonment, and the hawker or pedlar was to forfeit all his stock and be whipped as a common rogue.

Still the cry went up News! More News! and still the warring sectaries, mountebank astrologers, and frenzied politicians flooded the country with pamphlets and, as if the gates of passion had not been opened wide enough, the unfortunate Charles was sent to his doom on Tuesday, the 30th January, 164$\frac{8}{9}$. Sober men of all parties were shocked at the deed, and hastened to dissociate themselves from it, while the Royalist press became ten times more bitter than before. The Roundheads were split into two camps, and the Independents, who had now gained the ascendency, were assailed on all sides. Once again the old weapon of repression was brought from the armoury, and on the 20th September, 1649, Parliament passed the most drastic Act against the book-trade that had been known since the Star Chamber decree of 1637. In the preamble attention was called to the "assumed boldness" of the weekly pamphleteers, who, it was stated, "took upon them to publish, and at pleasure to censure the Proceedings of Parliament and Army, and other affairs of State," and to the licentiousness of printing which, in this country and in foreign parts, "hath been" and "ought to be" restrained.

This Act closely followed the model set before it in the Star Chamber decree of 1637, to such a pass had the reformers come. The first clause enacted that no persons were to write, print, or sell scandalous or libellous books under a penalty of ten pounds or forty days' imprisonment for the author, five pounds or twenty days for the printer, two pounds or ten days for the bookseller or stationer. The buyer of any book or pamphlet declared to be seditious was immediately to hand it over to the Lord Mayor, or to some Justice of the Peace of the County, under a penalty of one pound. No news-sheet was to be printed or sold without license, all such licenses to be obtained from the Clerk of the Parliament or the Secretary of the Army. No seditious books or pamphlets were to be sent either by post or carrier under a penalty of forty shillings for every copy found. For the better discovery of malignant (read Royalist) booksellers, magistrates were entrusted with full powers for searching any packs or packages which they might suspect of containing books or pamphlets of a seditious character. The clauses relating to printing contain a surprise. Printing was restricted to the City of London and the two universities,

"Provided, That this clause shall not be construed to extend to the Printing Press now used in the City of York, nor to the printing press now used in Finsbury for the printing of *Bibles and Psalms.*" This last was the press set up by William Bentley for printing the edition of the Bible authorised by the Assembly of Divines, which the Stationers' Company had so much resented that, in 1646, they passed a resolution : *no journeyman printer of this company who shall work at the printing house in Finsbury, ever to have any pension or gift whatsoever from the Company.* The Act further decreed that every printer should enter into bond in £300 to be of good behaviour, and no printer was to set up a press or to import any press or letters without first acquainting the Company of his intention.

Such were the conditions under which the book-trade was carried on from the time of the meeting of the Long Parliament until Oliver Cromwell became Lord Protector, and when it is remembered that the whole of that period was one of warfare and political unrest, the wretched character of the work produced is not to be wondered at. By far the largest part of the output of the press consisted of political and theological pamphlets, amongst which the writings of John Milton and James Howell shine out like stars in the night. Dramatic literature there was none, and the only poetry worth speaking of was the collection of Sir John Suckling's verse in 1646, and Herrick's *Hesperides* in 1647-8.

The art of printing in England at this period sank to its lowest point. Practically all the presses in London were busy turning out news-sheets as fast as they could print them, and any old type and blocks that could be secured for love or money were used to print them with. The largest printing house in London during this period was that of Miles Flesher and his partners in Little Britain. They also held the King's printing house by virtue of a mortgage executed by Robert Barker. The little good work done was mainly done by them. The press of Felix Kyngston was also a busy one, and his best work was creditable. Richard Cotes was also one of the largest printers of this time, while much of the hack work was

B

turned out by Bernard Alsop, Andrew Coe, and Thomas Brudenell. William Dugard, the head-master of Merchant Taylors' School, set up a press about this time, which will be noticed later on, and William Bentley's press at Finsbury turned out some well printed Bibles in miniature founts.

A marked improvement took place in the book-trade after 1650. The fury of partisan passions had spent itself. The Civil War was practically at an end, and men began to return to their old pursuits and their books. In 1652 the first announcement of the proposed Polyglot Bible was issued. The first volume appeared in September, 1654, the second in 1655, the third in 1656, and the last three in 1657. The printer was Thomas Roycroft of Bartholomew Close, and the type was supplied by the four recognized type founders, the double pica and italic used in the Dedication being that cut by John Day in the sixteenth century. The editor was Brian Walton, Bishop of Chester, and the work received every encouragement from Oliver Cromwell. This undertaking raised Roycroft's printing house to a leading position amongst the London printing houses, and John Ogilby's splendid reprints of the classical authors also came from this press. In 1653, Izaak Walton gave to the world his *Complete Angler*. In 1655 appeared the first volume of Sir William Dugdale's *Monasticon Anglicanum*, and in the same year William Dugard printed a folio edition of Sir Philip Sidney's *Arcadia*. But perhaps the best evidence of the revival of the book-trade is found in the two lists of books published by Humphrey Moseley with Brome's *Five New Plays*, in 1653, and Sir Aston Cokain's *Dianea* in 1654. The first of these contains one hundred and thirty five items, and the second, one hundred and eighty. Another important publisher of this time was Thomas Whitaker. On the 7th March, 165⅔, the whole of his copyrights were transferred by his widow and Alexander Brome, whom she had married, to Humphrey Moseley, Richard Thrale, Joshua Kirton, and Samuel Thompson. They fill upwards of four pages of the Stationers' Register, and, in addition to such classics as Tacitus, Aristotle, and Plutarch, included Bacon's Essays, Thos. Jones'

Catalogue of Manuscripts at Oxford and Cambridge, Camden's Britannia, Selden's Titles of Honour, Bede's Rerum Anglicarum Scriptores, besides the chief theological treatises and many school books. Henry Herringman's entries in the Registers also became more numerous year by year.

With the outbreak of the Civil War all the official printing, such as Acts and Orders of Parliament, Proclamations and the like, was farmed out by the Parliament and the Council of State to those of their supporters who made the best offer. Their number was large, and it is difficult to understand how the appointments were made. We find Joseph Hunscot, Edward Husbands, and John Wright, senior, successively printing for the Parliament. In 1653, Giles Calvert, Henry Hills, and Thomas Brewster were "printers" to the Council of State, Henry Hills and John Field were styled printers to the Parliament of England, while William Dugard and Henry Hills were printers to his Highness the Lord Protector. Later on we meet with Thos. Collins and Abel Roper as printers to the Council of State. Again, in 1660, John Macocke and John Streator were appointed printers to the Parliament, while John Macocke and Francis Tyton were also printers to the House of Lords. The most interesting of these appointments is that of Giles Calvert. The son of a Somersetshire clergyman, he espoused the cause of the Quakers, and became their first publisher. No evidence can be found that leads us to suppose that he joined their ranks, but the correspondence preserved at Devonshire House shows that he was in sympathy with them. He boldly placed his imprint on their writings, and this at a time when the writers and the printers were thrown into prison for their share in the publications. This appointment of Giles Calvert as one of the official "printers," shows clearly that he stood well with Cromwell and those in power, and accounts for his being able to publish Quaker writings as boldly as he did. Several of the men mentioned above were not "printers" by trade, they gave out the work to others, and shared the profits.

During the continuance of the Commonwealth, both printers and booksellers would seem to have had a quiet time. It had to be something extremely virulent to rouse the anger of the Government. One noticeable feature of the time was the great reduction that took place in the number of news-sheets. Many, of course, died of inanition, but there is no doubt that the clause of the Act of 1649, which compelled all news-sheets to be licensed by the Clerk of the Parliament, had a salutary effect. The *Intelligencer* and the *Newes* became the two official papers and were the forerunners of the Oxford and London Gazettes.

With the Restoration the book-trade found itself once more under the heel of the oppressor. Monk's victory was marked by the publication of books and pamphlets, attacking the monarchy in the most violent manner. The old animosities were once more raked up, and the Government determined, if possible, to put a stop to this, and were ably seconded by the Company of Stationers for purely personal reasons. Early in 1660 the Company had passed the following resolution : "The table remarking the great want of a law to restrain the exorbitances of printing and to secure property in copies; and being informed that the Parliament before their adjournment had appointed a committee for that purpose, of which, Mr. Prynne is chairman, and a bill having been presented to him, but nothing therein done, Mr. Warden Crooke is earnestly desired to solicit the business with Mr. Prynne or otherwise as occasion may offer."

Meanwhile, certain of the printers, amongst whom were Roycroft, Hodgkinson, and other important men, were advocating severance from the Company, and the formation of a distinct Company of Printers. The reasons they put forward were that the old Company had become mainly a Company of Booksellers, and was grown so large that none could be Master or Warden until he was well advanced in life, and therefore unable to keep a vigilant eye on the trade.

The Government adopted two methods of dealing with the book-trade. They appointed an Official Surveyor of the Press, and they passed an Act for preventing the frequent abuses in printing, etc., known as 14 Charles II, cap. 33. The person chosen as Surveyor of the Press was Sir Roger

L'Estrange, whose only recommendation to the post was that he was an adherent of the Royal party and had suffered for his loyalty. He knew nothing about printing or bookselling, but he was a sycophant and time-server, and carried out his duties with unnecessary cruelty. The Warrant creating Sir R. L'Estrange Surveyor of the Press is here given as it appears in the State Papers :—

CHARLES R.

WHEREAS in contempt of our laws and authority many treasonous, seditious, and unlicenc'd Pamphlets, Libells, and Papers, are dayly printed vented and dispersed by the obstinate and implacable Enemies of Our Royall person and Government, for redresse and remedy hereof, Our Will and Pleasure is that you prepare a Grant for our Royall signature for the erecting and constituting of an Office for the surveying of the Imprimery, and Printing Presses, and for the preventing of the inconveniences aforesd. And it is Our Will and Pleasure that you prepare a grant for Our Royall signature of ye said Office unto Roger L'Estrange, Esqr, of whose Loyalty and abilities Wee are well assured, and him to authorize and appoint to bee Our Surveyor of all the Imprimery and Printed Pictures and allsoe of all Books and Papers whatsoever hereafter to bee imprinted or reprinted, except Books concerning the Common-Laws of this Realme or Books of History concerning the State of this Realme or any other Books concerning Affairs of State, or concerning Heraldry Titles of Honor and Armes, or the Office of Earl Marshall, or Books of Divinity Phisick Philosophy Arts and Sciences and such other books and Papers as are granted by Our Letters Patents to Our proper and peculiar Printers and usually claimed and imprinted by them by virtue of the sd Letters Patents. To have and to hold the s^d Office or Offices of Our s^d Surveyor and Licencer for and during the terme of his naturall life to bee excersized by himselfe or his sufficient Deputie or Deputies which said Deputy or Deputies are from time to time to bee approved by the late Arch Bishop of Canterbury and Lord Bp of London or one of them and by Our Principall Secretaries of State or either of them with a sole Priviledge of writing, printing, and publishing all Narratives or relacons not exceeding two sheets of Paper and all Advertisements, Mercuries, Diurnals and Books of Publick Intelligence; and likewise of Printing or appointing to bee printed All Ballads, Maps, Charts, Portraictures and Pictures not formerly printed and all Breifs and Collections, Bills of Ladeing, Play-Bills, and Quacksalvers Bills, of Custom and Excise Bills, Post Office Bills, Auditors Bills, Ticquets and all formes or Blanks of Bonds, Bills, Indentures and Warrants, with power to search for and seize all unlicensed Books and Papers and all seditious, treasonable, schismaticall and scandalous Books and Papers and to seize and apprehend all and every the offenders therein and to bring them before one of our Principall Secretaries or the next Justice of Peace, to bee proceeded against according to law, together with all other Priviledges and Powers necessary, or conducting to our Service in ye Premisses, For which this shall bee your warrant, Given at our Court at Whitehall the 15th day of August 1663, in the 15th year of our reigne.

By His Maj^{ties} Command
Henry Bennet.

To Our Attorney or Sollicitor Generall.

Dom. S. Papers, Chas. II. Vol. 78. (96)

This document needs no comment. Nor is it necessary to say much about the Act of 1662, except that it was in a large measure a re-enactment of the Star Chamber decree of 1637, and the Act of 1649. York was again expressly mentioned as a place where printing might be carried on, and the printing house of John Streator was exempted from interference. Armed with ample power Sir Roger L'Estrange harassed the printers and booksellers without remorse. One of his unfortunate victims was Elizabeth Calvert, the wife of Giles Calvert, whom he imprisoned several times. Another, was John Twyn, a printer in Cloth Fair, who was tried for high treason and hanged at Tyburn for printing a pamphlet entitled *A Treatise of the execution of Justice*. That such men as Thomas Roycroft and James Fletcher should have acquiesced in a verdict which they must have known condemned a fellow printer to death, for so trivial an offence, is the saddest part of the story. There is, however, abundant evidence that Sir Roger L'Estrange met with great opposition from the trade, and ultimately gave up his office in disgust.

Subjected to unfair competition and merciless restriction, it is not much to be wondered at that the stationers, whether printers or booksellers, did not bear a very high character for commercial probity, and that George Wither's sketch of the "Dishonest Stationer" in his *Schollars Purgatory* was applicable to only too many of them. On the other hand, we may hope he also drew his companion picture of the "Honest Stationer" from some of his acquaintance.

The closing years of the period under review were marked by two great disasters, the outbreak of plague in London, in the autumn of 1665, and the great fire of 1666. By the first, trade in the City was brought to a standstill and printers and stationers were reduced to idleness. By the second, the chief printing houses and booksellers' shops, with all their contents, were destroyed, and the ashes of books and manuscripts were carried by the wind as far as Eton and Windsor. Happily for us the Thomason Collection was out of reach of the flames.

ABBREVIATIONS.

App. - - - - -	Appendix.
Arber - - - - -	Transcript of the Registers of the Company of Stationers.
B.M. - - - - - -	British Museum.
Bibl. Lind. - - - -	Bibliotheca Lindesiana.
Bodl. - - - - -	Bodleian.
Camb. Antiq. Soc. Comm. -	Cambridge Antiquarian Society's Communications.
Chan. Proc. - - - -	Chancery Proceedings.
D.N.B. - - - - -	Dictionary National Biography.
Dom. S. P. - - - -	Domestic State Papers.
Exchsq. K. R. - - -	Exchequer King's Remembrancer.
Edin. Bibl. Soc. Publ. - -	Edinburgh Bibliographical Society's Publications.
Harl. - - - - -	Harleian Manuscript.
Haz. - - - - - -	Hazlitt.
Hist. MS. Comn. - - -	Historical Manuscripts Commission.
Interr. - - - - -	Interregnum.
Lutt. Coll. - - - -	Luttrell Collection.
P.C.C. - - - - -	Prerogative Court of Canterbury.
P.R.O. - - - - -	Public Record Office.
Rep. - - - - - -	Report.
Sayle - - - - -	Early English Printed Books in the University Library, Cambridge.
Stat. Reg. - - - -	Stationers' Registers.
T.C. - - - - - -	Term Catalogues.

The Ames Collection of Title-pages is that at the British Museum catalogued under Title-pages (463 h. 4, 5).

The volumes of the Bagford Collection of Title-pages referred to in this work are Harl. MSS. 5915, 5919, 5921, 5923, 5927, 5928, 5929, 5932, 5936, 5949, 5963, 5965, 5967, 5973, 5990, now in the Printed Book Department.

A DICTIONARY OF THE BOOKSELLERS AND PRINTERS WHO WERE AT WORK IN ENGLAND, SCOTLAND AND IRELAND FROM 1641 TO 1667.

ADAMS (CHARLES), bookseller in London, (1) Marygold in Fleet Street; (2) Talbot, near St. Dunstan's Church, Fleet Street, 1654-62. Amongst his publications was an edition of the *Cynegeticon* of Gratius Faliscus, edited by Christopher Wase, 1654.

ADAMS (JOHN), bookseller in Oxford, 1610-71 (?). A stationer of this name leased a tenement in St. Mary's parish in 1610, and in 1637 a house to the North of the Schools Quadrangle was described as "lately" in the tenure of John Adams, bookbinder. [Madan, *Early Oxford Press*, p. 276.] His name is found on E. Brerewood's *Tractatus . . . . logici*, 1659.

ADAMSON (HUGH), bookseller (?) in London (?), 1643. Only known by the imprint to a pamphlet entitled *Sea-coale, Char-coale and Small Coale . . . . London: Printed for Hugh Adamson Ian. 27. Anno Dom. 1643.* His address has not been found.

ADDERTON (WILLIAM), bookseller in London; Three Golden Falcons in Duck Lane, 1628-71. Took up his freedom on June 30th, 1628. [Arber, iii. 686.] Made his first entry in the registers May 29th, 1629. Chiefly a publisher of theological literature. His name occurs for the last time in the Term Catalogue for Trinity, 1671. [Arber, *Term Catalogues*, vol. i. p. 78.]

ALLEN (BENJAMIN), bookseller and printer in London; The Crown, Pope's Head Alley, 1631-46. Took up his freedom on January 12th, 1631. [Arber, iii. 686.] He was the publisher of much of the political and theological literature of the period, including some New England Tracts on Church and Church government. Henry Archer's *Personall Reign of Christ* bears the imprint "Printed and sold by Benjamin Allen." There are many references to him in Hazlitt's Collections. His will, dated May 5th, 1646, was very short and mentioned no names, but legacies were left to his wife and to a son and daughter. This will was proved on May 15th in the same year by his widow, Hannah Allen. [P.C.C. 57 Twisse.]

ALLEN (HANNAH), bookseller and printer in London; The Crown, in Pope's Head Alley, 1647–50. The widow of Benjamin Allen. The last entry by her in the Registers was on September 2nd, 1650. She dealt chiefly in theological literature. She afterwards married Livewell Chapman, *q.v.* [Stationers' Registers, Liber E, fol. 249.]

ALLEN (JOHN), bookseller in London, (1) Rising Sun in the New Buildings in Pauls Church Yard, between the two North Doors; (2) Little Britain. 1656–67. Amongst his early publications were some astrological tracts; but in 1659 he wrote and published two pamphlets against the practice of judicial astrology. The second of these, entitled *Judicial Astrologers totally routed*, contains on the last leaf a list of 14 books sold by him. [B.M. 718 d. 31.] His name occurs in the Hearth Tax Roll, 1666, as living in Little Britain. [P.R.O. Lay Subsidy $\frac{252}{32}$.]

ALLEN (NATHANIEL), bookseller in London; Angel & Bible in Lumber [*i.e.*, Lombard] Street, 1642–43. Took up his freedom as a stationer on August 4th, 1634. [Arber, iii. 687.] His name is found on C. Herle's *Independency on Scriptures*, 1643.

. ALLESTRY, ALLESTRYE, or ALLESTREE (JAMES), bookseller in London, (1) Bell in St. Paul's Churchyard, 1652–64; (2) Rose & Crown, St. Paul's Churchyard, 1664–66; (3) Rose & Crown, in Duck Lane, 1667–69; (4) Rose & Crown, St. Paul's Churchyard, 1669–70. Was a relative, perhaps brother, of Richard Allestry the divine (1619–81), and father of Jacob Allestry, poetical writer (1653–86). Details of his early life are wanting, and the first heard of him as a bookseller is in the year 1652, when he is found in business at the Bell in St. Paul's Churchyard, in partnership with John Martin. In 1660 they were joined by Thomas Dicas, and at one time Timothy Garthwaite seems to have been associated with them. At this time James Allestry was one of the largest capitalists in the trade, and his shop was the resort of the wealthy and the learned. Amongst the State Papers is a series of interesting letters written by him to Edward, second Viscount Conway, on the subject of books. About 1660 he was appointed bookseller and publisher to the Royal Society, and either altered his sign or removed to other premises, known as the "Rose & Crown." As a publisher he was interested in the chief and most important ventures of the time, such as the Duchess of Newcastle's · Plays and Poems, the second part of Butler's *Hudibras*, and Ray's *Catalogus Plantarum*. Allestree employed the best printers of the day, much of his work being done by Thomas Roycroft, the printer of Walton's Polyglott. In the Great Fire of 1666 his premises were destroyed, and he was almost ruined. During the rebuilding of St. Paul's Churchyard he moved into Duck Lane, and there, by the help of his kinsman, Dr. Richard Allestry, who gave him the publishing of some sermons, he made a new start, returning to the Churchyard and resuming business under the old sign about 1669; but he did not live long afterwards, his death taking place on November 3rd, 1670. Smyth, the Secondary of the Poultry Compter, to whom we owe so much valuable information respecting the London book-sellers of his day, records in his *Obituary* (p. 89): "Die Jovis hora 8ª ante merid. obiit Jacob Allestry bibliopola in coemiter D. Paul's, Lond. Sepult Lunae 7 Novᵣ. Fitz-Williams capellan. Episcop. Winton. concionem facit funeb."

ALSOP, or ALLSOPP (BERNARD), printer in London, (1) with T. Creed, at the sign of the Eagle & Child; (2) Garter Place, in Barbican, 1617; (3) By Saint Anne's Church neere Aldersgate, 1618; (4) The Dolphin, in Distaff Lane, Old Fish Street, 1621; (5) Grub Street, in Honey Suckle Court, neere to the Flying Horse, 1641; (6) Grub Street, neere the Upper Pump, 1650 (1602–50). A native of Derby. Was apprenticed to Humphrey Lympenny, stationer of London, for eight years from Christmas, 1601, but in 1603 he was transferred for the remainder of his term to William White. (Arber, ii. 259.) In 1616 he is found in partnership with Thomas Creed, a printer who had begun printing about 1580, and whose printing house was known by the sign of the Eagle & Child. Creed either retired from business or died in the following year, when Alsop appears to have succeeded to his printing materials, but whether he moved into new premises or whether the first and second imprints given above refer to the same place is not clear. Nine years later he entered into partnership with Thomas Fawcett, or Forsett. In the year 1626 they were summoned before the High Commission for being concerned in printing Sir Robert Cotton's *Short View of the Long life and reign of Henry the Third*. Alsop admitted that he had purchased the manuscript of Ferdinand Ely, a secondhand bookseller in Little Britain. He and his partner only printed one sheet. They were also the printers of much of the dramatic literature of Beaumont and Fletcher, Decker, Greene, and other writers. Bernard Alsop was one of the twenty master printers allowed by the Act of 1637, but his partner was not mentioned. In 1641 he was sent for by the House of Commons for printing the Hertfordshire Petition. [Commons Journals, January 25th, 1641. *See* GREENSMITH, J.]. On the outbreak of the troubles with the King, Alsop and Fawcett printed several news-sheets, the best known being the *Weekly Accompt of certain Special & Remarkable Passages from Both Houses of Parliament*, which first appeared on August 3rd, 1643, and in the same year they were committed to the Fleet Prison for printing a pamphlet entitled *His Majesty's Propositions to Sir John Hotham and the Inhabitants of Hull*. They petitioned the House of Lords for their release, declaring that the pamphlet was printed by their servants during their absence. Beyond the imprisonment, which lasted for some months, no further punishment followed. [Lords' Journals, v. 214, 533.] Bernard Alsop was reputed by his contemporaries to have printed pamphlets on Scotch affairs, using Evan Tyler's imprint. Fawcett appears to have retired from the partnership about 1644. Nothing is known as to the date of Bernard Alsop's death, but in 1653 his widow, Elizabeth Alsop, is found carrying on the business. Creed's type and ornaments, when they came into Alsop's hands, had been in use many years and were getting into bad condition, but his successor used them during the whole of his life. Consequently his later books are very poor specimens of typography, and his news-sheets were printed in the roughest possible manner.

ALSOP, or ALLSOPP (ELIZABETH), printer in London; "At her house in Grub Street near the Upper Pump," 1653–56. Is believed to have been the widow of Bernard Alsop. The last book entry to her was on April 22nd, 1656.

ALSOP, or ALSOPP (THOMAS), bookseller in London; Two sugar loaves over against St. Antholin's Church, at the lower end of Watling Street, 1657. His name is found in the following book: *Poems by Hugh Crompton, The Son of Bacchus and Godson of Apollo. Being a fardle of Fancies, or a medley of musick, stewed in four ounces of the Oyl of Epigrames.* [Hazlitt, *Handbook*, p. 130.]

ANDERSON (ANDREW), printer at Edinburgh, 1653–57; at Glasgow, 1657–61; again at Edinburgh on the north side of the cross, 1661–76. Son of George Anderson. Succeeded heirs of G. Anderson in 1653. Removed to Glasgow about July, 1657, by invitation of the Town Council, who offered him one hundred marks per annum as a pension. He returned to Edinburgh in the summer of 1661, and in 1663 was appointed printer to the town and college on the death of G. Lithgow. In 1671 he was appointed King's Printer for forty-one years, and took several partners. Andrew Anderson died in June, 1676, being succeeded by his widow, Agnes, and his son, James. Most of his type and ornaments had been in use in the printing offices of Edinburgh for many years, and were in a very worn condition, his productions and those of his successors being among the poorest and most slovenly that came from the press of Scotland. Ninety-three issues have been traced to his press. [H. G. Aldis, *List of books printed in Scotland before 1700 . . . . with brief notes on the printers and stationers.* Edinburgh Bibliographical Society Publications, 1905.]

ANDERSON (GEORGE), printer at Edinburgh, "in King James his college, 1637–38; at Glasgow in Hutshisons Hospitall in the Trongate," 1638–47. Commenced printing in Edinburgh in 1637, having acquired a considerable part of the printing materials of Robert Young, *q.v.* In 1638 Anderson removed to Glasgow, taking a press with him. He worked chiefly for the General Assembly, but in 1644 he printed the Rev. John Row's Hebrew Grammar and Vocabulary, probably one of the earliest books in that language, printed in Scotland. George Anderson is believed to have died in 1648. He left a son, Andrew Anderson, who ultimately succeeded to the business. [H. G. Aldis, *List of books printed in Scotland before 1700.*]

ANDERSON (Heirs of GEORGE), printers in Glasgow, 1648, and in Edinburgh, 1649–53. On the death of George Anderson in 1647 the Town

Council of Glasgow agreed to continue his pension to his widow and children so long as they continued to carry on the business; but in 1649 they had removed to Edinburgh, and in 1653 were succeeded by Andrew Anderson. [H. G. Aldis, *List of books printed in Scotland before 1700.*]

ANDERSON (WILLIAM), bookseller in London, 1660. His name occurs on the following ballad: "*Admire not Noble Sir, that you should hear.*" [Bibl. Lind. Catal. of Eng. Ballads, No. 810.] His address has not been found.

ANDREWS (ELIZABETH), bookseller in London; White Lyon near Pye Corner, 1663-64. The widow of John Andrews, *q.v.*

ANDREWS (HENRY), bookseller (?) in London, 1642. His name is found in the imprint to an eight-page pamphlet published in 1642, entitled, *Newes from Black-Heath concerning the meeting of the Kentish Men*, etc., etc. . . . . *London, Printed for Henrie Andrews*, 1642, E. 144 (13). His address has not been found.

ANDREWS (JOHN), bookseller in London; White Lyon near Pye Corner 1654-63. Appears to have dealt chiefly in the ephemeral literature of his time, such as ballads, broadsides, and all kinds of pamphlets. His will was proved on March 12th, 166⅔: by this he divided the residue of his goods, books, quires, etc., between his wife Elizabeth and his three children, Elizabeth, Mary, and John. [P.C.C. 35 Laud.]

ARCHER (EDWARD), bookseller in London; Adam and Eve in Little Britaine, 1656. Publisher of plays, of which he issued a catalogue in 1656, "more exactly Printed then ever before." This list he added to a comedy called the *Old Law*, the joint production of Massinger, Middleton, and Rowley. He may have been a descendant of the Thomas Archer, bookseller, who flourished between 1603 and 1634. [W. W. Greg, *List of Masques, etc.*, App. II.]

ARDING (WILLIAM), (?) bookseller in London, (?) 1642. This name occurs in the imprint to a pamphlet entitled *Propositions for Peace* [E. 152 (1).] The printing is so bad that it might very possibly be a mis-reading of Harding, as there are one or two stationers of that name noted in the Registers of the Company of Stationers [Arber, ii. 238; iii. 687]. Again it might be the name of a Lincoln bookseller, as portions of the tract refer to that place.

ARMSTRONG (WILLIAM), (?) bookseller in Cambridge, 1647. A pamphlet entitled *Animadversions upon a declaration of the proceedings against the xi. members*, bears the imprint, Cambridge, Printed for Will. Armstrong. Anno. Dom. 1647. [E. 398 (4).]

ASH (FRANCIS), bookseller and bookbinder of the City of Worcester, 1644-51. The earliest mention of this bookseller is an entry in the Register of Apprenticeships, 1605-60, at Stationers' Hall, where, under date of December 7th, 1646, it is recorded that Francis Rea, the son of Ann Rea, of Churchill, co. Worcester, had put himself apprentice to Francis Ash for seven years, the indenture bearing date January 6th, 1644. Francis Ash is said to have been a Papist, and to have done a large trade in Popish books and pictures in the West of England. In a pamphlet entitled *A second beacon fired by Scintilla* written by a London bookseller, Michael Sparke, Sen., *q.v.*, are some interesting particulars relating to Francis Ash, in which it is stated that he was largely employed in obtaining "pictures" for the English Bible, and that he went to France, and there commissioned Hollar to engrave them. In the *Historical Catalogue of the British and Foreign Bible Society*, the Edinburgh editions of the Bible of 1633 are noted as containing these pictures in the New Testament. See Nos. 367, 368. Clement Barksdale's *Nympha Libethris*, 1651, 8°., has this imprint, "*London, Printed for F. A. at Worcester*," and in stanzas 56 and 67 the author refers to Ash's skill as a bookbinder. Ash is believed to have died either during, or soon after the siege of Worcester (September, 1651).

ASSIGNS OF JOHN BILL, *see* BILL (JOHN), Assigns of.

ASSIGNS OF JOHN MORE, *see* MORE (J.), Assigns of.

ASTON (JOHN), bookseller in London; Cat-eaten-streete (Cheapside, re-named in 1845 Gresham Street), at the signe of the Bul's Head, 1637-42. Took up his freedom February 6th, 1637 [Arber, iii. 688], in which year he published Thomas Heywood's *True Description of His Majesties Royall Ship Built this Year 1637 at Woollwitch in Kent.* 4to.; and a satire on women called *A Curtaine Lecture,* 1637. 12°. In 1641 he was imprisoned for a short time for printing the *Preamble with the protestation made by the whole House of Commons, 3 May, 1641.* [B.M. 669, f. 3 (2), Commons Journals.]

ATKINSON (HENRY), bookseller in London; Staple Inn Gate in Holborn, 1642-59. Took up his freedom October 3rd, 1631 [Arber, iii. 686]. Amongst his publications was Richard Kilburne's *Brief survey of the County of Kent,* 1657.

ATKYNS (RICHARD), patentee of law books, 1639-77. The printing of books of common law was created a monopoly by letters patent, granted by King Edward VI to Richard Tottel, and renewed to him by Queen Elizabeth (January 12th, 1 Eliz.). After his death, *i.e.,* on March 20th, 159⅔, it was granted to C. Yetsweirt for thirty years. He only enjoyed it for a short time, and at his death, in 1598, the reversion was granted to Thomas Wight and Bonham Norton, for the remainder of the term. They, however, surrendered it in consideration of a new grant which was made on March 10th, 159⅞, for thirty years [Patent Rolls, 41 Eliz., 4th part]. That patent expired on March 10th, 1628. It was no doubt put up to the highest bidder, and was next granted by James I (January 19th, 15 James I) to John More, Esquire, for forty years. A few months afterwards More assigned his printing rights to Miles Fletcher, *q.v.,* and his partners, John Haviland and Robert Young, for an annuity of £60 and a third of the profits. John More died August 17th, 1638, leaving this annuity, etc., to his daughter Martha, then the wife of Richard Atkyns, who thus became patentee by right of his wife. Miles Fletcher attempted to evade paying this legacy, and in 1639 purchased the stock and premises of Charles More, son of John More, for a sum of £930, and subsequently sold his rights to the Company of Stationers. But Atkyns and his wife brought an action against Fletcher and the Company in the Court of Chancery. The outbreak of the Civil War stopped the case, but at the Restoration they recommenced proceedings, and were successful, Miles Fletcher being held to have bought of Charles More wrongfully, and being compelled to pay up all arrears up to 1643, and since the Restoration, to Richard Atkyns and his wife. [P.R.O. Chan. Proc. Before 1715. Reynardson, Bund. 31, 126.] At one time Henry Twyford and John Streator, *q.v.*, were two of the assigns of R. Atkyns, whose name does not appear in any law book before 1677. Richard Atkyns is chiefly remembered as the author of a work entitled *The Origin and Growth of Printing*, 1664, in which he put forward the theory that the art of printing was introduced into England and begun at Oxford by a certain Frederick Corsellis in 1468, and that the *Exposicio sancti Jeronimi* was printed by him. This story has long since been proved to be unfounded, and the date in the *Exposicio* has been proved to the satisfaction of all bibliographers to be a misprint for 1478. Atkyns subsequently fell into distress, partly, it is believed, by the vagaries and extravagances of his wife, and was committed to the Marshalsea for debt. He died without issue on September 14th, 1677, and was buried in the church of St. George the Martyr, Southwark. [D.N.B.]

AUSTIN (JOHN), bookseller in London, 1642. His name occurs on the following broadside: *A List of the names of such persons who are thought fit for their accommodation, and the furtherance of the service in Ireland, to be entertained as reformadoes.* [Bibl. Lind. *Catalogue of English Broadsides*, No. 29.] His address has not been found. He may be identical with John Aston.

AUSTIN, or AUSTEN (ROBERT), printer in London, (1) Old Bailey, 1643; (2) Addlehill, Thames Street, 1649–50. 1642–56. Took up his freedom November 7th, 1636. [Arber, iii. 688.] He is chiefly worthy of notice as the printer of George Wither's *Campo-Musæ*, 1643, and the same author's *Vox Pacifica* in 1645. In 1643, in company with Andrew Coe, he printed some numbers of a news-sheet entitled *A Perfect Diurnal of the Passages in Parliament.* There was another publication bearing a very similar title, *A Perfect Diurnall of some Passages in Parliament*, of which Francis Coles and Lawrence Blacklock were the publishers. Both claimed precedency, but the Stationers' Company apparently refused to recognise the *Perfect Diurnal* of Austin and Coe, as no entry of it is found in the registers, whereas that of Coles and Blacklock was regularly entered and continued to run for several years. Austin was also interested in other news-sheets. On November 3rd, 1643, he started *Informator Rusticus, or The Country Intelligencer*, which does not seem to have got beyond its first issue. In the following January he began another, entitled *Occurrences of certain speciall and remarkable passages in Parliament and the affaires of the Kingdome*, which was still in existence in 1646.

BADDELEY (RICHARD), bookseller in London; Within the Middle Temple Gate, 1650–53. Was probably a native of Durham, as on October 29th, 1650, he took as an apprentice Richard Baddeley, son of Richard Baddeley of that city. [Stationers' Company Register of Apprenticeships, 1603–66.] He published a *Letter to a Gentleman in the Country*, 1653, attributed to John Milton. [Masson's *Life of Milton*, vol. 4, p. 520.]

BADGER (GEORGE), bookseller in London; In St. Dunstan's Churchyard at his shop turning up to Cliffords Inne, 1641; (2) St. Dunstan's Church-yard, Fleet Street, 1641–51. Was probably a relation of Richard Badger and Thomas Badger. His widow married Theodore Crowley. [Stationers' Registers, Liber F, p. 160.] Both the addresses given above relate to the same house, which had previously been in the possession of H. Taunton, stationer.

BADGER (RICHARD), printer in London; (?) White Swan, at the foot of Addling Hill, near Baynard's Castle, 1602–42. According to the entry in the Registers of the Company of Stationers, Richard Badger was the son of John Badger, of Stratford-upon-Avon. [Arber, ii. 261.] The parish registers of the town do not confirm this, the only entries of a Richard Badger being Richard, son to George Badger, born September 14th, 1580, and another son of the same name, born August 17th, 1585. There is no mention in the Registers of any son born to a John Badger. [Stratford-on-Avon Parish Registers, Parish Register Society, 1897.] R. Badger came to London and was apprenticed to Peter Short, a printer, on March 25th, 1602, for eight years, and took up his freedom in April, 1610. He then joined George Miller, *q.v.*, another Stratford man, who had succeeded to the printing business of Richard Field, also a native of Stratford, and the printer of Shakespeare's *Venus and Adonis* and *Lucrece*. How long he remained with Miller is unknown, but Sir John Lambe states that about 1630 Richard Badger succeeded to the printing office formerly kept by Valentine Simmes. [Arber, iii. pp. 699–704.] Badger was admitted a master printer on June 12th, 1629, and in 1639 spoke of himself as "printer to the Prince his Highness." He was also spoken of as printer to Archbishop Laud, for whom he is said to have printed "Bibles with superstitious pictures" [*True Informer*, No. 34, June 8th, 1644.] Timperley (p. 488) mentions a copy of Laud's speech at the trial of Bastwick as printed on vellum by Richard Badger. He had a good assortment of letter, and his workmanship was far above the average. Amongst his devices is found the "Anchora Spei," successively used by T. Vautrollier, R. Field, and George Miller. The date of his death is unknown, but he had a son, Thomas Badger, and he was also probably related to George Badger.

BADGER (THOMAS), printer in London; (?) Lucrece without Newgate, over against St. Sepulchre's Church (the printing house of the Purfoots), 1639–46. Son of Richard Badger. Printed as the assign of Thomas Purfoot the second, and on that printer's death in 1639 was elected a master printer in his place, and in all probability took over the old printing office as it stood. He was certainly in possession of the types, initial letters, and ornaments used by the Purfoots. Amongst the notable books that came from his press was James Howell's *Dodona's Grove*, 1640, and Sir H. Vere's *Elegies*, 1642. [*Domestic State Papers*, Charles I, vol. 446 (54); Arber, iii. 702.]

BAILEY, or BAILY (GEORGE), bookseller (?) in London, 1642. His name appears in the imprint to a broadside *To the Honourable the knights*, etc. [B.M., 669, f. 4 (49).] He may have been a relative of Thomas Bailey, the bookseller of Middle Row, Holborn, and perhaps carried on business with him.

BAILEY, BALEY, or BAILY (THOMAS), bookseller in London; (?) Middle Row, neer Staple Inn, Holborn, 1617–42. Published the *Earle of Essex his speech in the Artilrie garden, July 28th, 1642*. 4°. [E 200. (54).] Is probably identical with the bookseller in Middle Row, Holborn, who in 1634 had published a second edition of Samuel Rowland's *Night Raven*.

BAILY (T.), *see* Bailey (T.).

BAKER (JOHN), bookseller in London; Ship in St. Paul's Churchyard, 1653. Smyth in his *Obituary*, p. 36, has this entry: "Novem. 16, 1653, John Baker, bookseller, died." Shirley's masque of *Cupid and Death*, which was presented before the Portuguese Ambassador upon March 26th, 1653, and apparently printed before the end of that year, has the imprint, "London: Printed according to the Authors own Copy, by T. W. for J. Crook and J. Baker, at the sign of the Ship in St. Paul's Church yard, 1653." There was another bookseller of this name.

BAKER (JOHN), bookseller in London, (1) Peacock in St. Paul's Churchyard, 1659-66; (2) Peacock in Little Britain, 1667-70; (3) Three Pigeons, St. Paul's Churchyard, 1670-84. The Register of Apprenticeships at Stationers' Hall records a John Baker, son of Michael Baker, stationer, as bound to George Thomason on September 6th, 1647. He was out of his time in 1655. In 1659, in partnership with Edward Brewster, he published a Greek edition of *Hesiod* for the use of schools, which was printed for them by D. Maxwell. The title-page, printed in red and black, is preserved in the Ames Collection of title-pages in the British Museum, No. 2867.

BALDEN (RICHARD), bookseller (?) in London, 1642. His name occurs on the title-page of a pamphlet entitled *An Uprore at Portsmouth*, 1642. [Hazlitt, ii. 489.] His place of business is not indicated.

BALEY (T), *see* Bailey (T.).

BALLARD (WILLIAM), bookseller in Bristol; Bible in Corn Street, 1651-53. His name is found on Robert Purnell's *Way to Heaven discovered*, 1653. [E. 1489 (2).]. He was a dealer in Welsh books. [Rowland's *Cambrian Bibliography*, p. 156.]

BANKS (THOMAS), bookseller in London, (1) Blackfriars, on the top of Bridewell Stairs; (2) In the Old Bailey, 1641; (3) At the sign of the Seal in Westminster Hall, 1641-49. Took up his freedom on June 26th, 1637. [Arber, iii. 688.] Dealt chiefly in theological and political tracts and broadsides. In 1647 and at other times he had a stall in Westminster Hall, distinguished by the sign of the "Seal," and he was associated with another stall-holder there, Mistress Breach, in the publication of the Rev. John Cotton's *Controversie concerning liberty of conscience*, 1649. [*Library*, N.S., October, 1905, pp. 382-3.]

BARBER (JOSEPH), bookseller in London; The Lamb, in the New Buildings, St. Paul's Churchyard, 1653-58. Was associated with Samuel Speed in the publication of Sir P. Temple's *Man's Master Piece*, 1658.

BARKER (CHRISTOPHER), the Third, printer, 1640–80, son of Christopher Barker the second, and grandson of Robert Barker, the King's Printer. In 1643 he was sequestered for carrying the printing presses to the City of York, and the inference is that he was also the printer of the documents that were printed subsequently at Nottingham, Shrewsbury, and Bristol. At the Restoration, Christopher Barker the third, and John Bill the second, were restored to their moiety of the King's Printing Office, but Barker immediately assigned his moiety over to Sawbridge, Hills, Kirton, Roycroft, and Mearne, for an annuity of £100 a year, and appears to have given up printing, although his name continued to appear in the imprints of books down to the expiration of the patent in 1680. [*Library*, October, 1901. *The King's Printing House under the Stuarts*.]

BARKER (ROBERT), King's printer, Northumberland House, Aldersgate Street, 1570–1645. The eldest son of Christopher Barker the first, printer to Queen Elizabeth. He was probably born at Sudely, near Datchet, co. Bucks, was made free of the Company of Stationers on June 25th, 1589, and held a partnership in the Royal Printing House until his father's death in 1599. He is said to have married Rachel, a daughter of William Day (afterwards Bishop of Winchester), by whom he had a large family. On the accession of James I, Robert Barker held the office of King's Printer by virtue of the reversionary patent granted to his father, and afterwards obtained the reversion for his eldest son Christopher the second, and a further reversion of thirty years to his second son, Robert, on the death of Christopher and himself. In 1605 and 1606 he was Master of the Company of Stationers. Robert Barker was the printer of what is known as the "Authorised" version of the Bible in 1611. It has been generally supposed that he bore the whole cost, but there is little doubt that he was financed throughout by Bonham Norton, John Norton, and John Bill, in return for a share in the profits of the office. The value of the office at that time is said to have been £30,000. In 1615 his son Christopher the second married Sarah, the eldest daughter of Bonham Norton. Soon afterwards they were in financial difficulties, and assigned their interest in the King's

Printing House to Bonham Norton and John Bill. In 1618 Robert Barker brought an action in the Court of Chancery to recover possession, stating that according to the agreements the assignments were only for one year. This Norton denied, and a series of law suits extending over many years followed. Down to the year 1616 the imprints bore Robert Barker's name only. In 1616 they bore the names of Robert Barker and John Bill, and after July, 1617, until May, 1619, they ran "Bonham Norton and John Bill." Barker was successful in his first suit, and a decree was pronounced in his favour, but John Bill was held to have been a bonâ fide purchaser, and accordingly the imprints were altered again to Robert Barker and John Bill. But in 1620 Norton ejected Barker from the office, and the imprints were again changed to Bonham Norton and John Bill, and they continued thus until October 20th, 1629, when a final decree was pronounced in favour of Robert Barker, and they became for the third time Robert Barker and John Bill. In the course of this dispute the statement was made that the King's Printing House was situated at Northumberland House, Aldersgate Street, and subsequently at Hunsdon House, Blackfriars. The death of John Bill in 1630 necessitated a further change in the imprints, which then became Robert Barker and the assigns of John Bill. In 1634 Robert Barker mortgaged his moiety of the office to Miles Fletcher and his partners, and in 1635 he was committed as a debtor to the King's Bench Prison, where he died in 1645. His will, if he made one, has not been found. Of the five sons borne him by his wife Rachel, Christopher the second and Robert the second were already dead. Of the rest, Mathew only is subsequently heard of. The King's Printing House, when it was in the hands of Christopher Barker, was rich in all forms of type, ornaments, initial letters, including the handsome pictorial initial letters once used by John Day, and many others previously in the office of H. Bynneman. As various editions of the Bible, Prayer Book and Statutes show, it turned out some very fine books. To this stock Robert Barker succeeded, but the beauty of his black letter printing was marred by careless workmanship. The Bible of 1611 is, of course, the chief glory of his press. It was printed, like all previous folio editions, in great primer black letter, and had an elaborate engraved title-page, the work of Cornelis Boel, and also an engraved map of Canaan, partly the work of John Speed.

[*Library*, N.S., October, 1901. *King's Printing House under the Stuarts* . . .]

BARLEY (RICHARD), bookseller in Dover, 1654. Only known from the imprint to a pamphlet entitled, *An Antidote against Anabaptisme* .... By Jo. Reading, B.D. ... London. Printed by Tho. Newcomb, for Simon York and Richard Barley, dwelling in Dover, 1654. 4°. [Ames Collection of Title-pages, No. 2,410.]

BARLOW (WILLIAM), bookseller in London; Without Aldersgate, 1658. His name occurs in the imprint to a work called *Fundamenta chymica*, by L. C. Philomedico Chemicus, 1658. 8°. Only known by the title-page preserved amongst the Bagford fragments. He may have been a descendant of Timothy Barlow, bookseller (1616-18).

BARTLET (JOHN), senior, bookseller in London, (1) Gilt Cup, Goldsmiths' Row, Cheapside, 1619-37; (2) Gilt Cup near St. Austines Gate, 1641; (3) In St. Faith's Parish, 1643-44; (4) In the new buildings on the South side of Pauls, neer St. Austine's-Gate, at the sign of the Gilt-Cup, 1655; (5) At the Golden Cup in Pauls Church Yard over against the Drapers, 1657; (6) Gilt-Cup in Westminster Hall, 1658. Took up his freedom in the Company of Stationers on July 26th, 1619, and set up in business at the Gilt Cup in Goldsmiths' Row, Cheapside, his chief publications being sermons and other theological works. He was one of the victims of Laud's persecution, being apprehended in December, 1637, and brought before Sir John Lambe on a charge of having given William Prynne's servant some of the writings of Dr. Bastwick and Mr. Burton to be copied. He was ordered by the Privy Council to shut up his shop, and as he did not obey the order quickly enough, he was imprisoned in the Compter in Wood Street for three months, until he had entered into bond of £100 not to use his trade in Cheapside, to quit his house within six months, and not to let it to anyone but a goldsmith under a penalty of £600. He was afterwards brought before the Privy Council on the Archbishop's warrant, and sent to the Fleet prison, where he remained six months. [*Domestic State Papers*, Charles I, vol. 374, 13, etc.; vol. 378, 86; vol. 501, 18; *Domestic State Papers*, 1643 (4).] He afterwards moved into St. Paul's Churchyard, where his imprint appears in four varieties, though probably all relating to the same house. He had a son, John, who held a stall in Westminster Hall under the same sign, but probably it belonged to the father also. John Bartlet the elder appears to have died between 1657 and 1660. [*Library*, N.S., October, 1905, pp. 384-5.]

BARTLET (JOHN), the Younger, bookseller in London, Westminster Hall, 1657. His name is found in the imprint to a broadside entitled *An Elegy on the death of the Rt. Hon. Robert Blake, Esq.*, 1657. [Lutt. Coll. I, 10.] Several other books have the Bartlets' Westminster Hall imprint between this date and 1660, and the stall was probably jointly held by father and son. [*Library*, N.S., October, 1905, pp. 384–5.]

BARWICK (HENRY), bookseller (?) in London, 164$\frac{1}{2}$. A pamphlet entitled *The Prince of Orange his Royall Entertainment to the Queen of England* .... [E. 138 (17)] bears the imprint "First imprinted at the Hague in Holland, and now Reprinted in London for Henrie Barwicke 1641."

BASSET (THOMAS), bookseller in London, (1) St. Dunstan's Churchyard, Fleet Street; (2) George, near St. Dunstan's Church, Fleet Street; (3) Westminster Hall, 1659–93. A dealer in law books, chiefly remembered for the Catalogue of Law Books which he published in 1673. Jacob Tonson was one of his apprentices. A list of 13 books published by him in 1659 follows the preface to *Hermaelogium, or An Essay at the rationality of the art of Speaking*, 1659. 8°.

BATEMAN (THOMAS), bookseller (?) in London, 1659. His name occurs in the imprint to a pamphlet entitled: *Letter from Maj. Genl. Massey to an Hon. Person in London*, 1659. 4°.

BATES (THOMAS), bookseller in London, (1) Maidenhead on Snow Hill, Holborn Conduit, 1645; (2) Old Bailey. 1640–47. May probably be identified with the person of that name whose address is given in a contemporary pamphlet as Bishop's Court, in the Old Bailey, and at whose house, in 1641, there was a dispute between Henry Walker the ironmonger and a Jesuit. He was the publisher of much popular literature, broadsides, ballads, and lampoons, as well as many political pamphlets. On December 13th, 1641, he, in company with John Wright, sen., published the *Diurnal or the Heads of all the Proceedings in Parliament*. Another news-sheet which they produced was *Mercurius Civicus*, probably the first illustrated newspaper, its front page having every week a portrait of some celebrity. It began on May 4th, 1643, and ended on December 10th, 1646, quite a long life for a news-sheet. Bates and Wright were also the publishers of *The True Informer*, and Bates was also associated with F. Coles, *q.v.*, in the issue of the *Diurnall Occurrences* in 1642. In connection with this he was imprisoned for a short time in the year 1642 for publishing false reports on the Army. [*Library*, N.S., April, 1905, pp. 184 *et seq.*; Commons Journals, June 8th, 1642.]

BATT (M.), bookseller in London, 1642. His name occurs on several political pamphlets such as the following: *True and exact relation of the Proceedings of His Majesty's Army in Cheshire, Shropshire, and Worcestershire.* [October 5th], 1642. [Hazlitt, iv. 19; E. 126 (43).]

BEAL (G.), (?) bookseller in London, (?) Old Bayley and neer Temple Bar, 1648. The following political pamphlets of the year 1648 have the imprint, London, Printed for G. Beal, and are to be sold in the Old Bayley, and neer Temple Bar (1) *A great and bloudy fight at Colchester* .... 1648. [E. 453 (18)]; (2) *Two petitions of the Lord Mayor* .... 1648. [E. 453 (45).]

BEALE (JOHN), printer in London; (?) Fetter Lane [the printing house of Robert Robinson], 1612–41. This printing house belonged from 1587–97 to Robert Robinson. After his death his widow married Richard Braddock, who continued the business till 1609, when it was bought by Thomas Haviland and William Hall. Two or three years later it was sold by Hall to John Beale, who took into partnership for a short time Thomas Brudenell. Sir John Lambe, from whose notes on the London printing houses this notice is compiled, says; "Master John Beale succeeded his partner Master William Hall about 15 yeares since (*i.e.*, 1620), never admitted (of great estate but a very contentious person) he tooke soll to furnish ye pore with bread and doth not do it. He bought Hall [out] and took Thomas Brudenell to be his partner for £140, which Brudenell had much a doe to recover." [Arber, iii. 699–700.] Beale was a relation by marriage to Humphrey Robinson, *q.v.* [Excheq. K. R. Bills and Answers, Lond. and Midd., 34.] Towards the close of his life he was afflicted with blindness, but appears to have still carried on business with S. Buckly, *i.e.*, Stephen Bulkley, *q.v.*, afterwards the Royalist printer, at York and elsewhere, for their names appear together in the imprint to Lewis de Gand's *Sol Britannicus*, 1641, 8°. [B.M. 1137, a. 13]. John Beale

D

died on September 17th, 1643, and on March 16th, 164⅔, his copies were transferred to Humphrey Robinson. [Stationers' Registers, Liber F.] He printed some important works, including Speed's *Theatre*, 1611; Bacon's *Essays*, 1612 and 1639; Record's *Ground of Arts*, 1618; an edition of *Cicero*, 1628; and B. Jonson's *Bartholomew Fayre*, 1631.

BEAUMONT (ROBERT), bookseller in London; Little Britain, 1650. Was in partnership with Lawrence Sadler, *q.v.*, and their names are found in the imprint to a medical book entitled *De Rachitide sive morbo puerili*, by Francis Glisson, 1650. 8°. He was probably dead before 1660, when another edition of the book appeared with Sadler's name only.

BECKE (H.), bookseller in London; In the Old Bayley, 1643-48. His name occurs in the imprint to the following pamphlets: *Protestation of the Two and Twenty Divines for the setling of the Church*, 1643 [*i.e.*, March 10th, 164⅔, E. 92 (24)]; *A bad and Bloody Fight at Westminster*, 1648. [E. 443 (17)]; and *Sad newes out of Kent*, 1648. [E. 443 (41).]

BECKETT (JAMES), bookseller in London; Inner Temple Gate, Fleet Street, 1636-41. Took up his freedom August 1st, 1636 [Arber, iii. 688], and in the same year published T. Heywood's *Challenge for beautie*. His first registered publication was the same author's play of the *Royall King and the loyall subject*, 1637. [Arber, iv. 376.] He was also the publisher of J. Kirke's *Seven Champions of Christendome*, 1638; F. Lenton's *Great Britain's Beauties*, 1638; T. Middleton's *Mad World my masters*, 1640; L. Sharpe's *Noble Stranger*, 1640; J. Shirley's *Humorous Courtier*, as well as a romance called *Marianus* in 1641, after which no more is heard of him. Amongst his other publications were T. Decker's *English Villanies seven several times Prest*, 1638; H. Peacham's *Truth of our Times* and *Valley of Varietie*, both in 1638; R. Braithwaite's *Epitome of all the lives of the Kings of France*, 1639 [Hazlitt, i., p. 48], and John Taylor's *Woman's Sharpe Revenge*, 1640. Only three of his publications were entered in the Registers before 1640.

BEDELL (GABRIELL), bookseller in London; Middle Temple Gate, Fleet Street, 1646-68. Is first met with on November 7th, 1646, when, in partnership with Mercy Meighen, *q.v.*, the widow of Richard Meighen, he made an entry in the Registers of the Company of nineteen books which had formerly belonged to R. Meighen. Twelve of these were plays. Later, however, they appear to have dealt principally in law books. In 1650 they took Thomas Collins, *q.v.*, as third partner. In 1654 Mercy Meighen died, and G. Bedell is found in partnership with R. Marriot, T. Garthwayte, and J. Crooke, but eventually he and T. Collins settled down together, and a list of 86 books, arranged under subjects, published by them in 1656 occurs at the end of T. Goffe's *Three excellent Tragedies.* Gabriell Bedell died on February 27th, 166⅞ "by taking a cup of poyson, as is reported." [Smyth's *Obituary*, p. 77; W. W. Greg, *List of English Plays*, p. 42.]

BEE (CORNELIUS), bookseller in London; Little Britain, 1636–7½. Was the son of Thomas Bee, citizen and haberdasher, of London, whose will was proved May 28th, 1621. [P.C.C. 33 Dale.] He appears to have been a man of some capital, and joined Laurence Sadler, *q.v.*, in 1637 in the publication of the *Atlas Major.* [*Domestic State Papers*, Charles I, vol. 371, 95.] He is frequently mentioned in the domestic correspondence of the Commonwealth period, and Doctor Worthington in his diary notes [vol. i., p. 185] that the library of John Hales was purchased by Cornelius Bee for £700. His great publication was the *Critici Sacri* in 9 vols. folio, 1660. He had thought of issuing a tenth volume, and he greatly resented the publication of Matthew Poole's *Synopsis* of the critical labours of biblical commentators. Lawsuits resulted, the result being given in favour of Poole. Bee thereupon abandoned his projected tenth volume. [*Domestic State Papers*, Charles II, vol. 244, 27; *Case betwixt Mr. Poole and Mr. C. Bee* (1677?). *Vindication of Mr. Poole's design* (1677?)]. Cornelius Bee lost between £6,000 and £10,000 by the great fire. He married a sister of Lancelot Toppyn, bookseller, *q.v.*, and his wife died in 1654. One of his daughters married James Fletcher or Flesher, son of Miles Fletcher or Flesher, and another married Nathaniel Hooke, bookseller, *q.v.* Cornelius Bee died on January 2nd, 167½, and was buried at Great St. Bartholomew. [Smyth, *Obituary*, p. 93.]

BEESLEY (WILLIAM), (?) bookseller in London; Charles Street, Covent Garden, near the Peates (?) 1641. His name occurs on the imprint to a pamphlet entitled *Beaten Oyle for the lamps of the Sanctuarie.* [E. 163 (14).]

BELL (HENRY), bookseller and printer (?) in London, 1660–61. There were two booksellers in London of this name during the seventeenth century. The earlier one is believed to have died about 1639 or 1640. The name of the second is found on the title-page of a work on the life and death of Charles I, called the *Royal Martyr*, published in 1660. [B. M. Gren, 3544.] He was also associated with Peter Lilliecrap, the printer, *q.v.*, in issuing a theological pamphlet called the *Female Duel*, by T. Toll, in 1661. [B.M., E. 1813 (2).] His address has not been found.

BELL (JANE), bookseller and printer in London; East end of Christchurch, 1650–59. Succeeded Moses Bell. Printer of popular literature such as *Amadis de Gaul* and *Reynard the Fox*. Hazlitt notes an edition of *Sir P. Sidney's Ourania* printed by her in 1655 with a curious list of books. [Hazlitt, i. 30.] Most of her type was old.

BELL (MOSES), bookseller and printer in London; neere Christ-Church [Newgate Street], 1628–48. Took up his freedom July 25th, 1624. [Arber, iii. 685.] Started as a bookseller with Henry Bell, possibly a brother, who died about 1639. He was also associated with Benj. Green, *q.v.*, in 1632. Henry and Moses Bell assigned over all their copies to John Haviland and John Wright, sen., on September 4th, 1638. [Arber, iv. 434.] After this, Moses Bell began printing on his own account. He died about 1649, and was succeeded by Jane Bell, *q.v.*, probably his widow.

BELLAMY, or BELLAMIE (JOHN), bookseller in London, (1) South entrance, Royal Exchange; (2) Two Greyhounds, Cornhill; (3) Three Golden Lyons, Cornhill. 1620–54. A noted publisher of Americana. A native of Oundle, in Northamptonshire. [Price, J. *The City Remonstrance Remonstrated*. 1646. E. 345 (18).] He served his apprenticeship with Nicholas Bourne, stationer, *q.v.*, and took up his freedom in February, 1620. For some time afterwards he continued to work for Bourne, and several books, including Richard Braithwaite's volume of verse entitled *Time's Curtaine Drawne*, bear Bellamy's name as publisher, but were sold at Bourne's shop. Some time during the year 1622 he set up for himself at the Two Greyhounds in Cornhill, and began to publish books relating to New England. The first was *A Sermon preached at Plymouth in New England Dec. 9th 1621. Together with a preface shewing the state of the contree, and condicon of the inhabitants,* which he entered on the Register on March 22nd, 162½, and published shortly afterwards. In the same year he also published Patrick Copland's *Virginia's God be thanked, a sermon of thanksgiving for the happie successe of the affayres in Virginia ; A Brief Relation of the Discovery and Plantation of New England, and The Relation or Journal of the beginning and proceedings of the English Plantation settled at Plymouth in New England,* edited by G. Mourt. In 1623 he moved to his third address, and from there issued *Good Newes from New England .... Written by E. W.,* which bore the date 1624 on the title-page. In 1630 he published *The humble request of his Majesties loyal subiects the Governor & the Company late gone to New England, to the rest of their brethren in and of the Church of England,* and very shortly afterwards the Rev. J. Cotton's sermon, *Gods promise to his plantation.* Bellamy also published William Wood's *New Englands Prospect,* 1634, 1635, and 1639; Governor Winslow's *Hypocrisie Unmasked ....* 1646; Thomas Hooker's *Survey of the summe of Church Discipline,* 1648; John Cotton's *The Way of Congregational Churches Cleared,* 1648, and Thomas Sheppard's *Clear Sunshine of the Gospel,* 1648. John Bellamy took an active part in the political and religious controversies of the time. On the outbreak of the Civil War he took up arms for the Parliament and was given the rank of colonel. He also represented the Ward of Cornhill on the Common Council, and when the split took place between the Presbyterians and Independents he published *The humble Remonstrance and Petition of the Lord Mayor Aldermen & Commons of the City of London,* which was printed for him by Richard Cotes in 1646. This led him into a pamphlet war with the opposite party, and he wrote *A Vindication of the humble remonstrance,* and in answer to a further attack, *A Justification of the City Remonstrante and its Vindication.* [B.M. E. 350 (23).] In these pamphlets are some interesting biographical details concerning the publisher. Bellamy appears to have retired from business about 1650, and settled at Cotherstock, or Cotterstock, in his native county of Northamptonshire, where he died about January 20th, 165⅔. By his will, which was dated January 14th, 165⅔, he left the bulk of his property to his brothers and sisters and their children. Special mention was made of his house and two shops in St. Paul's Churchyard, London, one of which, the White Lion, was then in the occupation of Philemon Stephens, stationer, *q.v.,* and he bequeathed a certain number of books to form a standing library for the ministers of Cotherstock. The will was proved on February 7th, 165⅔. [P.C.C. 92, Alchin.]

BELLINGER (JOHN), bookseller in London; Cliffords Inn Lane in Fleet Street, 1642–78. Son of William Bellinger, citizen and girdler of London; apprenticed on August 24th, 1642, to Humphrey Tuckey, *q.v.*, for eight years. [Stationers' Register of Apprenticeships.]

BENINGTON (EDWARD), bookseller (?) at Oxford, 1647. A pamphlet entitled: *A Gallant speech spoken by His Highness James Duke of York* [E. 399 (37)] has the imprint, "Printed at Oxford for Edward Benington, for the publike use of Great Brittain, Anno 1647." This appears to be one of the pamphlets printed by John Harris, *q.v.*, and to which he added names that cannot be identified as stationers. The Thomason copy of this pamphlet is apparently incomplete and mis-bound with a portion of another.

BENSON (JOHN), bookseller in London, (1) St. Dunstan's Churchyard, Fleet Street, 1641; (2) Chancery Lane. 1635–6?. Was chiefly a publisher of ballads and broadsides. In 1647 he was associated with John Saywell, *q.v.*, in the publication of Francis Quarles' *Hosanna, or Divine poems on the Passion of Christ*, which was entered on May 29th, 1647. [Stat. Reg., Liber F, p. 95.] In 1651 he began to issue music books in partnership with John Playford, *q.v.* He died on January 23rd, 166?. [Smyth's *Obituary*, p. 73.]

BENTLEY (WILLIAM), printer in London; Finsbury, 1646–56. This printer is first heard of in 1646, when the Westminster Assembly of Divines proposed the issue of a new and cheap edition of the Bible. As no printer in London except Bentley would undertake the work, it was given to him, whereupon the Company of Stationers immediately issued an order that "no journeyman printer of the company who should work at the printing house in Finsbury should ever have any gift or pension whatsoever from the company." In the Act of 1649, and that of 1652, this printing house was specially mentioned as being exempt from their provisions, but, nevertheless, Bentley met with strong opposition from Hills and Field, who claimed the exclusive right of Bible printing as successors to Robert Barker and his assigns. In November, 1656, Bentley printed a broadside entitled *The Case of William Bentley printer at Finsbury . . . . touching his right to the printing of Bibles and Psalms* [B.M. 669, f. 20 (24)], in which he undertook to furnish octavo Bibles with marginal notes better printed and corrected than any other edition at two shillings per volume as against the official price of 4s. 6d. He further stated that he had already finished five several editions. Two of these, dated 1646 and 1648, are amongst those in the collection of the British and Foreign Bible Society. In 1659 William Kilburne wrote a pamphlet entitled *Dangerous errors in several late printed Bibles*, which was printed at the Finsbury press, and was clearly written as a puff. *See* FIELD (JOHN).

BERRIMAN (THOMAS), bookseller (?) in London; Great St. Bartholomews, 1642. *Exceeding Joyfull Newes from the Earl of Bedford*, 1642 [E. 113 (17)] has the imprint, "London printed, for Thomas Berriman dwelling in Great St. Bartholomew, August 23, 1642."

BEST (JOHN), printer in London; Three Crowns, Giltspur Street, 1660–65. A printer of broadsides, ballads, and popular literature. In 1664 he printed for William Crook *The History of the Life and Martyrdom of St. George* . . . . by Thomas Lowick, gent. ; Geo. Swinnock's *Christian-Man's-Calling*, 1663–65, and a broadside, *The King's Majestys Love to London* [*London's modest answer*]. [B.M. C. 20 f. 2 (60).]

BEST (RICHARD), bookseller in London; Gray's Inn, Holborn, 1640–53. Took up his freedom March 30th, 1640. [Arber, iii. 688.] He dealt chiefly in political pamphlets and law books, but amongst them is found Jo. Tatham's *Fancies Theatre*, 1640.

BIARD (JOHN), bookseller (?) in London, 1643. This name occurs in the imprint to a political squib, printed without date, but probably in 1643, *A Brief Dialogue between Zelotophit . . . . and Superstition . . . . London. Printed for John Biard*. [E. 140 (5).]

BILCLIFFE (JOSEPH), bookseller in London; Great Piazza, Covent Garden, 1661–63. Mentioned in "Mercurius Publicus" for April, 1661, as agent for certain "lozenges." He was also an agent for the receipt of letters for the Postmaster-General, but from a notice that appears in *Mercurius Publicus* of June 18th, 1663, he seems to have abused his trust.

BILL (JOHN), the First, Assigns of (1630–60). In his will, proved on May 12th, 1630, John Bill made especial mention of James Burrage, and desired him to continue the same employment in the printing office he then had. He also mentions a William Garrett. But there is no evidence that these were the assigns referred to. One of his executors was Martin Lucas, who, with Robert Barker, was fined £300 for leaving the word "not" out of the seventh commandment in the edition of the Bible printed in 1632, but Lucas was not a printer. In all probability the real printers and assigns were Miles Fletcher, John Haviland, and Robert Young, who controlled so many of the London printing houses at that time.

BILL (JOHN), the Second, printer in London; (?) Hunsdon House, Blackfriars, 1630–80 (?). The son of John Bill, the King's Printer, who died in 1630, and who by his will left all his estate and terme in his part of the King's Printing Office to his son. During the Commonwealth, Henry Hills, and John Field, q.v., were appointed printers to the State, and it was said that John Bill the second and Christopher Barker the third, q.v., sold to them the manuscript copy of the last translation of the Bible. On the Restoration, Christopher Barker the third and John Bill the second were restored to the position of King's Printers. John Bill the second continued to enjoy his share of the profits of the office during his lifetime, and his successors till the end of the Stuart period. [Plomer, *Wills*, p. 53 ; *Library*, N.S., October, 1901, pp. 353–75.]

BIRD (HENRY), bookseller (?) in London, 1641. His name is given as one of the "better sort of freemen" of the Stationers' Company, in a list of those who had paid their respective proportions of the poll tax on August 5th, 1641. [*Domestic State Papers*, Charles I, vol. 483, 11.]

BIRD (THEOPHILUS), bookseller in London, 1656. Associated with A. Penneycuicke in publishing Ford and Decker's masque, *The Sun's Darling*, 1656. His name appears at the end of the Epistle Dedicatory.

BISHOP (GEORGE), printer in London; (?) Warwick Court, Warwick Lane, 1641–44. In partnership with Robert White, q.v. Their work included the following news-sheets : *Certaine Informations from several parts of the kingdom*, 1643; *Kingdoms Weekly Intelligence*, 1643, and *Mercurius Britanicus*.

BISHOP (RICHARD), printer in London; St. Peter's Pauls Wharf, 1631–53. Took up his freedom March 29th, 1637, having in 1634 bought the business of William Stansby, printer, for £700. According to Sir John Lambe's Memoranda [Arber, iii. 700, etc.] this was originally John Day's business, being subsequently divided up between Peter Short and John Windet, Stansby having bought Windet's share.

BISSE (JOHN), bookseller in London; Bell in St. Paul's Churchyard, 1649–53. Only known through the entry in Smyth's *Obituary*, p. 35: "July 6. [1653] John Bisse, bookseller, died."

BLACKLOCK, *see* Blaiklock.

BLACKMORE (EDWARD), bookseller in London, (1) Blazing-Starre, St. Paul's Churchyard, 1620; (2) South door of Paul's Church; (3) Angel, St. Paul's Churchyard. 1618–58. Dealt chiefly in popular literature, such as Melton's *Astrologaster*, 1620, which contains his Blazing-Star address. He died September 8th, 1658. [Smyth's *Obituary*, p. 48.] The *Weekly Intelligencer* of November 25th, 1651, contains advertisements of two books issued by him.

BLADEN (WILLIAM), bookseller in London; Great North-doore of Pauls at the sign of the Bible, 1612–24; address unknown, 1640–42; printer in Dublin, 1630–63. First met with in 1612 as a bookseller in London in partnership with John Royston. In 1618 certain stationers of London formed themselves into a society "to trade in the city of Dublin by vending and selling of books and other commodities . . . . to be transported out of England thither, and there to be sold," the books stocked for this purpose being known as the Irish "stock." They appointed William Bladen their factor in Dublin. He was admitted to the Franchise of the city in January, 16⅜, by special grace and on payment of a fine of £10 English money. In April, 1637, he was elected Sheriff for the following year. Meanwhile the trading venture of the London stationers had turned out a failure, and the partnership was dissolved in 1639, when William Bladen bought the stock for £2,600. His name first appears in imprints in 1641. In 1647 he filled the office of Lord Mayor of Dublin, and during the Commonwealth he acted as State Printer. His death took place in Dublin, in July, 1663, and he was buried on August 1st in St. Werburgh's Churchyard. Bladen's will was proved in the Prerogative

Court in August, 1663. His wife, " Elinor," was the principal beneficiary. He directed all his stock in his shop, printing house, and warehouse, both in Dublin and in London, together with his interest in his then dwelling-house and printing house, to be sold unto some person having served 7 years to a printer, stationer or bookseller. He mentions his "son, Dr. Thos. Bladen." Probably this was the editor of Clarke's *Praxis*. He also left a son of the same name, who is believed to have come to London and set up as a bookseller. [Information supplied by Mr. E. R. McC. Dix.; *Library*, July, 1907.]

BLAGRAVE (ROBERT), bookseller at Oxford, 1656–62. Son of John and Lydia Blagrave. His will was proved 1662. His imprint is found in Caius' *Suetonius Tranquilus*. [Information supplied by Mr. Madan.]

BLAGUE (JOHN), bookseller in London, (1) Pope's Head Alley, 1652; (2) Golden Ball in Cornhill, near the Poultry, 1652. 1642–52. John Blague, son of Benjamin Blague, barber-surgeon of London, apprenticed on October 30th, 1642, to John Burroughes for eight years. [Stationers' Registers, Apprenticeships.] Partner with Samuel Howes, *q.v.* They published jointly H. Whitfield's *Strength out of Weakness* . . . . 1652, and Phillip Barrough's *Method of Physick*, 1652.

BLAIKLOCK, or BLACKLOCK (JOSEPH), bookseller in London. Turk's Head, Ivy Lane, 1639–60. Took up his freedom April 29th, 1639. [Arber, iii. 688.] Chiefly a publisher of theological literature. He issued in 1651 an edition of the *Imitatio Christi* under the title of *The Christian's Pattern* [Harl. 5927, 501.] His name is found in the imprint to C. Ducket's *Sparks from the Golden Altar*, 1660.

BLAIKLOCK, BLAKELOCK, or BLACKLOCK (LAWRENCE), bookseller in London, (1) Sugar Loaf next [near] Temple Bar; (2) Middle-Temple-Gate. 1638–53. Took up his freedom March 5th, 1638. [Arber, iii. 688.] Amongst his publications were Fr. Beaumont's *Poems*, 1652; W. Bosworth's *Chaste and lost lovers*, 1651, and H. Mill's *Poems*, 1639. During the Civil War, in company with Fr. Coles, and Lawrence Chapman, he printed a news-sheet called the *Perfect Diurnall of some passages in Parliament*, 1643–49. The last heard of him is in 1653, when he issued a law book, Young, W., *A Vade Mecum, etc.*

BLAKELOCK, *see* **Blaiklock.**

BLOME (JACOB), bookseller in London; Knight Rider Street, 1619–61. Took up his freedom March 26th, 1618. [Arber, iii. 688.] Was originally in partnership with George Edwards, but on June 4th, 1621, they assigned over their copies to Geo. Hodges. [Arber, iv. 54.] In 1631 Blome obtained from Ralph Mabb the copyright of Guillim's *Display of Heraldry*, but he does not seem to have re-issued it until 1660.

BLUNDEN (HUMPHREY), bookseller in London; Castle in Cornhill, 1635–52. Took up his freedom June 15th, 1635. [Arber, iii. 688.] Before the Civil War he is found publishing plays and books of a popular character. In 1639 he issued Robert Davenport's comedy, *New Trick to cheat the Devill;* and in 1640 J. Johnson's *Academy of Love*. During the Civil War he issued a large number of political pamphlets, and was associated with John Partridge in the publication of many of the writings of William Lilly, the astrologer. But his chief claim to notice at that period was as editor of a news-sheet called *Speciall Passages and certain informations from several places*, the first number of which appeared on August 16th, 1642. It became popularly known as "Blunden's Passages" [*Mercurius Civicus*, June 8th, 1643.] Nothing more is heard of him after 1652.

BOAT (MARMADUKE), bookseller in London, 1642. Took up his freedom August 4th, 1640. [Arber, iii, 688.] Associated with Andrew Coe in publishing *Master Pyms Speech in Parliament* [March 17th], 1641. 4°. [B.M. E. 200 (37)], and *Master Hollis his Speech in Parliament*, March 21st, 1642. His address has not been found.

BODDINGTON (GEORGE), bookseller in London; In Chancery lain neer Serjants-Inn. 1648. His name is found on the imprint to James Beaumont's *Psyche or Loves Mysterie*, a poem printed in folio by John Dawson in 1648.

BODVELL or BODRELL (PETER), bookseller in London and Chester. 1664–70. Was apprenticed to Thomas Brewster, *q.v.*, and was one of the witnesses at his trial in February, 1664. [See *An Exact Narrative*, B.M. 1132, b. 57.] He is mentioned again in some Chancery proceedings brought by the Stationers' Company against certain Chester booksellers in the year 1699. John Minshull, one of the defendants, stated that he was apprenticed to a London bookseller, Mr. Peter Bodrell or Bodvell, who was burnt out in the great fire of 1666, and then removed to Chester, where he died before John Minshull's term of apprenticeship was complete. [*Library*, 2nd Series, No. 16, pp. 373-83.] Peter Bodrell was associated with Edward Fowkes or Foulkes, *q.v.*, in publishing the Book of Common Prayer in the Welsh tongue in 1664. [Rowlands, *Cambrian Bibliography*, p. 191.] There is a memorial to a Peter Bodvell in St. Michael's Church, Chester (*see* Fenwick's *History of Chester*, 1896, p. 316).

BOLER (JAMES), bookseller in London; Marygold in Fleet Street, 1641-49. Son of James Boler, who died in 1634. [Arber, iv. 435.] Published a book on needlework called *The Needles Excellency*, 1640, and his imprint is found in a pamphlet entitled *Humble Advice . . . . of certaine ministers . . . . of Banbury . . . . Oxon and of Brackly . . . . Northampton.* 1649. 4°.

BOND (WILLIAM), bookseller (?) in London, 1641-2. Several political pamphlets issued in the years 1641 and 1642 have the imprint: "London, Printed for W. Bond," but his address is not given. He may possibly have been a relative of Charles or John Bond, stationers, of London. [Arber, iii. 685, 687; E. 131 (9); E. 181 (32).]

BOSTOCK (ROBERT), bookseller in London, (1) King's Head, St. Paul's Churchyard; (2) St. Faith's, Southwark, 1650. 1629-58. Took up his freedom December 5th, 1625 [Arber, iii. 686], and appears to have dealt chiefly in theological literature. During the Civil War he took an active part on behalf of the Parliament, and was appointed by the Committee of Sequestrations one of its Treasurers. At this time he was busily engaged in the publication of political pamphlets, one of the most noted of which is undoubtedly *The Kings Cabinet Opened*, consisting of the Royalist papers that were captured at the battle of Naseby. In 1645, and again in 1646, he was in trouble for publishing pamphlets relating to the disputes between England and Scotland. [*Domestic State Papers*, Charles I, vol. 510, 125; vol. 513, 30, 39; Hist. MS. Comm., 6th Report, App., pp. 111], and on June 5th, 1650, he was bound over in £500 not to print seditious pamphlets. [*Domestic State Papers*, 1650.] He died suddenly in the street at Banbury on December 11th, 1656 [Smyth, *Obituary*, p. 43], and his copyrights, fifty-four in number, were transferred to George Thomason. [Stationers' Company Registers, Liber F, p. 23.]

BOULTER (ROBERT), bookseller in London, (1) Turk's Head in Cornhill, 1666 ; (2) Turk's Head in Bishopsgate Street, near the Great James, 1667. Was one of the three publishers of the first edition of Milton's *Paradise Lost*, 1667. The first imprint given above is found on the title-page of one of the Rev. T. Doolittle's treatises on the great plague published in 1666, and the second in an edition of Sir Walter Raleigh's *Judicious and select Essays*, published by him in 1667.

BOURDEN, *see* Burden.

BOURKE (THOMAS), printer at Waterford and Kilkenny, Ireland, 1643-48. The authorised official printer of the Catholic Confederation. Sir J. T. Gilbert describes him as a "native printer." In 1643 he is found at Waterford, where he continued until 1645, when he appears to have moved to Kilkenny, where in that year was printed Henry Burkhead's *A tragedy of Cola's Furie, or Lirenda's Miserie*, of which there is a unique copy in the British Museum. The books that came from the Kilkenny press bore no printer's name, but Bourke's name is found on a broadside printed there entitled *Declaration by the Confederate Catholics' Council*, 1648. [*Library*, N.S., October, 1901. *Irish Provincial Printing*, by E. R. McC. Dix.]

BOURNE (NICHOLAS), bookseller in London ; South entrance, Royal Exchange [Cornhill], 1601-57. Son of Henry Bourne, citizen and cordwainer of London, put himself apprentice to Cuthbert Burby, bookseller, for seven years from March 25th, 1601. Burby died between August 24th and September 16th, 1607, and by his will left Nicholas Bourne the offer of his stock on favourable terms and gave him the lease of the premises in Cornhill in consideration of his true and faithful service. Mistress Burby assigned over her late husband's copyrights to Nicholas Bourne on October 16th, 1609. These consisted mainly of theological works, and we have it on the evidence of John Bellamy, *q.v.*, one of his apprentices, that he would not allow them to sell play-books [see *A Justification of the City Remonstrance and its Vindication*, E. 350. (23).] Nicholas Bourne was Master of the Company in 1643 and again in 1651. He died in 1657. [Plomer, *Wills*, p. 42.] A list of 58 books, etc., printed for him occurs at the end of Robert Witbie's *Popular Errours*, 1651, 8°. [B.M. E. 1227.] It contains a few works relating to English trade and fishery rights.

BOURNE (THOMAS), bookseller in London; Bedlam [*i.e.*, Bethlehem
Hospital], 1628–71. Took up his freedom January 15th, 1623. [Arber,
iii. 685.] Smyth in his *Obituary*, p. 91, thus records the death of this
bookseller " 19 June 1671. Thomas Bourne bookseller at Bedlam (my
old acquaintance) died hora 8 p^t merid. ; his corps carried from Lorimer's
Hall to Bottol. Bishopsgate, Thurs., June 22, and there buried, with the
service of the common prayer, though he died a recusant." The only book
in which his name has been found is an edition of the *Articles of
Visitation of the Bishop of Chichester*, in the year 1628. [B.M. 5155, c. 13.]

BOWDEN (WILLIAM), bookseller (?) in London, 1641. His name occurs
in the imprints to several political pamphlets of the year 1641 ; but none
of them give his address [E. 181 (1).]

BOWEN (PENYELL), bookseller (?) in London. Only known from the
record of his death in Smyth's *Obituary*, p. 91. "Penyall Bowen, stationer,
once apprentice to Octavian Pulleyn, sen., bookseller in St. Paul's
Churchyard, dying of a veyne broken was buried at St. Butolph's without
Aldersgate."

BOWLER (J.), *see* Boler (J.).

BOWMAN (FRANCIS), bookseller and printer (?) in Oxford and London,
1634–47. Published books in Oxford between 1634 and 1640. He is
believed to have left Oxford about the year 1641. Several books are found
printed in London in 1647 by *F. B.* These initials are found in G. Pretis'
Oranta the Cyprian Virgin ; Thomas Stanley's *Poems and Translations*,
and also in Sir Robert Stapylton's *Musaeus or the loves of Hero and Leander*.
The copyright of this last work belonged in the first place to Henry Hall,
printer at Oxford, and was transferred by him on March 4th, 164⅘, to
Humphrey Moseley. There is no other printer or bookseller in London
at that date to whose name the initials apply, and the probability is that
the printer of these books was Francis Bowman. [F. Madan, *Early Oxford
Press*, pp. 278, 306, 313.]

BOWMAN (THOMAS), bookseller (?) of Oxford, 1664. Had a son, Thomas
Bowman. Mentioned in a lease of property in Oxfordshire, dated 1664.

BOWTELL (STEPHEN), bookseller in London; Bible in Pope's Head Alley, 1643–64. Amongst his publications, which were chiefly of a political character, was a curious piece of Americana from the pen of Nathaniel Ward, under the pseudonym of Theodore de la Guard, entitled *The simple Cobbler of Aggawam in America* . . . . 1647. 4°.

BOYDELL (ROBERT), bookseller in London. In the Bulwarke neere the Tower, 1650–55. His name is found on the following work: Foster, N. *Briefe Relation of the late Horrid Rebellion*, 1650, and his death is recorded in Smyth's *Obituary*, p. 40, "March 16, 165⅚, Mr. Boyden, bookseller, by yᵉ Tower died."

BRADFORD (NEHEMIAH), (?) bookseller in London, 1659. Only known from the imprint to a pamphlet entitled *Dialogue between Riches, etc.* London. Printed for Nehemiah Bradford, MDCLIX. [E. 999 (2).]

BRADLEY (DANIEL), (?) bookseller in London, 1642. His name is found on the imprints to several political tracts and broadsides of the year 1642. He may have been related to the George and John Bradley, stationers, who took up their freedom on December 1st, 1628, and September 15th, 1631. [Arber, iii. 686.]

BREACH (   ), Mrs., bookseller in London; Westminster Hall, "at the foot of the stone stairs going up to the Court of Requests," 1649–75. Was associated in 1649 with Thomas Banks, *q.v.*, who also kept a stall in the Hall, at the sign of the Seal, in publishing the Rev. John Cotton's *Controversie concerning libertie of conscience*, 1649. In 1675 she was in trouble for selling a pamphlet entitled *A Letter from a Person of Quality to his Friend in the Country*. One of the witnesses described Mrs. Breach as a fat woman. She must have been a familiar figure in the Hall throughout the Civil War, Commonwealth and the Restoration. [*Hist. MSS. Comm.*, 9th Report App. p. 66a; *Lords' Journals*, vol. xiii. 17; *Library*, N.S., No. 24, pp. 380–390.]

BREWSTER (A   ), bookseller in London; Three Bibles at the West end of St. Paul's, 1666–81. Appears to have succeeded Thomas Brewster, at this address.

BREWSTER (EDWARD), bookseller in London, (1) The Star, West end of
Paul's, 1621–3; (2) The Great West Door of St. Paul's, 1624; (3) The
Bible near the North door of Paul's, 1627–34; (4) Bible in Paul's Churchyard, 1635; (5) Bible on Fleet Bridge, 1640–47. Dealt exclusively in theological books. Treasurer of the English Stock of the Company of Stationers
from 1639 to 1647. Under date October 7th, 1647, Smyth in his *Obituary*,
p. 24, states "Mr. Brewster, stationer, buried." He left a son Edward.

BREWSTER (EDWARD), bookseller in London; Crane in St. Paul's
Churchyard, 1654–99. Son of the preceding. Master of the Company of
Stationers, 1689–92. [Arber, v. lxvi.] A list of books published by him in
1655 will be found in S. Birckbek's *Treatise of the four last things.*
[E. 1460 (2).]

BREWSTER (THOMAS), bookseller in London, (1) Three Bibles under
Mildred's Church in the Poultry, 1649; (2) Three Bibles in Paul's Churchyard, 1659. 1649–64. What relation, if any, this bookseller was to the
two preceding has not been discovered. In company with Giles Calvert
and Henry Hills he was appointed official printer to the Council of State
on the accession of Cromwell, but he only held the appointment until the
end of 1653, after which the name of Henry Hills is found alone or in
conjunction with John Field, *q.v.* Thomas Brewster had as partner for a
short time G. Moule, *q.v.* In 1654 he published an edition of the Bible in
Welsh. [Ballinger, *Bible in Wales*, p. 10.] In 1664, in company with Simon
Dover and Nathan Brooks, he was tried at the Old Bailey for having caused
to be printed two pamphlets, the one entitled *The Speeches of some of the late
King's Justices;* the other, *The Phœnix of the Solemn League and Covenant.*
One of the witnesses against him was his servant, Peter Bodvell, *q.v.*
Brewster was condemned to pay a fine of 100 marks and to stand in the
pillory on two days. [*An Exact Narrative of the Tryal . . . . of John Twyn,*
etc. 1664.] In a note in *The Newes* of April 28th, 1664, he is said to
have died shortly afterwards. A list of books on sale by Thomas Brewster
occurs at the end of Robert Purnell's *Little Cabinet*, 1657. [E. 1575.] It
consists mainly of theological books and pamphlets against the Quakers.

BRIDGES, BRUGES, or BRUGIS (HENRY), printer in London; Sir John
Oldcastle, Py-Corner, 1660–83. He is mentioned in a list of booksellers,
printers, and stationers against whom search warrants were granted in 1664

[*Domestic State Papers*, Charles II, vol. 99, 165] and again as a printer in the survey of the press made on July 24th, 1668, but the number of his presses is not given. [Plomer, *Short History of English Printing*, pp. 224, 225.] In 1670 the Company of Stationers ordered that his press and materials should be defaced, and himself indicted for printing a Popish book entitled *Think well on't*. [Records of the Stationers' Company.] The name of Michael Brugis is found in the imprint to a political tract of the Commonwealth period.

BRIGGS (PHILIP), bookseller in London, (1) Dolphin, St. Paul's Church-yard, between the two north doores, 1655; (2) Mermaid Court near Amen Corner, Pater-Noster Row, 1671. 1655-72. His name is found on Edmond Ellis's *Dia Poemata*, 1655. Peter Lilliecrap, *q.v.*, printed several things for him. [Hazlitt, H. 183, ii. 585, iii. 30, ii. 260.]

BROAD (ALICE), printer at York; Stonegate over against the Star, 1660-67. Widow of Thomas Broad. Printed several books for Francis Mawbarn, *q.v.*

BROAD (THOMAS), printer at York, (1) At Mistris Rogers house on Stone-gate, over againste the Starre, 1644; (2) In Stone-Gate over against the Starre, 1644; (3) Near Common-Hail Gate, 1649-60. On the occupation of the City of York by the Parliament's army, Thomas Broad was appointed printer in the place of Stephen Bulkey. His death took place about 1660, when he was succeeded by his widow, Alice Broad.

BROCAS (ABISHA), bookseller in Exeter, 1655-74. Mentioned in an advertisement of patent medicines in the "Newes" in 1663. Published the following books: Tickell (J.), *Sum and substance of religion*, a broadside, 1655 [816. m. 22 (28)]; Fullwood (F.), *General Assembly*, 1667.

BROCKLEBANK (RALPH), bookseller in York; In the Minster Yard, 1647. Only known from the imprint to a tract entitled *An Answer to the Poysonous Sedicious Paper of Mr. David Jenkins*, 1647, 4°, printed for him by Thomas Broad, of which there is a copy in the York Minster Library. [Davies, *Memoir of the York Press*, p. 79.] It was issued the same year in London by Robert Bostock.

R

BROME (HENRY), bookseller in London, (1) Hand, in Paul's Churchyard, 1657; (2) Gun, Ivy Lane, 1660–66; (3) Gun, St. Paul's Churchyard, or (4) Gun in Ludgate Street at the West End of Paul's, 1669; (5) Star, Little Britain, 1666–69. Publisher of broadsides, poems, plays, and general literature. According to the best authorities he was in no way related to Alexander or Richard Brome, the playwrights, though he published the works of both of them, and wrote a preface to Richard Brome's play *The Queens Exchange*. A list of 42 works published by him in 1664 will be found at the end of the *Songs and Poems* of Alex. Brome, which he published in that year. Another list for the year 1667 was issued with Sir P. Rycant's *Present State of the Ottoman Empire*, of which there is a unique copy—once belonging to Samuel Pepys—in Magdalene College, Cambridge. The date of his death is unknown, but he left a son, Henry, who succeeded him in business.

BROOKE (NATHANIEL), bookseller in London, (1) Angel, Cornhill; (2) At the Angel, in the second yard going into the Exchange from Bishopsgate Street. 1646–77. This bookseller must not be confused with Nathan Brooks, who was tried and convicted at the Old Bailey in 1664 for publishing seditious books. An extensive list of Nathaniel Brooke's publications will be found in Gray's Index to Hazlitt.

BROOKE (SAMUEL), bookseller in London, 1661. Hazlitt records the three following works as bearing this bookseller's name: *Catalogue of Peeres of the Realm*, 1661; Will. Ramsay, *Man's Dignity*, 1661; *Perfect List of the Knights*, 1661; none of which appear to be in the British Museum. [Hazlitt, ii. 86, 511; iii. 188.]

BROOKE (WILLIAM), bookseller in London; Black Swan Inne Yard in Holborn, 1661. Publisher of a curious romance entitled *The Princess Gloria or the Royal Romance*, 1661, the unsold copies of which were reissued in 1665 by Edward Man.

BROOKS (NATHAN) (?) bookseller in London; Bunhill near Moor Fields, next door to the Feathers, 1664. Must not be confused with Nathaniel Brooke, bookseller. He was perhaps the Nathan Brookes, son of Edward Brookes, of Onelip, co. Leicester, who was apprenticed to Randall Taylor for 8 years from March 25th, 1650. [Stationers' Register of Apprenticeships, 1605–66.] Nathan Brooks was tried and convicted with Thomas Brewster, and Simon Dover, in 1664, for publishing seditious books. In the indictment he is described as a "bookbinder" of Moorfields, but was found guilty of publishing the books. He was condemned to stand in the pillory at the Exchange and in Smithfield on two successive days, and to be confined during his Majesty's pleasure. [*An Exact Narrative of the Trial of J. Twyn* .... 1664.] His address appears in the *Domestic State Papers*, Charles II, vol. 113 (7).

BROUN (SAMUEL), *see* Browne (Samuel).

BROWN (JAMES), printer in Aberdeen, 1650–61; "Market Place at the Townes Armes." Son of William Brown, Minister of Innernochtie. Succeeded Raban, in 1650, occupying the same house, and was appointed printer to the Town and University. Died July, 1661. Succeeded by John Forbes. [H. G. Aldis, *List of books printed in Scotland before 1700*, p. 109.]

BROWN (P.), (?) bookseller in London, 1656. Is only known from the imprint to the first edition of the Rev. Henry Beesley's collection of sermons entitled, Ψυχομαχία, *or the Soules Conflict* .... 1656, of which the title-page is preserved in the Ames Collection, No. 2553. His place of business is not given.

BROWN, or BROUN (ROBERT), stationer in Edinburgh; The Sun, on the north side of the street, over against the Cross, 1649–85 (?). Probably the Robert Brown, "my prenteiss," to whom Robert Crombie, *q.v.*, in 1645 left his "best stand of cloaths." One of the six booksellers who in 1671 successfully appealed to the Privy Council against Anderson's attempted enforcement of his monopoly. His will was registered May 7th, 1685. [H. G. Aldis, *List of Books printed in Scotland before 1700*, Edin. Bibl. Soc. Publ., 1905, p. 109.] *See also* Swintoun (G.) and R. Brown.

BROWNE (JOHN), bookseller in London; Guilded Acorn in Paul's Church-yard, 1652–61 (?). According to Hazlitt (iii. 43) he was the publisher of the Rev. Samuel Clarke's *Martyrologie . . . of England*, 1652, folio; Hazlitt had apparently seen a copy of this work, as he gives the collation, but no copy of it appears to be in any of our national libraries. Browne was afterwards in partnership with William Miller.

BROWNE (SAMUEL), bookseller and printer in London and at the Hague.
(1) Fountain, St. Paul's Churchyard, 1639; (2) St. Paul's Churchyard, at
the sign of the White Lyon and Ball, 1641–43; (3) Hage.   Samuel
Browne English bookeseller dwelling in the Achter-Om at the signe
of the English Printing Press, 1643–60; (4) At the sign of the Queen's
Arms near the little north door of St. Paul's Church, 1661–65.   (1638–65.)
Took up his freedom June 3rd, 1633. [Arber, iii. 687], his first registered
publication being an edition of Herodian's *History of Greece* in Greek and
Latin, entered on February 3rd, 163⅞.   At the outbreak of the Civil War,
having strong royalist sympathies, he left the country and settled at the
Hague, where he printed and published much royalist literature, including
an edition of the *Eikon Basilike* in 1649, Jeremy Taylor's *Martyrdom of
King Charles*, 1649, and a broadside ballad entitled *Chipps of the Old
Block*, in 1659. [Lutt. Collection, ii. 40.]   Returning to England at the
Restoration, he settled at the sign of the Queen's Arms in St. Paul's
Churchyard, and in partnership with a Frenchman named John de l'Ecluse,
q.v., issued several French books.   He died of the plague in the autumn
of 1665, and Smyth, in his *Obituary*, p. 66, has the following notice of
him : "Aug⁴. 1665, Mr. Brown, once a bookseller at yᵉ Hague, who
married the daughter of Mr. Nath. Hall of yᵉ Exchequer, died at yᵉ Pest
House, ex peste, about this time."

BRUDENELL, or BRUDNELL (JOHN), printer in London; Maiden-
Head-Alley, near Newgate, 1660–66.   Appears to have succeeded Thomas
Brudenell.   He was ruined by the Fire of London. [Plomer, *Short
History*, p. 225.]

BRUDENELL or BRUDNELL (THOMAS), printer in London; Newgate
Market, 1621–60.   Is first heard of as partner with John Beale, in 1621.
[Arber, iii. 699–700.]   He afterwards set up for himself as a printer
in Newgate Market, taking as partner Robert White.   A feature of their
business was the printing of astrological works, this being one of the
few houses in London that stocked astrological signs.   They issued a
duodecimo edition of the Bible in 1647, and appear to have had an
extensive assortment of letter of varying merit, notably two founts of great
primer roman and italic used in the latter half of Sprigges' *Anglia Rediviva*,
which they printed in 1647.   In 1651 Thomas Brudenell brought an action

against the executors of John Partridge, a London bookseller, to recover a debt for printing various books, chiefly the writings of William Lilly, the titles, prices and quantities being set out at length. [*Library*, N.S., January, 1906.]

BRUGIS or BRUGES (HENRY), *see* Bridges (H.).

BRUISTER, *see* Brewster.

BRYSON (JAMES), printer in Edinburgh; a little above the Kirk Style at the signe of the Golden Angel, 1638–42. A bookseller who commenced printing in 1639 in succession to the heirs of A. Hart. He rented his house from Hart's widow. He was probably a relative of Robert Bryson, *q.v.* Died in April, 1642, his widow continued the bookselling business. Device: headpiece with I.B. in centre; and many of Hart's ornaments. Some of his ornaments were afterwards used by G. Lithgow and A. Anderson. [H. G. Aldis, *List of books printed in Scotland before 1700*, p. 110.] *See* also Bryson, R. and J.

BRYSON (ROBERT), printer in Edinburgh; at the signe of Jonah, 1637–45. A bookseller who commenced printing in 1640. Apparently had some connection with R. Young, *q.v.* His inventory discloses an extensive stock of books and the list of debtors includes several booksellers, among them "Mr. Cruik [Crooke] and Mr. Hope, buiksellars at Londone." Wife, Isobel Herring; children, Samuel, Isobel, Helen. Died 1645. Ornaments: tailpiece with monogram R.B. and several formerly in possession of Finlason and Young. [H. G. Aldis, *List of books printed in Scotland*, p. 110.]

BRYSON (Heirs of R.), booksellers in Edinburgh, 1646. Only known by the imprint of a book, No. 1241, in Mr. Aldis's *List of books printed in Scotland before 1700.*

BRYSON (R. and J.), printers in Edinburgh, 1641. Some official papers were printed (apparently by Robert Bryson) in their joint names in 1641, and at the end of that year, or in 1642, they petitioned unsuccessfully to have the recent appointment of Young and Tyler, *q.v.*, as King's Printers set aside in favour of themselves. [H. G. Aldis, *List of books printed in Scotland before 1700*, p. 110.]

BUCK (JOHN), printer and bookbinder at Cambridge, 1625–68.   One of the Esquire Bedells, was appointed printer December 16th, 1625, and was in partnership first with his brother, T. Buck and Leonard Green, and afterwards with T. Buck and Roger Daniel.   Although his name drops out of the imprints after 1635, he continued to have an interest in the printing office until 1668. [Camb. Antiq. Soc. Comm., vol. v, p. 304; Harl. MSS. 5929 (405).]

BUCK (THOMAS), printer and bookbinder at Cambridge, 1625–70.   Was appointed by Grace, July 13th, 1625.   He had several partners, including Leonard Greene, John Buck, Roger Daniel.   From 1640 to 1650 his name disappears from the imprints of Cambridge printed books, but in 1651–2 he appears to have become once more printer to the University for a brief space.   He is said to have resigned in 1653, but he continued to retain an interest in the office up to the time of his death in 1670.   The bindery of the brothers J. and T. Buck is distinguished for the beauty of its stamps, and the skill shown in decorative treatment.   Dr. Jebb, speaking of the remarkable bindings executed by the ladies of Little Gidding, says that "a Cambridge bookbinder's daughter that bound rarely " was engaged to teach them the art, and Mr. Cyril Davenport in an interesting article on the same subject shows the resemblance between the stamps used on Little Gidding books and those found on books bound by or for the Cambridge printers.   He concludes that the "bookbinder's daughter" came either from the University printers themselves, or from some Cambridge bindery which they patronised. [*Bibliographica*, Vol. II, pp. 129 *et seq.*]

BUCKLEY (S.), *see* Bulkley (Stephen).

BUCKNELL (THOMAS), bookseller (?) in London; Golden Lion, Duck Lane, 1651–52.   His name is found on Samuel Sheppard's *Epigrams: Theological, Philosophical and Romantick*, 1651.

BULKELEY, *see* Bulkley.

BULKLEY, BULKELEY, or BUCKLEY (STEPHEN), printer in London, York, Newcastle-on-Tyne, and Gateshead, 1639–80.   One of the sons of Joseph Bulkley, bookseller, of Canterbury.   He was apprenticed to a London printer, Adam Islip, for eight years from February 2nd (Candlemas Day), 163?, and took up his freedom February 4th, 1639.   Stephen

Bulkley then appears to have joined John Beale, *q.v.* Their initials are found in a book entitled *The Secretary in Fashion,* a translation by John Massinger, dated 1640. They also printed Lewis De Gand's *Sol Britannicus,* 1641, a pamphlet written in praise of King Charles, but in this instance Bulkley's name is printed Buckley, a mistake which also occurs in the spelling of the name in the Register of Apprenticeships at Stationers' Hall. In this same year, 1641, Stephen Bulkley printed for two London booksellers a book entitled *The Masse in Latin and English,* a translation by James Mountaine of Du Moulin's *Anatomie of the Masse,* of which three issues are known. Two political pamphlets have also been traced to Bulkley's London press, in consequence of which he was ordered to appear before the House of Commons as a delinquent, but fled to York, taking his press and letters with him. At York his first issue was Sir B. Rudyard's speech, which he printed on July 23rd, 1642. In 1646 he moved to Newcastle, where he remained till 1652; from thence he went to Gateshead, and it is said that during this time he was thrown into prison and plundered of his goods for his loyalty. He returned to Newcastle in 1659 and remained there till 1662, when he returned to York and set up his press in the parish of St. Michael le Belfrey. In 1666 he was in trouble for printing a book called *An Apology of the English Catholics.* In a letter to the Secretary of State written at this time, Bulkley is described as getting "but a poore livelyhood, a man well beloved amongst the ould cavaleers and an object of charity." He died in the month of February, 16⅚, and was succeeded in his printing house by his son John. [Register of Apprenticeships, Stationers' Hall; Davies' *History of the York Press; Domestic State Papers,* Charles II, vol. 175, 28; *Library,* January, 1907.]

BULL (JOHN), bookseller in London; Grub Street, 1624–43. Is first heard of in 1624, when he published Sir Henry Wotton's *Elements of Architecture.* Nothing more is heard of him until after 1640, when he appears to have dealt chiefly in political pamphlets and broadsides. [Gray's *Index to Hazlitt;* Bibl. Lindes, *Catalogue of Broadsides,* 19, 26.]

BURDEN, or BOURDEN (W.), bookseller in London; Cannon Street, near London Stone, 1657. Issued Henry Bold's volume of verse called *Wit a sporting in a pleasant Grove of New Fancies .... 1657.* 8°. [B.M. 11630, a. 24], also an edition of Jo. Tatham's *Fancies Theatre* under the title of *The Mirrour of Fancies,* 1657. [Hazlitt, H. 592.]

BURDET (SAMUEL), bookseller (?) in London, 1660. Only known from the imprint to a broadside entitled *The Phanaticks Plot Discovered* [August 9th], 1660. [B.M. f. 25 (67).]

BURROUGHS (JOHN), bookseller in London, (1) Golden Dragon neare the Inner Temple-Gate; (2) Next door to the King's Head in Fleet-Street. 1641–52. Associated with John Franke. They were chiefly publishers of theological and political pamphlets. John Burroughs was clerk to the Company of Stationers in 1652. [Arber, v. lxxv.]

BURTON (RICHARD), bookseller in London. (1) Horseshoe West Smithfield; (2) Horseshoe at the hospitall gate in Smithfield. 1641–74. Took up his freedom November 2nd, 1640. [Arber, iii. 688.] Chiefly a publisher of ballads. [Bibl. Lind. *Catalogue of a collection of English Ballads,* 45, 786, 821, 997.]

BURTON (SIMON), bookseller in London; Next the Mitre taverne, within Algate, 1640–41. Only known from the imprint to Richard Crashawe's *Visions or Hel's Kingdome,* a translation from the *Visions of Quevado.* Hazlitt records [iii. 62] another translation from the same author, under the title of *Hell Reformed,* issued by the same publisher in 1641.

BUTLER (JAMES), bookseller (?) in London, 1644. Known only by a broadside entitled *Two Imcomparable Generalissimos.* [Hazlitt, H. 667.]

BUTLER (ROBERT), bookseller in London; Gray's Inn Gate, 1663. Only known from an advertisement in *Mercurius Publicus,* June 4th, 1663.

BUTLER (THOMAS), bookseller in London; Lincoln's Inn Fields near the Three Tuns by the Market Place, 1656–59. Published two books by William Blake, the author of *Silver Drops,* viz., *The Yellow Book,* 1656, and *Trial of the Ladies,* 1657.

BUTTER (NATHANIEL), bookseller in London, (1) Pyde Bull, St. Austins Gate, 1608; (2) Cursitors Alley, 1660. (1605–64). The son of Thomas Butter (1581–90). Admitted a freeman February 20th, 160¾. [Arber, ii. 736.] Entered his first publication in the registers December 4th, 1604. Two editions of *King Lear* bear his name and the date 1608, one without any address and the other with that of the Pyde Bull. That without address has the well-known "Heb Ddien, heb ddina ddim" device, the other the winged horse used by George Snowden and afterwards by Nicholas Okes, who took over the business of the Snowdens some time in the year 1608. In 1622, in conjunction with William Shefford, Butter published a sheet entitled *News from most parts of Christendom*, and from that time made journalism his chief business. In 1630 he began a series of half-yearly volumes of collected foreign news under titles such as the *Swedish Intelligencer*. Charles I granted to Butter and N. Bourne the right of publishing all matter of history or news, they paying the sum of ten pounds yearly to the repair of St. Paul's. On May 21st, 1639, Butter made over the copyrights of all ´plays in his possession to Miles Fletcher, or Flesher, devoting himself entirely to the issue of news-sheets. He is last heard of in the Registers on December 3rd, 1663, when he made over to Thomas Rookes, *q.v.*, his copyright in Dr. Halliday's *Sermons*. [Registers, Liber F, p. 274.] He died in the following February, and his death is thus recorded by Smyth in his *Obituary*: "22 Febry 166⅔. Nath: Butter an old stationer, died very poore." [D.N.B. ; *Library*, N.S., No. 26, pp. 163–6 ; *Domestic State Papers*, 1638–9, p. 182.]

BYFIELD (ADONIRAM), bookseller in London, (1) Bible in Pope's Head Alley near Lombard Street, 1657; (2) Three Bibles in Cornhill next door to Pope's Head Alley, 1660 (1657–60). Son of the Puritan divine of this name. Apprenticed to Ralph Smith for seven years from May 7th, 1649. [Stationers' Register of Apprenticeships, 1605–66.] Amongst his publications was Samuel Morland's *History of the Evangelical Churches*, 1658. f°. [B.M.]

CADE (JOHN), bookseller in London, (1) Globe in Cornhill; (2) At the Royal Exchange. (1664–78). Nothing is known of the early publications of this bookseller, but in 1678 he is found selling Saxton's maps. [Arber, *Term Catalogues*, i. 304.]

CADWELL (J   ), printer in London, 1659–62. Son of Edward Cadwell of London, draper; apprenticed to Roger Norton, *q.v.*, for seven years from June 23rd, 1646. He was evidently in a small way of business, the only two books found with his imprint being an allegory called the *Voyage of the Wandring Knight*, 1661, printed in black letter, and *A Brief account of ancient Church-Government*, 1662, 4°., ascribed to Obadiah Walker. His type and ornaments were of the poorest. His address has not been found.

CALVERT (ELIZABETH), bookseller in London, (1) Black Spread Eagle, St. Paul's Churchyard, 1664–66; (2) Little Britain, 1666–67; (3) Black Spread Eagle, Barbican, 1667–73. The widow of Giles Calvert, *q.v.* During her husband's lifetime she was imprisoned for selling what was considered a treasonable book, and was in prison at the time of his death. After his death she continued to publish books that offended the authorities. In 1667 the Mayor of Bristol laid an information against her for sending books to certain Bristol booksellers about the Fire of London, and she was again arrested and imprisoned in the Gatehouse for some weeks. In the same year Samuel Mearne seized a private press of hers in Southwark, at which was printed a book entitled *Nehushtan*. After Sir Roger L'Estrange's retirement from the post of censor, she appears to have been left unmolested. The last year in which her name appears in the *Term Catalogues* is 1673. [*Domestic State Papers*, Charles II, vol. 43, 21; vol. 76, 29, 30; vol. 77, 49; vol. 209, 75; vol. 248, 88; Arber, *Term Catalogues*, vol. i.]

CALVERT (GEORGE), bookseller in London, (1) Half-Moon in Watling Street neare Paule's stump, 1650; (2) Half-Moon in the new buildings in Paul's Churchyard, 1655–66; 1675–82; (3) Bible in Jewen Street, 1667; (4) Golden Ball in Little Britain, 1669–74. 1648–82. Son of George Calvert, of Meere, in the county of Somerset, "clerk," and brother of Giles Calvert, *q.v.* Apprenticed to Joseph Hunscott, for eight years from Michaelmas, 1636. [Stationers' Register of Apprenticeships.] In conjunction with Thomas Pierrepoint, he issued in 1655 a folio edition of Sidney's *Arcadia*, and miscellaneous works. This edition was printed for him by W. Dugard. He published two other editions in 1662 and 1674, the first printed by Henry Lloyd, for W. Dugard, the second without printer's name. After the great fire he moved to the Bible in Jewin Street.

CALVERT (GILES), bookseller in London; Black-Spread-Eagle, St. Paul's Churchyard, 1639–64. Son of George Calvert, of Meere, in the county of Somerset, "clerk," and brother of George Calvert, *q.v.* He was first apprenticed to William Lugger, bookseller, for nine years from June 30th, 1628, but for some reason not stated his indentures were cancelled, and he took out fresh indentures on June 11th, 163½, for the remainder of his term, seven years, with Joseph Hunscott. [Stationers' Register of Apprenticeships.] He took up his freedom on January 25th, 1639. [Arber, iii. 688.] He is chiefly noted as the publisher of the early Quaker literature, but so far as is at present known he was not openly of that society. On Cromwell's accession to power Giles Calvert, with Henry Hills and Thomas Brewster, was appointed official "printer" to the Council of State. This appointment shows that he was in favour with the Government, and explains how it was that he was able to publish Quaker books without restraint. On only one occasion, in 1656, does he appear to have been questioned, but nothing serious seems to have followed. [*State Papers*, 1656, p. 308.] In 1661 he was arrested and thrown into prison for publishing a pamphlet entitled *The Phœnix of the Solemn League and Covenant*, but he was released after a few weeks' confinement. He is believed to have died about April, 1664, and was succeeded in his business by his widow, Elizabeth Calvert.

CALVIN (JAMES), (?) bookseller in London, 1642. Only known from a pamphlet entitled *Prologue & epilogue to a comedie presented at the entertainment of the Prince his Highnesse, by the scholars of Trinity College, Cambridge, in March last.* 1641. By Francis Coles. [E. 144. (9).]

CAMPLESHON (LEONARD), bookseller in York, Stonegate, 1661. Alice Broad printed for him the *Good Husbands Jewel* .... The Fifth edition. [B.M. 779. b. 1.]

CARTWRIGHT (RICHARD), bookseller in London, (1) Bible in Duck Lane neere Smithfield ; (2) Hand and Bible, Duck Lane. 1627–47. Took up his freedom June 15th, 1615, his first publication being a sermon preached by Matthew Brookes at Paul's Cross at Christmas, 1626, entitled the *House of God.* [B.M. 3932 f. 27.] He died on November 17th, 1647. [Smyth's *Obituary*, p. 25.] By his will he desired to be buried in the Church of Little St. Bartholomew. He mentions his brother Samuel Cartwright, and left the half of his stock to his wife and the other half to his son-in-law, Thomas Smith. One of his executors was Thomas Slater, *q.v.* The will was proved on April 11th, 1648. [P.C.C. 59, Essex.]

CARTWRIGHT (SAMUEL), bookseller in London, (1) Bible in Duck Lane ; (2) Hand and Bible in Ducke Lane. 1623–50. Brother of Richard

Cartwright, and evidently in business with him. Took up his freedom October 16th, 1622. [Arber, iii. 685.] Amongst his publications was an English edition of Mercator's *Atlas*, of which he held a half share with Michael Sparke. He died August 17th, 1650. [Smyth's *Obituary*, p. 29.]

CAVE (JOHN), ? bookseller in London, 1642. Only known from the imprint to the two following pamphlets, *Parliaments censure on Sir Richard Gurney*, 1642, and *True news from Portsmouth*, 1642.

CHANTLER (JAMES), bookseller in Newcastle, 1653–8. On November 10th, 1653, a daughter of James Chantler, "bookseller," was baptised at the Cathedral Church. On November 23rd (a fortnight later), Elizabeth, his wife, was buried there, and on June 6th, 1658, James Chantler, bookseller, himself was buried. There is no other record of him. (Information kindly supplied by Mr. Richard Welford).

CHAPMAN (LAURENCE), bookseller in London, (1) Upper end of Chancery Lane, next Holborn; (2) Against Staple Inn; (3) Next doore to ye Fountain Tavern in yᵉ Strand neare the Savoy. 1620–55. Took up his freedom February 9th, 1618. [Arber, iii. 684.] During the Civil War he was associated with Lawrence Blaiklock and Francis Coles in the publication of the *Perfect Diurnal*, and also issued *The Scottish Dove*. Amongst his other publications may be noticed Inigo Jones's work on *Stone Henge*, 1655, folio.

CHAPMAN (LIVEWELL), bookseller in London, (1) Crown in Pope's Head Alley, 1651–61; (2) In Exchange Alley in Cornhill, 1665. Son of Edward Chapman, of London, scrivener. Apprenticed to Benjamin Allen November 6th, 1643, for seven years. Married, between 1650 and 1653, the widow of Benjamen Allen. [Stat. Reg., Liber E, f. 249.] In 1655 Chapman was apprehended for printing seditious pamphlets, and amongst the Thurloe State Papers [vol. 4, p. 379] is an interesting letter from Col. Barkstead, in which he says that Chapman "is the owner or at least a sharer in the private press, that hath and doth soe much mischiefe . . . ." He is said to have been the compiler of a notorious tract entitled *The Phoenix of the Solemn League & Covenant* in 1661, for the publication of which Thomas Brewster, Giles Calvert and others were punished. Amongst his other publications may be noticed an edition of Sir John Harrington's *Oceana*, published in 1655.

CHAPMAN ( ), Mrs., (?) bookseller in London, 1662. Perhaps the wife of Livewell Chapman, *q.v.* Mentioned in the *State Papers* [Charles II, vol. 67, 161], as having "managed" the printing of a pamphlet called *The Face of the Times*, written by Sir Harry Vane and printed with his *Epistle General* in 1662.

CHATFIELD (STEPHEN), bookseller in London, (1) In the middle of St. Dunstan's Churchyard in Fleet Street, 1654; (2) Under St. Dunstan's Church in Fleet Street, 1654. Only known from the imprint to the second edition of a book entitled *Festorum Metropolis* ... by Allan Blayney, 1654. The first imprint is from the Bagford fragments [Harl. 5919 (294)], and belongs evidently to a different book or a different edition of the work noted.

CHETWIN, or CHETWIND (PHILIP), bookseller in London ; Next to the Black Horse in Aldersgate, 1670 (1656–74). Married the widow of Robert Allot, 1626–36, and so became possessed of certain copyrights in various Shakespeare quartos. In 1663 he published the third folio, and followed it up with a re-issue in 1664, to which he added the seven spurious plays, no doubt with a view to increasing the sale. His address has not been found before 1670. [Arber, *Term Catalogue*, vol. i.]

CHIDLEY (SAMUEL), bookseller (?) in London ; Bow Lane at the signe of the chequor, 1652. Only known from the imprint to a pamphlet entitled *A Cry against a crying Sinne*, 1652, 4°. [Hazlitt, *Handbook*, i. 112.]

CHILDE (THOMAS), printer in London ; Dogwell Court, Whitefriars, 1660–66. In partnership with Leonard Parry, *q.v.* They carried on a small business, printing chiefly political tracts and broadsides. They were ruined by the Fire of London. [*Domestic State Papers*, Charles II, vol. 243, 126.]

CHISWELL (RICHARD), bookseller in London, (1) Two Angels and Crown, Little Britain; (2) Rose and Crown, St. Paul's Churchyard, 1666–1711. This eminent publisher was born in the parish of St. Botolph's, Aldersgate, on January 4th, 1639. The entry of his apprenticeship and the date of his taking up his freedom have not been found, but he was evidently in business as a bookseller before Lady Day, 1666, as his name is found in the Hearth Tax returns for the parish of St. Botolph's for the half-year ending on that day. [P.R.O. Lay Subsidy $\frac{242}{32}$.] No book entry occurs in the Registers under his name before 1667, and the bulk of his work lies outside the period covered by this dictionary. He died in 1711, and was buried in St. Botolph's. [D.N.B.; Arber, *Term Catalogue, passim.*]

CHRISTOPHER (EDWARD), bookseller in London, 1642–43. Associated with Robert Wood, *q.v.*, in publishing political broadsides and tracts. His place of business has not been found.

CHURCHILL (WILLIAM), bookseller in Dorchester, 1659–88. His name is found on the following work:—Usher (J.), *Eighteen Sermons*, 1659. E. 1004. Later dates in *Term Catalogues*, vols. i and ii.

CLAPHAM (TH.), (?) bookseller in London (?) 1642. His name is found on the imprint to a pamphlet entitled *Newes from the City of Norwich*, 1642. [E. 114 (15).]

CLARKE (JOHN), bookseller in London, (1) Under St. Peter's Church in Cornhill; (2) Entring into Mercers' Chappell at the lower end of Cheapside; (3) Under Creechurch. 1620–69. Took up his freedom March 23rd, 16$\frac{19}{20}$. [Arber, iii. 685.] Dealt almost entirely in theological literature. Smyth records his death in the *Obituary* (p. 82), 29th July, 1669; "Old John Clark, Bookseller under Creechurch (once in Cornhill), my old acquaintance, died this day, *plenus dierum et senii infirmitatum.*" A catalogue of 61 books, all theological, on sale by him in 1652 is given at the end of a work entitled *Sacred Principles Services and Soliloquies*, 1652.

CLARKE (JOHN), junr., bookseller in London; Lower end of Cheapside entring into Mercers' Chapel, 1651–90. Admitted a freeman September 1st, 1628. [Arber, iii. 685.] Son of the preceding.

CLARKE (ROBERT), bookseller in London; Rose in Ivy Lane, 1646–65. Took up his freedom December 2nd, 1639. [Arber, iii. 688.] Mentioned in the will of his brother Edmund Clarke, of St. Faith's parish [P.C.C. 152 Hyde], proved on December 9th, 1665, who bequeathed him and his wife Elizabeth the sum of 20s. a piece to buy them rings, and left bequests also to their children. Robert Clarke was the publisher of the *Genealogie of all Popish Monks*, 1646, 4°.

CLAVELL (ROBERT), bookseller in London, (1) Stags Head, near St. Gregory's Church in Paul's Churchyard ; (2) Stag in Ivy Lane. 1658–1711. Son of Roger Clavell, late of the Isle of Purbeck, co. Dorset, gent., apprenticed to Richard Royston for seven years from March 11th, 1649, and took up his freedom on March 11th, 1656. He was Master of the Company of Stationers in the years 1698 and 1699. Robert Clavell, in partnership with John Starkey, founded and edited the periodical bibliography called *Mercurius Librarius*, which began in Michaelmas term, 1668, and was afterwards succeeded by the *Term Catalogues*. [Arber, *Term Catalogues*, i. viii.]

CLIFTON (FULKE), bookseller in London, (1) On New Fish-street Hill under St. Margaret's Church, 1620 ; (2) The Lamb, New Fish-street Hill, 1623-40 ; (3) Old Bailey, 1641-44. Took up his freedom March 29th, 1615. Chiefly a publisher of broadsides and political pamphlets, amongst which the following piece of Americana may be noticed : *A Proportion of Provisions needful for such as intend to plant themselves in New England.*

CLOWES (JOHN), printer in London ; Over against the lower pump in Grub Street, 1647–60. One of the many small printers who set up in defiance of the authorities. His type was very bad, and his press-work most careless. In conjunction with Robert Ibbitson he printed several numbers of the news-sheet, *The Perfect Occurrences*, between 1647 and 1649.

CLUTTERBUCK (RICHARD), bookseller in London, (1) Little Britain, at the sign of the Golden Ball, 1637; (2) Gun, near St. Botolph's, Little Britain, 1641 (1633-48). Took up his freedom March 1st, 163⅞ [Arber, iii. 687], dealt chiefly in popular literature such as Jo. Davenport's *Witches of Huntingdon*, 1646, 4°. [E. 343 (10)], and Jas. Oxenham's *True Relation of an apparition*, 1641, 4°. [E. 205. (6).] He died November 22nd, 1648. [Smyth's *Obituary*, p. 26.]

COATES, *see* Cotes (R.).

COE (ANDREW) the elder, printer in London, 1642-44. Took up his freedom February 6th, 163⅞. [Arber, iii. 688.] Shared with R. Austin and John Clowes the printing of the *Perfect Diurnal of the Passages in Parliament* between 1642 and 1643. He was also the printer of many political pamphlets, in which he was associated with Marmaduke Boat. His type, ornaments, and initials were old and worn, and his press-work bad. He died between April 12th and July 30th, 1644, and was succeeded by his son Andrew and his widow Jane. The position of his printing office has not been found.

COE (ANDREW), the younger, printer in London, 1644–67. The son of Andrew Coe. After his father's death, in 1644, carried on the business in partnership with his mother, Jane Coe, *q.v.* They continued to print the *Perfect Occurrences.*

COE (JANE), printer in London, 1644–47. Widow of Andrew Coe, senr. Carried on the business after his death with her son, Andrew Coe, junr.

COKE, *see* Cooke (William).

COLE (PETER), bookseller and printer in London, (1) Glove in Cornehill neere the Royal Exchange, 1637–42; (2) Glove and Lyon in Cornhil neare the Royal Exchange, 1643; (3) Printing Press in Cornhill near the Royal Exchange, 1643–65; (4) Living in Leaden-Hall, and at the sign of the Printing Press, 1660–65 (1637–65). Took up his freedom January 11th, 163⅞, and was originally a bookseller, amongst his earliest publications being Captain John Underhill's *Newes from America,* 1638, 4°, printed for him by John Dawson, who did most of his printing at this time. Some time in 1643 Cole himself added printing to his bookselling business. It appears from the Records of the Stationers' Company that, as agent for the Company, he had seized a press and letters in Bell Alley, over against Finsbury, and he gave his word that they should not be used in a disorderly way, but in June of the same year an order was made by the Committee of Examinations " that the keys of the room where the printing presses and materials of Peter Cole now are shall be restored to him, he entering bond in 1000 li not to remove the said presses or dispose of them without first acquainting this Committee and the Master and Wardens of the Company of Stationers and have their consent thereto. And that hereafter he do not presume to print with the said presses any book, pamphlet or paper not licensed according to the Ordinance of Parliament of the 14th of this present June." [*Domestic State Papers,* Charles I, vol. 498, 96.] A list of 30 books, chiefly theological, printed and sold by him in 1651, will be found in F. Glisson's *Treatise of the Ricketts,* at the end of the Preface. His death is thus recorded by Smyth in his *Obituary* (p. 70): "Decr. 4. 1665. Peter Cole, bookseller and printer in Cornhill, hanged himselfe in his warehouse in Leadenhall; reported to be distracted." His will was proved on December 22nd. By this he left the bulk of his property to his brother Edward's children, but made special bequests to Elizabeth Ridley, the youngest daughter of John Ridley, citizen and stationer of London, and to Samuel Thompson. [P.C.C. 153. Hyde.]

COLEMAN STREET PRESS, 1643 (?)—January 17th, 164⅘. On January 17th, 164⅘, a secret press was discovered in the house of Nicholas Tew, stationer, *q.v.*, at the above address, at which the following items were printed. (1) A slip of paper commencing *Alas pore Parliament, how art thou betrai'd?* written by some Independent against Ld. Gen. Essex and Ld. of Manchester, and scattered about the streets at night, December 9th, 1644. Identified by the officers of the Co. of Stationers, as printed in a letter similar to that used in other books which Tew confessed were printed at this press. (2) [*A copie of a Letter, Written by John Lilburne . . . . To Mr. William Prinne, Esq.*] Printed about January 15th, 164⅘. (3) *An Answer to nine arguments, Written by T. B. Written long since by . . . John Lilburne, 1645, i.e.,* January 17th, 164⅘. In addition to the above, the undermentioned books are believed to have been printed at this press. (4) *Man's Mortalitie . . . . By R. O. Amsterdam.* Printed by John Canne, 1643. (5) *The Compassionate Samaritane . . .* The second edition, 1644, *i.e.,* January 5th, 164⅘. [*Library*, N.S., October, 1904; *Secret Printing during the Civil War*, pp. 374–403.]

COLES (AMOS), printer in London; (?) Ivy Lane, 1649–51. In partnership with Thomas Mabb, *q.v.*

COLES, COULES, or COWLES (FRANCIS), bookseller in London, (1) In the Old Bailey; (2) At the halfe-bowle in the Old Bailey; (3) Lamb, in the Old Bailey; (4) Wine Street, near Hatton Garden. 1626–81. Took up his freedom July 1st, 1624. [Arber, iii. 685.] Chiefly celebrated as a publisher of ballads, in which he was associated with T. Bates, W. Gilbertson, T. Vere, and Jo. Wright. His ballads were invariably illustrated with curious woodcuts. He was also associated with Lawrence Blaiklock in publishing the news-sheet called *The Perfect Diurnal.* It is likely that there was more than one publisher of this name and that the above imprints may refer to father and son.

COLLINGS (R.), *see* Collins (R.).

COLLINS (ARTHUR), bookseller (?) in London, 1641. Described as one of the "better sort of freemen" of the Company of Stationers, in a list of those who had paid their respective proportions of the poll-tax on August 5th, 1641. [*Domestic State Papers,* Charles I, vol. 483 (11).]

COLLINS (JAMES), bookseller in London, (1) King's Arms, Ludgate Street; (2) King's Arms in Ivy Lane, 1666; (3) King's Head, Westminster Hall, 1667–70 (1664–81). Dealer in all kinds of literature. A list of seven books printed for and sold by him at his shop in Westminster Hall in 1667 occupies the recto of the last leaf of J. Glanvill's *Some Considerations about Witchcraft.* In this list is mentioned *The Compleat Angler,* and Bishop Hall's works in three folio vols. [*Library,* N.S., No. 24; Arber, *Term Catalogues,* vol. i, *passim.*]

COLLINS (JOHN), bookseller in London; Neer the church in Little Britain, 1651–54. His name is found on Sir A. Weldon's *Court and character of King James,* 1651, and in John Turner's *Commemoration . . . . of the . . . . Gunpowder Plot,* 1654. Smyth in his *Obituary* (p. 67), records his death :—"15 Septr., 1665. Collyns, bookseller ag^st ye church in Little Britain died *ex peste.*"

COLLINS (MATHEW), bookseller in London; Three Black Birds, Cannon Street, 1660–64. Only known from the imprints to two publications, the first a broadside, *The True Effigies of the German Giant,* 1660 [Bodleian]; and Daniel's *Copy Book,* 1664. [Hazlitt, H. 227, iii. 287.]

COLLINS (RICHARD), bookseller in London, 1630 (?)–48. His name is found on a political pamphlet entitled *A Declaration concerning the King . . . . 1648.* [E. 473 (17).] He may be identical with the Richard Collins, stationer, who took up his freedom January 30th, 1628. [Arber, iii. 686.]

COLLINS (THOMAS), bookseller in Northampton; Near All Hallows Church, 1651. His name is found on the imprint to a pamphlet entitled *A Patterne of Universall Knowledge* .... *Translated into English by Jeremy Collier*. [E. 1304 (1).]

COLLINS (THOMAS), bookseller in London; Middle-Temple-Gate in Fleet Street, 1650–67. In partnership with Gabriell Bedell between 1650 and 1655, when they issued several plays. In 1660, in .conjunction with Abel Roper, he held the office of printer to the Council of State, and on April 24th a sum of £88 was paid to them for printing proclamations, etc. [*Calendar of State Papers*, 1659–60, p. 598.]

CONIERS (JOSHUA), bookseller in London, (1) Black Raven in the Long Walk, near Christchurch; (2) Black Raven, Duck Lane. 1662–88. His name, in company with that of Henry Marsh, is found on a book of anecdotes called *Fragmenta Aulica or Court and State Jests* .... by T. S. Gent. 1662. [B.M. 12316 a. 27.] At the end is an advertisement of a history of the Civil Wars, also published by him. After the fire Coniers appears to have moved to Duck Lane. In his reprint of the *Term Catalogues*, Mr. Arber has given his first name as "Joseph," instead of "Joshua."

CONSTABLE (FRANCIS), bookseller in London and Westminster, (1) White Lion, Paul's Churchyard, 1616–24; (2) In St. Paul's Church Yard at the sign of the Crane, 1631; (3) Under St. Martin's Church in Ludgate, 1637; (4) King Street [Westminster] at the sign of the Goat, 1640; (5) Westminster Hall, 1640. 1613–47. Took up his freedom July 2nd, 1614. [Arber, iii. 684.] His first registered publication was *Hymens Triumphes*, entered on January 13th, 161$\frac{3}{4}$. He published large numbers of plays, in which he was associated for some years with Humphrey Moseley. He died August 1st, 1647. [Smyth's *Obituary*, p. 24.] It is probable that he rented a stall in Westminster Hall very much earlier than 1640, the date given above, but that is the first appearance of the Hall in the imprint of any book. It occurs in the *Sparagus Garden*, a comedy by Richard Brome, published in that year. [*Library*, N.S., No. 24, p. 382; W. W. Greg, *List of English Plays and Masques*.]

CONSTABLE (RICHARD), -(?) printer in London, Smithfield, 1649–50. Believed to have been brother or nephew of Francis Constable, *q.v.* He is mentioned amongst those who were bound over, in 1649, not to print seditious books. [*Calendar of State Papers*, 1649–50, pp. 522, 523.]

CONVERT (G.), *see* Calvert (Giles).

COOKE, or COOK (THOMAS), (?) bookseller in London, 1642. His name is found on a pamphlet entitled *Instructions from the House of Commons* . . . . 1642. [E. 111 (13).] A stationer of this name took up his freedom June 1st, 1635. [Arber, iii. 687.]

COOKE (WILLIAM), bookseller in London; Near Furnivall's Inn Gate in Holborn, 1632–41. A publisher chiefly of law books, but also shared with Andrew Crooke, the copyrights in several plays, including William Habington's *Queene of Arragon*, 1640, and several of those of James Shirley. He was also associated with M. Walbancke in the publication of Sir Henry Spelman's *De Sepultura*, 1641. The last heard of him is in 1641, when he issued Sir Ed. Coke's *The compleate Copy-Holder*, with a preface from his own pen.

COOPER, *see* also Cowper.

COOPER (THOMAS), journeyman bookseller, 1665. Only known from the following notice of his death in Smyth's *Obituary*, p. 67 :—"Septem. 11. 1665. Tho. Cooper, journeyman bookseller to Mr. R. Royton [*i.e.*, Richard Royston], died *ex peste.*"

COSSINET (FRANCIS), bookseller in London, (1) Golden Anchor in Tower Street at Mincheon lane end; (2) Tower Street at the corner of Mincing Lane; (3) Anchor & Mariner in Tower Street. 1658–69. Dealt in seafaring books and Quaker literature. A list of seven books published by him in 1659 will be found at the end of the second edition of J. Heydon's *Advice to a Daughter*, which he published in that year. [B.M. 8415, a. 11.]

COTES (ELLEN), printer in London; Barbican, Aldersgate Street, 1653–70 (?). Widow of Richard Cotes, *q.v.* At the time of the Survey of the press made in 1668 she employed three presses, two apprentices and nine pressmen. [*Domestic State Papers*, Charles II, vol. 243, p. 181.]

COTES (NATHANIELL), (?) bookseller in London, 1660. Only known from the imprint to a pamphlet entitled *Mr. Pryne's Letters and Proposals* [August 17th], 1660. E. 1040 (4).

COTES (RICHARD), printer in London; Barbican, Aldersgate Street, 1635-52. In partnership with his brother, Thomas Cotes, until the death of the latter in 1642, when he succeeded to the business, and in the same year was appointed the official printer to the City of London. He died on January 13th, 165¾. [Smyth's *Obituary*, p. 31.] His will was dated December 18th, 1652, and is an interesting document. He left a son, Andrew, under age, to whom he bequeathed a sum of money and his rights in Parkinson's *Herbal*. He also left bequests to Andrew Crooke, Michael Sparke, Anthony Dowse, and his apprentice, William Godbid. The residue he left to his wife, Ellen Cotes. One of his daughters was married to Thomas Williams, bookseller, of Little Britain. [P.C.C. 4 Bowyer.] His widow, Ellen, carried on the business for some years.

COTES (THOMAS), printer in London; Barbican, Aldersgate Street, 1620-41. Brother of Richard Cotes. Took up his freedom January 6th, 1606. He held the printing house originally established about 1560 by John Charlewood, printer to the Earl of Arundel, under the sign of the Half Eagle and Key. On the death of Charlewood in 1593, James Roberts married his widow and succeeded to the printing office and printed several Shakespeare quartos. About 1608 Roberts sold the business to William Jaggard, who eventually took his son Isaac Jaggard into partnership, and it was at this press that the first folio edition of Shakespeare was printed. On the death of Isaac Jaggard, his widow Dorothy assigned over the business and all the copyrights to Thomas and Richard Cotes, on June 19th, 1627. Thomas Cotes died in 1641. His will was dated June 22nd and proved on July 19th. He desired to be buried in the parish church of St. Giles, Cripplegate, of which he was the clerk. He had two sons, James and Thomas. His sister Jane was the wife of Robert Ibbitson, *q.v.*, and he mentioned a brother living in Yorkshire. His brother Richard Cotes was to have the printing house and all the implements on payment of £100. [Arber, iii. 700-704; iv. 182; *Library*, N.S., April, 1906, p. 149; P.C.C. 87, Evelyn.]

COTTON (GILES), (?) bookseller in London, 1648. His name is found in the imprint to a pamphlet entitled *His Majesties Declaration*, 1648. [E. 475 (4).]

COTTON (RICHARD), (?) bookseller in London, 1641. Only known from the imprint to the following pamphlet, *L. F. Lord Keeper His Speech Before the King's Majesty* . . . . which reads, "Printed and are to be sold by Richard Cotton, 1641." An R. Cotton was living near the King's Arms in Little Britain in 1660 and published *The Traytors Tragedy* [B.M., E. 1035. (6).] *See* also COTTON (Robert).

COTTON (ROBERT), bookseller (?) in London, 1641. Only known from the imprint to an official document, *Expresse commands from both Houses of Parliament*, which reads: London, Printed for Robert Cotton, 1641. This may be a misprint for Richard, *q.v.*, or *vice versa*.

COTTON (SAMUEL), (?) bookseller in London, 1652. Only known from the imprint to two political pamphlets: (1) *A declaration of the L. Admiral Vantrump* . . . . [June 25th], 1652 (E. 668, 14), and *A Letter sent from the Court of* . . . .*the King of France* . . . . [June 29th], 1652. [E. 668 (21).] His address is not given.

COTTRELL (JAMES), printer in London; Black & White Court, Old Bailey, 1649–70. Set up as a printer about 1649. During the Commonwealth he printed a good many pamphlets that offended the authorities. In 1664 he was arrested with others for illegally printing law books, *see* Fletcher (M.). At the time of the survey of the press made in July, 1668, he employed two presses, two compositors and no apprentices, so that we may infer that his business was not a large one. [Thurloe, *State Papers*, vol. 3, pp. 738–9; *Domestic State Papers*, Chas. II, vol. 243, p. 181.]

COULES (FRANCIS), *see* Coles (Fr.).

COURTNEY (JOHN), bookseller in Salisbury, 1650–64. His name occurs on the following: W. Creede, *Judahs purging* . . . . n.d., 4° [B.M. 694 k. 5. (6)]; George Ditton, *Symbolum Apostolicum* [a broadside], n.d. [B.M. 669 f. 14 (84)]; J. Priaulx, *Confirmation Confirmed*, 1662, 4°. [B.M. 226 g. 18 (5).]

COWLES (F.), *see* Coles (F.).

COWLEY (THOMAS), bookseller in London; Greyhound in St. Paul's Churchyard, 1640–70. Took up his freedom March 26th, 1640. [Arber, iii. 688.] His name is found on an edition of Peter du Moulin's *Anatomy of the Masse*, translated by James Mountaine, and printed by Stephen Bulkley in 1641 in London under the title of *The Masse in Latine and English with a Commentary*. Of this a copy is in the Bodleian, and the title-page only is preserved among the Ames Collection of title-pages in the British Museum. [No. 1678.] Thomas Cowley died in 1670, and left a legacy of £100 to the poor of the Stationers' Company. [Timperley, p. 546.]

COWPER (THOMAS), (?) bookseller in London, 1638–41. Only known from documents in the *State Papers*, in which he declared that he had imported large numbers of foreign bibles, prayer books and psalters, which were seized by the Stationers' Company and not returned to him. [*Domestic State Papers*, vol. 478 (54).] He may be identical with the Thomas Cooper, *q.v.*, described in 1665 as a journeyman bookseller to Richard Royston, whose death is recorded in Smyth's *Obituary*, p. 67.

CRAGGS (JAMES?), bookseller in London; Next door to the Harp and Ball near Charing Cross, c. 1667. Only known from a letter sent by Lodowick Lloyd to Robert Francis, in which an appointment is made at the above house. [*Domestic State Papers*, Charles II, vol. 244 (136).]

CRANFORD (JOSEPH), bookseller in London, (1) Phœnix St. Paul's Churchyard near the little north door, 1653; (2) King's Head, Paul's Churchyard, 1658; (3) Castle & Lion in St. Paul's Church Yard, 1659; (4) The Gun, in St. Paul's Church yard, 1661 (1653–64). Dealt chiefly in theological literature. There was another bookseller of the same name with a shop in Norwich in 1659.

CREAKE (THOMAS), bookseller in London, 1642–60. Took up his freedom September 3rd, 1638 [Arber, iii. 688.] Associated with Christopher Latham in the publication of political pamphlets. His address is unknown.

CRIPPS (HENRY), bookseller at Oxford and London, (1) Oxford, 1620–40; (2) London: The first shop in Pope's Head-Alley, next Lombard Street, 1650–61. Very little is known respecting this bookseller. He is found publishing books at Oxford from 1620 to 1640, notably the first and second editions of Burton's *Anatomy of Melancholy*, 1621 and 1624, but between 1640 and 1650 he left Oxford and settled in London, where he joined Lodowick Lloyd, *q.v.*, in several ventures. His death took place about 1661, and he was succeeded by his widow, who continued the business for several years. [Madan's *Early Oxford Press*, pp. 278, etc.]

CRIPPS (Mrs.), bookseller in London ; First shop in Pope's-Head-Alley, 1661–64. Widow of Henry Cripps. The initials S.C. found in the imprint to C. Trenchfield's *Historical Contemplations*, 1664, may refer to her.

CROFT, or CROFTS (EDWARD), bookseller in London; Against St. Botolph's Church, Little Britain, 1666–67. His name occurs in the Hearth Tax Roll for the half-year ending Lady Day, 1666, as having premises in Little Britain. [P.R.O. Lay Subsidy, $\frac{252}{32}$.] His death is recorded in Smyth's *Obituary* (p. 77), under date December 29th, 1667 : "Edw. Croft bookseller against St. Buttolph's Church in Little Brittain died hora 5 *ante merid.* : his relict, remarried since to Mr. Blagrave, an honest bookseller, who live happily in her house in Little Brittain."

CROFTS (ROBERT,) bookseller in London, (1) Crown in Chancery Lane next the Rowles; (2) Crown in Chancery Lanc under Serjeants Inne, 1657–64. Dealt largely in plays and broadsides. [*See* Hazlitt, H. 163, H. 39, H. 79, iv. 160.]

CROMBIE (ROBERT), bookseller in Edinburgh, 1645. Probably the Robert Crumby, "servand, keeper of his buith," named in 1631 in the inventory of James Cathkin. Apprentice, Robert Brown, *q.v.* Died August or September, 1645. [H. G. Aldis, *List of books printed in Scotland before 1700*, p. 112.]

CROOKE (ANDREW), bookseller in London; Green Dragon in St. Paul's Churchyard, 1630–74. Took up his freedom March 26th, 1629. [Arber, iii. 686], and became one of the leading publishers of his day. He dealt largely in plays, in the publication of which he was associated with G. Bedell and W. Cooke, and he published the first authorised edition of Sir T. Browne's *Religio Medici.* A list of 17 plays by Beaumont and Fletcher sold by him is given at the end of the play *Wit without Money*, which he issued in 1661. He sometimes supplied books to Scottish booksellers. [*See* HILL (J.).] Andrew Crooke was master of the Stationers' Company in the year 1665–66. Smyth in his *Obituary*, p. 103, thus records his death: "Sep. 20. [1674.] Andrew Crooke bookseller, this evening died, being well the day before among his acquaintance in Little Britain, my old acquaintance." He left no will. Administration of his effects was granted to his widow on October 15th. [P.C.C., Admons.]

CROOKE (JOHN), bookseller in London, and King's Printer in Dublin, 1638–69, (1) Greyhound in St. Paul's Churchyard, 1638–39; (2) Ship in St. Paul's Churchyard, 1640–66; (3) Duck Lane, 1667–69; (4) Dublin, King's Printing Office, 1660–69. Brother of Andrew Crooke. He was associated with R. Sergier, J. Baker, and G. Bedell, and during this time issued several plays. In July, 1660, he was appointed Printer General in Ireland with a fee of £8 per annum and power to print all books and statutes, and he still retained his London business. Smyth in his *Obituary*, p. 80, thus records his death: "20th March 166⅞ Mr. John Crook bookseller in Duck Lane, brother to Andr. Crook, died this morning: buried at Botolphs Aldersgate, Mar, 23." He left no will, administration of his effects being granted to his widow Mary on April 20th. He was succeeded in the office of King's Printer in Ireland by Benj. Tooke, but in a book noted by Mr. E. R. McC. Dix in his *Books printed in Dublin*, under date 1671, the imprint runs: "Typis Regiis et impensis Mariæ Crooke." He left two sons, John and Andrew, both of whom were afterwards associated with the King's Printing House in Dublin. [Information supplied by Mr. E. R. McC. Dix; W. W. Greg, *List of English Plays & Masques*, Appendix 1, p. xxxvi.]

CROOKE (WILLIAM), bookseller in London; Three Bibles on Fleet Bridge, 1664–65. Published T. Lowick's *History of . . . St. George*, 1664. A list of seven books published by him is given at the end of *The Truth & Excellency of Christian Religion Demonstrated*, 1665, 4°.

CROSLEY (JOHN), bookseller at Oxford, 1664–1703. Was perhaps son or grandson of John Crosley, stationer in Oxford, who died February 12th, 16⅞. [Madan, *Early Oxford Press*, p. 276.] His imprint is found in M. Prideaux's *Easy & compendious Introduction, for reading all sorts of Histories*, 1664.

CROSSE (JOHN), English bookseller in Amsterdam; in the Calver Street, near the English Church, 1646. His imprint is found in John Featly's *Fountain of Tears*, 1646.

CROUCH (EDWARD), printer in London; Hosier Lane, Snow Hill, 1649–64. This printer is mentioned in the list of those bound over in 1649 not to print seditious pamphlets. [*Calendar of State Papers*, 1649-50, pp. 522, 523.] He was chiefly a printer of ephemeral literature such as the following broadside, *An elegy on the most execrable murther of Mr. Clun one of the comedeans of the Theator Royal*, 1664. [Lutt. Col. 1 (44).]

CROUCH, or CROWCH (JOHN), bookseller in London, 1635 (?)–1653. Two men of this name took up their freedoms in the Stationers' Company within a few years of each other, the earlier of the two on February 4th, 1635, and the other on December 2nd, 1639, but whether they were related is not known. The first was the publisher of several of Thomas Heywood's plays, and cannot be traced after 1640. The second was apparently in partnership with Thomas Wilson, *q.v.*, at the Sign of the 3 Foxes in Long Lane, and printed with him *Mercurius Democritus*, and also a pamphlet entitled *The Tyranny of the Dutch against the English*, in 1653. [Arber, iii. 687, 688.]

CRUMPE (JAMES), bookseller (?) and bookbinder in London; Little St. Bartholomews Well Yard, 1630–61. Took up his freedom on May 5th, 1628. He was the chief publisher of that voluminous writer Robert Younge, of Roxwell, in Essex.

CURTEYNE (ALICE), bookseller at Oxford, 1651. Widow of Henry Curteyn, *q.v.*

CURTEYNE (AMOS), bookseller in Oxford, 1665. His imprint is found in a little book of orthography called *The Vocal Organ . . . . Compiled by O. P. Master of Arts . . . .* Oxford. Printed by William Hall for Amos Curteyne, 1665. [B.M. G. 16589.]

CURTEYN (HENRY), bookseller at Oxford, 1625–51. The probate of his will is dated 1651. [Madan, *Early Oxford Press*, pp. 278, 299, etc.]

CUTLER (ROBERT), bookseller in London; Newgate Market near Butchers Hall, 1663–75. Gave a bond dated August 1st, 1663, that he would neither sell publish or dispose any unlawfull or unlicensed book. Henry Brome, *q.v.*, was one of the sureties. [*Domestic State Papers*, Charles II, vol. 78 (10).]

DAGNALL (STEPHEN), bookseller at Aylesbury, 165?. Only known from the imprint to *Severall proposalls for the general good of the Common-Wealth*, 165?. [E. 624. (7).]

DAINTY (THOMAS), bookseller in London; Parish of St. Michael in the Querne, 1623–52. Took up his freedom October 6th, 1623 [Arber, iii. 685], the earliest entry in the Register being on April 12th, 1639; but he published Martin Billingsley's *Coppie Book* in 1637. No other book is known to have been published by him, nor has any other book been found bearing his name, but there are many entries in the Stationers' Registers of this period showing that he had large dealings in books. For example, on November 3rd, 1647, he transferred fourteen copies under a bill of sale to the widow of Christopher Meredith, copies which had formerly belonged to Mr. Milborne deceased, presumably Robert Milbourne, or Milborne, *q.v.* These, with the exception of two, Jo. Clarke's *Dux Grammaticus* and Lord Carey's *Pacata Hiberniæ*, were all theological. Thomas Dainty died in 1652, and his will was proved in the P.C.C. on March 4th, 165½. [218, Bowyer.] A suit was afterwards commenced in the Court of Chancery against his estate, from which it would appear that towards the close of his life he gave up the trade of a bookseller for that of a coat-seller. [Chancery Proceedings. Mitford, 112, 81.]

DAKERS (ROBERT), printer in London; Angel Alley Aldersgate Street, 1666. Mentioned in the Hearth Tax Rolls for the six months ending Lady Day, 1666. [P.R.O. Subsidy Roll. $\frac{252}{33}$.]

DAKINS (JOHN), bookseller in London; Near the Vine Tavern in Holborn, 1650–65. Smyth, in his *Obituary* (p. 64), under date July 21st, 1665, records: " M. Daykyn bookseller, a recusant in High Holborn died there *ex peste*." This is probably the same with the above, whose name will be found on J. P. Camus' *Loving Enemie*, 1650, 12°. [E. 1336 (2).]

DALLAM (JOHN), bookseller in London; Shoe Makers Row, near Carter Lane, Blackfriars, 1641-48. Only known from the imprint to the following pamphlet, *The Humble representation of the Commissioners of the General Assembly*, 1648. [Harl. 5936. (409).]

DANCER (SAMUEL), bookseller in Dublin; Horse-shoe, Castle Street, 1662-68. The recognized publisher to the Irish Church Convocation, by which he was sent into England in February, 1666, to obtain the Royal assent to the adoption of the Book of Common Prayer approved by the Primate and Bishops of Ireland. A catalogue of books sold by him in 1663 is given at the end of Jeremy Taylor's *Discourse of Confirmation*. From this it appears that he dealt in statutes, proclamations, political pamphlets, and general literature. The date of his death appears to be unknown. [J. R. Garstin, *The Book of Common Prayer in Ireland*, 1871, pp. 10, 16; E. R. McC. Dix, *List of Books printed in Dublin*, part iii, 1651-75.]

DANIEL (JOHN), bookseller in London; Three Hearts in St. Paul's Church-yard, near the West-end, 1663. Only known from the imprint to a comedy called *Love a la Mode*, 1663, 4°. [B.M. 643. d. 38.]

DANIEL (ROGER), printer and bookseller in London and Cambridge. London, (1) Angell in Lumbard Street; (2) Angell in Pope's Head Alley, 1627-66; (3) In vico vulgo dicto Pater-noster Row, Aula vero Lovelliana, 1651; Cambridge: Augustyne Fryars, 1632-50. An edition of the *Whole Book of Psalms*, printed by the University printers in Cambridge in the year 1628, was to be sold "at London, by R. Daniell at the Angell in Lumbard Street." This seems to show that Roger Daniell was at work in London several years before he joined Thomas Buck as one of the University printers in that town. There is reason to believe that the shop with the sign of the Angel stood at the Lombard Street entrance to Pope's Head Alley, and that the first and second London addresses represent the same shop, and this is perhaps identical with "the first shop next Lombard Street," in Pope's Head Alley, afterward occupied by another University stationer, Henry Cripps, *q.v.* On July 24th, 1632, Roger Daniel was appointed one of the two printers to the University of Cambridge, and on August 21st of that year a formal deed of partnership was drawn up with Thomas Buck, *q.v.*, who, however, seems to have retired for a time from the business in 1640, as Roger Daniel's name alone figures in the imprints to Cambridge books from 1640 to 1650. In 1642 and 1643 he was in trouble with the House of Commons for printing certain things to which it took offence, and his patent as University printer was cancelled for neglect on June 1st, 1650, but he continued his business in London, and at the Restoration he petitioned to be reinstated as University printer, but without success. The last heard of him is in the year 1666. [R. Bowes, *Bibl. Notes on the University Printers .... in Cambridge*, Camb. Antiq. Soc. Com., vol. 5, pp. 283–362 ; Commons' *Journals*, ii. 733, 751, 900, 951 ; *Domestic State Papers*, Charles II.]

DARBY (CLEMENT), bookseller in London, 1659. Only known from the imprint to Richard Lovelace's *Lucaste*, printed for him by W. Godbid. His address has not been found.

DARBY (JOHN), printer in London ; Bartholomew Close, 1662–67. A printer in a small way of business whom Sir R. L. Estrange threatened to prosecute for having set up contrary to the Act of 1662. John Darby was constantly in trouble with the authorities for printing satires, lampoons, and other unauthorised literature, of which it is enough to mention Andrew Marvell's *Rehearsal Transposed*. [*Calendars of Domestic State Papers*, 1663–67.]

DAVENPORT (RALPH), printer in London ; St. Mary Magdalene, Old Fish Street, 1660–65. The following books came from his press : Burton (John), *History of Eriander*, 1661 ; Leigh (Edward), *Select & Choice observations concerning all the Roman & Greek Emperors*, 1663 ; Stevenson (M.), *Poems*, 1665. He died about September 17th, 1665, probably of the plague, having made a nuncupative will. [P.C.C. 27, Mico.]

DAVIES (JOHN), bookseller (?) in London, 1662. Only known from the imprint to the following pamphlet: *Strange and wonderfull visions and Predictions of William Juniper .... London : Printed for J. Davies and are to be sold by Simon Miller at the Star in St. Paul's Churchyard, 1662.*

DAVIES (THOMAS), bookseller in London, (1) Bible, over against the little North Door of St. Pauls Church, 1659; (2) Bible near North dore of St. Pauls, 1660; (3) Bible in St. Pauls Churchyard. 1656–60. Son of Humphrey Davies, of Cranbury, co. Warwick, gent., apprentice to William Holden for seven years from November 4th, 1641. Issued in partnership with Simon Miller and J. Crooke Parivale's *History of the Iron Age*, 1659, folio, a work notable for the portraits it contains. At the end is a list of ten books, chiefly theological, issued by him. He also dealt in school books. In 1660 Thedore Sadler, *q.v.*, joined him.

DAVIS (E   ), bookseller (?) in London, 1662. This name is found in the following book; Audley (Hugh), *The Way to be Rich* . . . . 1662.

DAVIS (JAMES), bookseller in London; Greyhound St. Paul's Churchyard, 1660–62. Published masques and plays on the subject of the Restoration. [Hazlitt, H. 513; I. 371.]

DAVIS (JAMES), bookseller in London; Little Britain, 1656. Only known from the entry in Smyth's *Obituary*, p. 43: "Augt 9th. [1656.] James bookseller in Little Britain, buried."

DAVIS (RICHARD), bookseller at Oxford; near Oriell College, 1646–88. A list of 25 books sold by this bookseller will be found on the last leaf of Zach. Bogan's *Meditations or the mirth of a Christian Life*. [1653.] This consists of classical, scientific and religious works, with one play, *The Amorous War*.

DAWES (GEORGE), bookseller in London; White Horse, over against Lincoln's Inn Gate in Chancery Lane, 1665–66. Dealer in law.books.

DAWKES or DAWKS (THOMAS), bookseller in London, 1635–67. Took up his freedom October 5th, 1635. [Arber, iii. 687.] In 1642 Felix Kyngston printed for him Humfry Vincent's *Professours Hurt to Profession*. [Harl, 5927 (106).] A Thomas Dawkes "printer" is noted in Arber's *Term Catalogues* as printing at various addresses in London between 1679 and 1689. This may be the same man.

DAWLMAN (ROBERT), bookseller in London; Brazen Serpent in St. Paul's Churchyard, 1627–59. Dealt solely in theological literature. After 1635 Luke Fawne was apparently in partnership with him. He died in 1659, and his copies were assigned to John Grismond, *q.v.*

DAWSON (GERTRUDE), printer in London, (1) Aldersgate Street; (2) Living in Bartholomew Close the second door from the Half-Moon Tavern's Alley, that goes into Aldersgate-Street, 1657 (1649–61). Successor to John Dawson. She was in possession of most if not all of the latter's initial letters and ornaments, but seems to have had a new fount of l.c. roman cut for her. The second imprint given above is found in a book called *Seaman's Secrets*, printed in 1657, the title-page of which is found in the Ames collection of title-pages at the British Museum (No. 2646).

DAWSON (JOHN), printer in London, 1634–48. Son of John Dawson, printer, who died about 1634, when he succeeded to the business. He had a large and varied assortment of letter, and some pictorial initials that are not without merit, while his presswork, particularly in his folios, shows care. He had amongst his ornaments a variation of the Aldine device, to which he added the letters I.D. on either side of the anchor stock (*see* Harl. 5963/182). He is believed to have died in 1648, being succeeded by Gertrude Dawson. The situation of his printing house has not been found, but it was possibly in Bartholomew Close, from which Gertrude Dawson afterward printed.

DAYKYN (M), *see* Dakin (J.).

DEACON (H), bookseller in London, 1660. His imprint is found in the following pamphlet: *The Tryall and Condemnation of Col. D. Axtell . . . .* London. Printed for H. Deacon, 1660. [E. 1046 (8).]

DEAVER, *see* Dewer or Dever.

DE PIENNE, *see* Pienne (Peter de).

DERRICKE, *see* Gilbertson.

DEVER, *see* Dewer (J.).

DEWER, or DEVER (JOHN), printer in London; Smithfield, 1646-47. Took up his freedom September 4th, 1626. [Arber, iii. 686.] Is found in partnership with Robert Ibbitson, *q.v.* Together they printed for T. Jenner a play called *The Royall Exchange*, 1646. A John Deaver is mentioned in the Registers in 1666, possibly the same.

DEXTER (GREGORY), printer in London; Near Christchurch Newgate St., 1641-43. Took up his freedom December 18th, 1639. [Arber, iii. 688.] In partnership with R. Oulton, *q.v.* He printed amongst other things, *A True Relation of the late Fight betweene S*^r *William Wallers Forces and those sent from Oxford* .... 1643. [B.M.]

DICAS (THOMAS), bookseller in London, (1) Bell in St. Paul's Churchyard; (2) Hen & chickens, St. Paul's Churchyard. 1660-69. In 1660 he joined James Allestree, *q.v.*, and John Martin. Smyth's *Obituary*, p. 80, has this record of him: "6 Febry. [1669] Tho Dicas bookseller, died at midnight of a consumption, much indebted. He was partner in some books with Mr. Martin and Mr. Alestry." Letters of administration of his effects were taken out in April by Thomas Johnson, the principal creditor. [P.C.C. Admon. Act Book, 1669.]

DOBSON (EDWARD), bookseller in London; Without Newgate, 1643-4. Only known from the following reference to him in a contemporary news-sheet: "By letters from Northampton we are advertised that Edward Dobson, alias Codpeece-Ned, some time a bookseller without Newgate, an abusive malignant, who had printed many scandalous pamphlets against the Parliament, was taken with a crucifix about his neck, by that garrison March 12. There is a warrant sent to bring him to London." [*True Informer*, No. 26, March 16-23, 1643, p. 190.] He published a pamphlet entitled *The Declaration Vindication & Protestation of Edward Dobson, Citizen & Stationer of London* .... *Bristoll* [*London*] *Printed in the Yeere M.DC.XLIIII*. 4°. [E. 257 (36)], November 6th. From this we learn that he was imprisoned (1) for selling a book about the Earl of Essex, first printed in 1600; (2) For beating Nicholas Tew, stationer, after which he escaped to Oxford; (3) On a false charge of carrying a saw to the Irish Lords.

DOD (EDWARD), bookseller in London ; Gun in Ivie Lane, 1646–57. In partnership with Nath. Ekins, *q.v.* They were the publishers of several of Sir Thomas Browne's writings. A list of 17 books on sale by them in 1657 occurs at the end of R. Bayfield's *Bulwarke of Truth*, published in that year. Amongst them is an edition of Lovelace's *Poems* and a work entitled *America*, by N. N. gent.

DOVER (J.), printer ; St. Bartholomew's Close, 1664–65. This may have been the widow and probably the successor of Simon Dover. The imprint is found in a medical work by William Drage of Hitchin, entitled *A Physical Nosonomy*, which has a second title-page entitled *Daimonomageia A Small treatise of sicknesses & Diseases from Witchcraft*, 1665. [B.M. 776, g. 3.]

DOVER (SIMON), printer in London, 1660–64. Tried at the Old Bailey in February, 166⅔, with John Twyn, Thomas Brewster, and Nathan Brooks. Dover's crime was printing a pamphlet entitled *The Speeches of some of the late King's Justices.* He was condemned to pay a fine of 100 marks, to stand in the pillory on two successive days, and to remain a prisoner during the King's pleasure. He is believed to have died in April, 1664, shortly after his conviction. [*An exact Narrative of the Tryal .... of John Twyn....* 1664 ; *The Newes*, April 28th, 1664.]

DOWSE (ANTHONY), bookseller in London ; Little Britain, 1641–72. Smyth in his *Obituary*, p. 95, says : " 8th April [1672.] Mr. Anthony Dowse stationer in Little Britain, died this day before noone ; buried at St. Butolph's Aldersgate y⁰ 13ᵗʰ, Dr. Meriton preached at his funerall." He is also mentioned in the will of Richard Cotes. No books have been found with his name.

DOWNES (THOMAS), bookseller in London ; Irish Warehouse Stationers Hall, 1609–58. Brother of Bartholomew Downes, bookbinder, who died in December, 1636. Appears to have had a share in the Irish Stock of the Company of Stationers. No books are found entered to him in the Registers after 1631, but in the University Library, Cambridge, there is a book dated 1635 bearing his address. He was Master of the Stationers' Company in 1642 and again in 1648. He died on February 19th, 1651, without issue [Smyth's *Obituary*, p. 46], and his will was proved on

March 9th. Bartholomew Downes also had a son Thomas, probably the Thomas Downes who took up his freedom December 5th, 1636. [Arber, iii. 688.]   Another DOWNES, a printer, is mentioned in the *Domestic State Papers*, Charles II, vol. 67 (161) about the year 1664.

DOWSE (JOHN), bookseller in London ; Great North Door of Pauls, 1664. Only known from an advertisement in the *Intelligencer* for that year.

DRADOUN (GEORGE), bookseller at St. Andrews, Scotland, 1654.   Named as a debtor in the inventory of Andrew Wilson, *q.v.* [H. G. Aldis, *List of books printed in Scotland to 1700*, p. 112.]

DRENNANE (JOHN), bookseller at St. Andrews, Scotland, 1645.   Named as a debtor in the inventory of Robert Bryson, *q.v.* [H. G. Aldis, *List of books printed in Scotland to 1700*, p. 112.]

DRING (PETER), bookseller in London, (1) The Sun in the Poultry, next door to the Rose Tavern, 1660–66 ; (2) Old Jewry, 1666.   Amongst his publications was George Alsop's *Character of the Province of Maryland*, 1666, described by Sabin [Vol. i. 118] as one of the rarest of Americana. It contains on the last two leaves a list of 13 books printed for and sold by him.   These included a romance called *Eliana* "by an English hand," one music book, two books on cookery, a jest book, and a commentary on . Chaucer.   On May 8th, 1666, he became surety for Thomas Johnson, printer, *q.v.*   [*Domestic State Papers*, Charles II, vol. 155, 70.]

DRING (THOMAS), bookseller in London ; George in Fleet Street, near St. Dunstan's Church, 1649–68.   Dealt principally in law books, but was also the publisher of some plays.   He died in 1668, his will being dated September 12th and proved on December 21st.   He left small bequests to John Place, bookseller, *q.v.*, and Thomas Bassett, bookseller, *q.v.*, the residue to his son Thomas, and the premises in Fleet Street in trust for his younger son Joshua.   Thomas Roycroft and John Bellinger were among the witnesses. [P.C.C. 154, Hene.]

DRIVER (THOMAS), bookseller in London ; near the Bishop's Head in S. Paul's Churchyard, 1661.   Only known from the imprint to Dr. Edward Sparke's *Scintillula Altaris*, 1661. [B.M. 4257 aaa. 42.]

DUDLEY (H.), (?) bookseller in London, 1461 [*i.e.,* 1641]. His name occurs on *A Discourse of divers petitions of high concernment and great consequence* .... *By John Spencer, Gentleman, 1641.* [E. 133 (1).]

DUGARD (WILLIAM), schoolmaster and printer in London; Merchant Taylors School; 1644-62. Born at the Hodges on the Lickhaynde in Shipley Yield, in the parish of Bromsgrove, in the County of Worcester, on January 9th, 1605; King's scholar at Worcester School, graduated M.A. at Sidney Sussex College, Cambridge, was successively usher of Oundle School in Northamptonshire, Master of the Free School in Stamford, co. Lincoln, Master of the Free School in Colchester, co. Essex, and in 1644 was appointed Master of the Merchant Taylors School in London. About this time he became a member of the Stationers' Company and set up a private printing press at the school. William Dugard's name first appears in the Registers of the Company on September 11th, 1648, when he entered a school book entitled *Rhetoricæ Elementa.* In 1649 he printed the first edition of the *Eikon Basilike,* and followed it with Salmasius' *Defensio Regia.* This roused the ire of the Council of State, which immediately ordered his arrest, seized his presses and implements, and wrote to the governors of the school directing them to dismiss him. The governors, however, contented themselves with desiring him to relinquish his press work. Sir James Harrington, author of *Oceana,* and John Milton interceded with the Council on his behalf, and persuaded him at the same time to give up the Royal cause. Upon this his presses were restored to him and he was appointed Printer to "His Highnes the Lord Protector." In addition to his official work, and also the writing, editing and printing of many school books, he printed John Milton's answer to Salmasius; an edition of Sir Philip Sidney's *Arcadia* and miscellaneous works, in 1655; a three volume quarto edition of Luther's *Table Talk,* and Selden's *Mare Clausum,* 1652. But he was again in trouble in 1651-2 for printing the *Catechesis Ecclesiarum.* This book and some others the Council of State ordered to be burnt. In 1661 W. Dugard was dismissed from his post at Merchant Taylors' School and set up a private school in White's Alley in Coleman Street. He died December 3rd, 1662. By his will he left £10 worth of his own books to Syon College and the rest of his property to his daughter Lydia. [P.C.C. 153, Laud.] From the numerous transfers noted in the Registers after his death, it is evident that William Dugard had an interest in a large number of copy-rights. His work as a printer will bear favourable comparison with the best of the period. His press was furnished with a good assortment of type, but how far he was his own compositor and pressman, and whether all the books bearing his name were really printed by him, are questions difficult to answer. [D.N.B.]

DUKESON (JAMES), (?) bookseller in London, 1660. Only known from the imprint to a broadside entitled *The Message of John Lambert Esq in answer to the Proclamation. London. Printed for James Dukeson, 1660.* [B.M. 190 g. 13 (145).]

DUNCAN, DUNKAN, or DUNCON (CHARLES), bookseller in London, 1636–46. Took up his freedom April 4th, 1636. [Arber, iii. 687.] First book entry March 8th, 163 9/40. [Arber iv. 501.] His place of business is unknown.

DUNCOMB, *see* Dunscombe.

DUNCON, *see* Duncan.

DUNKAN, *see* Duncan.

DUNMORE (JOHN), bookseller in London, (1) Kings Arms Little Britain; (2) Three Bibles, Ludgate Street. 1665–67. In partnership with Octavian Pulleyn, junr., *q.v.* They printed a French Liturgy and other French literature.

DUNSCOMBE, or DUNCOMB (ROBERT), bookseller in London, (1) Lilli-pot Lane [Sayle, ii. 1156]; (2) Golden Falcon in Cateaton Street, over against St. Lawrence Church; (3) Duck Lane, 1666 (1638–66). Sayle, in vol. ii. 1156, gives under Robert Dunscombe a theological work printed in 1638. Hazlitt gives two political tracts as printed for Robert Dunscombe in 1642. [ii. 454, 455.] Addresses 2 and 3 are found in the Ames Collection of title-pages (Nos. 3257 and 3280).

DUNSTER (THOMAS), printer and bookseller in London; Red Lion in Grub Street, 1650. Assisted Bernard Alsop, *q.v.*, to print a pamphlet entitled *A Brief Narration of the Plotting, Beginning and carrying on of*

*that Execrable Rebellion in Ireland. London: Printed by B. Alsop and
T. Dunster, And are to be delivered at Bernard Alsop's house in Grub Street,*
1650. [March 19th, 16⅘.] His imprint is also found again the same year
in *The Fallacie of the great water drinker, discovered by Mr. Tho. Peedle
and Mr. Thos. Corbie.* 1650. [Harl., 5921. 180, 181.]

ECCLESTON (CHRISTOPHER), bookseller in London; Middle shop under
St. Dunstan's church in Fleet Street, 1662–64. His name is found on the
two following books: *Sale's Epigrammatum. Being the choicest distichs of
Martial's Fourteen Books of Epigrams,* 1663, 8°. [B.M. 833. c. 4.]; Howel
(John), *Discourse concerning the precedency of kings,* 1664.

EDMONDS (WALTER), bookseller in London; Crown near Ludgate, 1638–
41. Took up his freedom March 26th, 1635. [Arber, iii. 687.] Mentioned
in a list of stationers, dated August 5th, 1641, as paying ten shillings as his
proportion of the poll tax. [*Domestic State Papers,* Charles I, vol. 483. 11.]

EDWARDS (THOMAS), (?) bookseller in London, 1642. Only known from
the imprint to a pamphlet entitled *The Scots resolution Concerning this
present Expedition . . . . London: Printed for Tho. Edwards.* His address
has not been found.

EELES (ROBERT), printer in London, 1646. Only known from certain
papers in the House of Lords, in which it is stated that he was employed
by a committee of the Lords to suppress seditious books, and had seized a
press and letters, belonging to William Larner, which had been used in
printing *London's Last Warning; A Remonstrance to the House of Commons; An Alarum to the House of Lords,* and all or most of Lilburne's
books. He further obtained the arrest of Richard Overton, a notorious
writer among the Independents. The Stationers' Company referred to him
as "a common printer and seller of unlicensed books," and did their best
to ruin him. [*Library,* October, 1904, pp. 390–91.]

EGLESFIELD (FRANCIS), bookseller in London; Marigold, St. Paul's
Churchyard, 1637–67. Took up his freedom July 4th, 1636. [Arber, iii.
687.] Became one of the largest and most important publishers of theological literature. At the end of David Dickson's *Short Explanation of the
Epistle of St. Paul to the Hebrews,* 1649, there is a list of 72 books published
by him, mostly Divinity, but including Herrick's *Hesperides.* [A. W. Pollard,

Library, October, 1901, p. 436.] This is one of the earliest book lists known, as they are seldom found before 1650. In 1660, in company with John Williams, he published an edition of the Book of Common Prayer, which was at once seized by the agents of Christopher Barker the third. Eglesfield and his partner excused themselves by saying that they did not know who was the King's printer. [*Domestic State Papers*, Charles II.] He received a bequest of a ring from Peter Parker, *q.v.*

EKINS (NATHANIEL), bookseller in London; Gun in St. Paul's Churchyard, 1641–60. Son of John Ekins, of Ringsted, co. Northampton, gent., apprentice to John Bellamy for eight years from July 7th, 1641. [Register of Apprentices, Stationers' Hall.] Partner with Edward Dod, *q.v.* In 1660 he was granted the office of licenser of Pedlars and Petty Chapmen. [*Domestic State Papers*, Charles II, vol. 25, 94.]

ELES (ROBERT), bookseller in London (?), 1651. Only known from the imprint to the following pamphlet : *True Speech delivered on the scaffold by James, Earl of Derby* .... 1651. His address has not been found. He may possibly be identical with Robert Eeles, *q.v.*

ELLIS (WILLIAM), printer in London; Thames Street, 1649–51. On June 3rd, 1650, a person of the name of Ellis was committed to Newgate for printing *Pragmaticus*. [*Domestic State Papers*, Interr., vol. 64, pp. 415–416.] He is further mentioned in that year as one of those giving security for good behaviour. [*Domestic State Papers*, 1649–50, pp. 522, 523.] The only thing traced to his press is a pamphlet in verse entitled *News from Newcastle*, 1651, a copy of which is in the Malone Collection in the Bodleian.

EMERSON (GODFREY), bookseller in London; The Swan Little Britain, 1637–46. Took up his freedom March 1st, 1613. [Arber, iii. 684.] He may be identical with the Godfrey Emonson or Edmondson who was publishing between 1623–37. His name occurs in the Churchwardens' Books of St. Botolph without Aldersgate as paying 26s. towards the restoration of the church in 1637. Amongst his later publications was a work on the subject of letter writing entitled *The Secretary in Fashion*, 1640, 4°., edited by John Massinger and printed, it is believed, by John Beale and Samuel Bulkley.

EMERY (JASPAR), bookseller in London ; In Paul's Church-yard at the signe of the Eagle and Child, neare St. Austin's Gate, 1629–41. Took up his freedom March 26th, 1629 [Arber, iii. 686], and at once began to publish plays, amongst his first entries in the register being Thomas Drew's *Duchess of Suffolk*, which he entered on November 13th, 1629. He was also the publisher of Thomas Heywood's *Life of Merlin*, issued in 1641. [B.M. 292. f. 35.]

ENDERBY (SAMUEL), bookseller in London ; Popes Head Alley, at the signe of the Starre, 1643–45. Son of Daniel Enderby of London, merchant tailor, apprentice to Nathaniel Newberry for eight years from March 5th, 163½. Took up his freedom August 27th, 1638. Published a few political pamphlets.

EUSTER or EWSTER (THOMAS), bookseller in London ; Gun in Ivy Lane, 1649. The publisher of Richard Lovelace's collection of verse entitled *Lucasta*, which was printed for him by Thomas Harper in 1649. William Dugard also printed for him the same year a little school manual entitled *The Plainest Directions for the true-writing of English . . . . By Richard Hodges . . . .* 1649. [E. 1377 (1).]

EVERSDEN (GEORGE), bookseller in London, (1) Over against the little North gate of S. Paul's Church, 1650 ; (2) Golden Ball, Aldersgate Street, 1652 ; (3) At the Mayden-head in St. Paul's Church Yard, 1656–65 ; (4) Adam & Eve, St. John's Lane, 1666–73. A list of 15 books published by him is given on the last leaf of J. Smith's *Mysterie of Rhetorique Unveil'd*, 1665. [B.M. 11805. b. 24.] With the exception of a medical work by Culpeper, and the *Life of Sir Thos. More*, these are all theological. This same list was reprinted without addition or alteration in the edition of the same work printed in 1673. The following are the references to his addresses in the order given : (1) Hoddesdon (J.), *Sion and Parnassus or Epigrams*, 1650 ; (2) T. More, *Vita & Exitus*, 1652 ; (3) Smith (J.), *Mysterie of Rhetorique unveil'd*, 1665 ; (4) Arber's *Term Catalogues*, vol. 1, p. 157.

EVERSDEN (HENRY), bookseller in London, (1) Gray-Hound in St. Paul's Churchyard ; (2) Under the Crown Tavern in West Smithfield. 1657–67. A list of 17 books published by Henry Eversden and three forthcoming

works, occurs on sigs. L. 7, 8 of Arminius' *Just Man's Defence*, 1657.
[B.M. 4257, a. 10.] With one exception, Will. Elder's *Pearls of Eloquence*,
all these are theological.

EWSTER, *see* Euster.

FAIRBEARD (SARAH), bookseller in London; At the North Doore of the
Royal Exchange, 1646. Only known from the imprint to the following:
The State of a Christian [a broadside]. [669, f. 10, 70.]

FALCONER, FAULKNER, or FALKNER (FRANCIS), bookseller in
London, (1) Under St. Margaret's Church, New Fish Street, 1614; (2)
Near St. Margarets Hill, Southwark, 1627 (1605–48). Son of Thomas
Falconer or Falkener, late of Stanton Harcourt, co. Oxon, yeoman,
apprentice to Andrew Wise for eight years from Midsummer, 1598. [Arber,
ii. 229.] Took up his freedom July 2nd, 1605. [*Ibid*, iii. 683.] Entered
The Jests of George Peele on December 14th, 1605. Amongst his other publi-
cations may be noted T. Brewer's *Merry Devil of Edmonton*, 1626, 1631;
N. Breton's *Pasquil's Mad Cappe*, 1626; J. Mason's *Tragedy of Muleasses*,
1632; Robert Greene's *Dorastus & Fawnia*, 1648. [Sayle, vol. ii, p. 670.]

FALCONER (JOHN), bookseller at Glasgow, 1659–62. Named among the
debtors in inventory of G. Lithgow, *q.v.* [H. G. Aldis, *List of books printed
in Scotland before 1700*, p. 112.]

FALKNER, *see* Falconer.

FARNHAM (EDWARD), bookseller in London, (1) Neere the Exchange,
1657; (2) Pope's Head Alley neere Cornehill, 1657–60. In partnership
with W. Hope, *q.v.*

FAULKNER, *see* Falconer.

FAWCETT or FORCET (THOMAS), printer in London, (1) Grub Street;
(2) Heydon Court in old Fish Street neere the upper end of Lambert Hill.
1621–43. Took up his freedom May 7th, 1621 [Arber, iii. 685.] Partner
with Bernard Alsop, *q.v.* In Sir J. Lambe's *Notes* [Arber, iii. 704], he is
described as the abler man, better workman and better governor. The
second address given above is from a title-page in the Bagford Collection
entitled, *True Character of Mercurius Aulicus*, a work of which no copy has
been traced.

FAWNE (LUKE), bookseller in London; Parrot in St. Pauls Churchyard, 1631–66. Took up his freedom March 26th, 1629. [Arber, iii. 687.] In partnership for some time with Robert Dawlman at the Brazen Serpent in St. Paul's Churchyard. Afterwards set up for himself at the sign of the Parrot. Dealt exclusively in works of divinity and was a strong supporter of the Presbyterian party. In 1652, in conjunction with five other booksellers, he published a pamphlet entitled *A Beacon set on fire or the humble information of certain booksellers stationers of London, to the Parliament & Commonwealth of England.* In this attention was directed to the Popish books that had been printed of late years, and to other books favoured by the Independents. The Independents replied with *The Beacons Quenched*, while Michael Sparke, *q.v.*, published on his own account *A Second Beacon fired by Scintilla.* These pamphlets were the object of much satire in the news-sheets of the time. Luke Fawne died without issue on March 20th, 166⅝. [Smyth's *Obituary*, p. 71.] In his will he left a bequest to his apprentice, Brabazon Aylmer, and nominated John Macock, *q.v.*, one of his executors. [P.C.C. 23, Mico.]

FEATHERSTONE (HENRY), bookseller in London; St. Anne's Blackfriars, 1609–47. Son of Cuthbert Fetherston. Apprenticed to Bonham Norton, September 29th, 1598, for nine years. [Arber, ii. 230.] Warden of the Company of Stationers in 1635 and 1639. Master of the Company in 1641. He was the publisher of *Purchas his Pilgrimage*, 1612. Seems to have given up publishing in 1627. He died March 18th, 164⅞. [Smyth's *Obituary*, p. 23.] George Thomason, *q.v.*, was one of the executors to his will. [P.C.C. 69, Essex.]

FELTON (JOHN), bookseller at Stafford, 1658. Only known from the imprint to the following work: *Iter Mediteranium. A True Accompt Given of the Proceedings of the Right Honourable Lord Glin, The Lord Chief Justice of England, and the Honourable Barron Hill one of the Barrons for the Exchequer, in their Summer Circuit in the Counties of Berks, Oxford, Gloucester, Monmouth, Hereford, Worcester, Salope and Stafford. Printed for the author John Lineall, and are to be sold by John Felton in Stafford,* 1658. 4°., 10 leaves. In verse. [Hazlitt, 1, 258].

FENNER (   ), bookseller at Canterbury, 1663. Mentioned in an advertisement of patent medicines in *The Intelligencer & Newes* of that year.

FERRIS (SAMUEL), bookseller in London, (1) In Cannon Street under St. Swithin's Church; (2) Cannon Street near London Stone, 1662–63. Was the publisher of some of Archbishop Usher's sermons (*see* Ames' Collection of Title-pages, 3058) and an edition of P. Boaistuau's *Theatre of the World*, 1663.

FIELD (JOHN), printer in London and Cambridge. London: (1) Addle Hill, neer Baynard's Castle, 1644; (2) St. Andrews in the Wardrope, 1649; (3) Seven Stars Fleet Street, 1659. Cambridge: Silver Street, 1655–68 (1635–68). Took up his freedom February 4th, 1635. [Arber, iii. 687.] Appears to have been originally a bookseller only, as in 1644 the imprint, found in several tracts by Adam Steuart, reads " London, Printed *for* John Field, and are to be sold at his shop on Addle Hill " [B.M. E. 20 (7); E. 274 (14).] On January 25th, 1649, he was joined with Edward Husbands, *q.v.*, as printer to the Parliament. [*House of Commons Journals*, vol 6, p. 349.] He was also appointed printer to Oliver Cromwell. On October 12th, 1655, Field was appointed by Grace printer to the University of Cambridge, and about the same time it was ordered by Cromwell that the copyright of the Bible should be entered to him and Henry Hills, *q.v.*, in the Stationers' Registers. This was opposed by John Streator and other printers on the ground that it would lay them open under the Act of September 20th, 1649, to be sued for 6*s.* 8*d.* on every copy they possessed. [*Domestic State Papers*, 1656, vol. 126, 92.] Field printed many editions of the Bible, notably a quarto edition in 1648, a duodecimo edition in 1652, and a 32mo edition in 1653, all of which were noted for the number and variety of the misprints, the general badness of the printing, and their excessive price. In connection with this William Kilburne wrote a pamphlet entitled *Dangerous errors in several late printed Bibles* .... " Printed at Finsbury, 1659." This pamphlet was written not so much out of zeal for the purity of the Bible, as on behalf of those whose trade had been injured by the monopoly given to Field and Hills by Cromwell. Field was also fiercely attacked in another pamphlet entitled *The London Printers Lamentacon, or, the Press ˙ opprest, and overprest*, the chief paragraphs in which are reprinted by Mr. Arber in his *Transcript*, vol. iii. 27, 28. In 1655 Field built a new printing office in Silver Street, Cambridge, the University having for that purpose taken a lease of the ground from Queens' College for a term of years; and by several renewals this continued to be the University Printing Office till about 1827, when the Pitt Press was commenced. It stood on the north side of Silver Street, on a portion of the site now occupied by the new Master's Lodge of St. Catherine's College. [Bowes, *Biographical Notes on the University Printers*, pp. 307, 308.] John Field died in 1668.

FIELDING (JACOB), (?) bookseller in London, 1652. His name is found on the imprint to a pamphlet entitled *A terrible and bloudy fight at Sea between the English and the Dutch.* 1652. This and its publisher are referred to in a paragraph in *Mercurius Democritus* for the week ending July 21st, 1652. He may have been a relative of William Fielding.

FIELDING (WILLIAM), (?) bookseller in London, 1642. His name occurs in the imprint to several political pamphlets in 1642. His address has not been found.

FIRBY (THOMAS), bookseller in London; near Grays Inn-Gate in Holbourn, 1657. Only known from the imprint to a pamphlet entitled *First Fruits and Tenths*, 1657.

FISHER (   ), barber & bookseller; Old Bailey. Smyth in his *Obituary*, p. 29, has the following entry:—"July 30, 1650. Mr. Fisher, barber and bookseller in Old Baily, died." In the same year the following imprint occurs on a pamphlet by A. Speed, *Privately Printed and sold Privatly at Mr. Fisher's house in King street.* [B.M. E. 599 (1).]

FISHER (WILLIAM), bookseller in London; Posterne Gate neer the Tower, 1657–63. Dealer in nautical books. In partnership for some time with William Lugger or Lugard, *q.v.* Fisher was also the publisher of Edward Cocker's *Art's Glory, or the Penman's Treasury*, 1659.

FLESHER, *see* Fletcher.

FLETCHER (HENRY), bookseller in London; Three Gilt Cups in Paul's Church Yard near the West End, 1656–61. Publisher of several of Sir John Harrington's works and miscellaneous literature.

FLETCHER (JAMES), printer in London; Little Britain, 1652–67. Son of Miles Fletcher. He married a daughter of Cornelius Bee the bookseller. In 1664 he, with his father, was proceeded against for illegally printing law books. In the survey of the press made in July, 1668, he is returned as keeping five presses, thirteen workmen and two apprentices. He died in 1670. [Smyth's *Obituary*, p. 89 ; Plomer, *Short History*, pp. 224, 225.]

FLETCHER, or FLESHER (MILES), printer in London ; Little Britain, 1611–64. Took up his freedom November 4th, 1611 [Arber, iii. 683], and in 1617 joined George Eld, who died in 1624. Fletcher then petitioned the Archbishop of Canterbury to be appointed a master printer in his place, and the request was granted. From this time his business prospered and he joined partnership with Robert Young, *q.v.*, and John Haviland. These three men were the largest capitalists in the trade for many years. They had a share in the King's Printing House, and they bought up the businesses of William Stansby, George Purslow and Edward Griffen. In 1629 John More assigned over to Miles Fletcher and his partners his patent for printing law books in return for a sum of £60 per annum and a third of the profits. In 1661 the Company of Stationers bought the remainder of the lease from Miles Fletcher and his son James for £200, but a lawsuit arose over this in 1664. [Chan. Proc. Reynardson, Bundle 31.] Miles Fletcher was Master of the Company of Stationers in the years 1652, 1653, 1662, and 1663. He was also a prominent man in the parish of St. Botolph without Aldersgate, serving as churchwarden with Richard Cotes, *q.v.*, in 1645, 1646, and 1647. He was assessed in the parish books in the sum of £1 14s. 8d. towards the restoration of the church, this being the largest sum paid by any stationer in Little Britain In March, 1637, Robert Young assigned over to him 80 works previously the copies of Benjamin Fisher. Miles Fletcher died November 13th, 1664. [Smyth's *Obituary*, p. 61.] By his will, which consisted of only a few lines, he left everything to his son James, no one else being mentioned. [P.C.C. 121, Bruce.] He made a gift of plate to the Company of Stationers. [Timperley, p. 543.]

FORBES (JOHN), the elder and the younger, booksellers and printers at Aberdeen ; above the Meal Market, at the Sign of the Town's Armes, 1656–1704. Succeeded James Brown, *q.v.*, from whose widow they purchased his printing materials in 1661–2. Became printers to the Town and the University, and occupied the house formerly rented by Raban and by Brown. The elder Forbes died in November, 1675, and the business was continued by his son. [H. G. Aldis, *List of Books printed in Scotland before 1700*, p. 113 ; Edinburgh Bibliographical Society, 1905.]

FORCET, *see* Fawcet (T.).

FORREST (EDWARD), bookseller in Oxford, 1625–82. There may have been two men of this name during this period, probably father and son. In 1669 an Edward Forrest is found in partnership with John Forrest, *q.v.* William Hall printed for him: Cowell (Jo.), *Institutiones Juris Anglicani*, 1664. [Ames Collect. 3213. *See also* F. Madan, *Chart of Oxford Printing*, pp. 29, 31.]

FORREST (JOHN), bookseller in Oxford, 1660–69. In partnership with E. Forrest, *q.v.*, in 1669. [Arber, *Term Catalogues*, vol. i. p. 11; F. Madan, *Chart of Oxford Printing*, p. 30.]

FOSTER (MARK), bookseller in York, 1642. Stephen Bulkley, the York printer, printed three broadsides for this bookseller in July, 1642: (1) *Sir B. Rudyard's Worthy speech .... in the .... H. of Commons .... July 1642*, [B.M. 190. g.]; (2) *The petition of Sir F. Wortley to the king on behalf of the Commons of York*. [190 g. 12. (13)]; (3) *The petition of divers baronets of the County of Lincoln*. [190 g. 12. (68).]

FOSTER (RICHARD), bookseller in York; Minster Yard, 1659. His name is found on a pamphlet entitled *The Rendezvous of General Monck*. 1659. [E. 1005. (11).]

FOULKES, *see* Fowkes.

FOWKES, or FOULKES (EDWARD), (?) bookseller in London, 1664. Associated with Peter Bodvell, *q.v.*, in publishing the Book of Common Prayer in Welsh, printed for them by S. Dover in 1664. He may have been a descendant of Thomas or Nicholas Fowkes, mentioned in Arber's *Transcript*, ii. 132. His address has not been found. [Rowland's *Cambrian Bibl.*, p. 191.]

FOWLER (HENRY), bookseller (?) in London, 1642. Hazlitt mentions several political tracts printed for him, none of which has been traced. [Hazlitt, ii. 680; iii. 283, 290, 292.]

FOWLER (ROBERT), bookseller (?) in London, 1641–42. Took up his freedom January 15th, 1621. [Arber, iii. 685.] Only known from a broadside
entitled *Some passages that happened the 9th March, between the Kings
Majestie and the Committee of both Houses, when the Declaration was
delivered. London printed for Robert Fowler.* 1641. [Hazlitt, ii. 94.]

FRANCK, *see* Frank.

FRANCKLING, *see* Franklin.

FRANK, or FRANCK (JOHN), bookseller in London; Next door to the
King's Head Tavern, Fleet Street, 1641–42. Associated with Jo. Burroughes
and Edward Husband in the publication of political broadsides.

FRANKLIN (J.), bookseller (?) in London, 1642. Only known from the
imprint to a pamphlet entitled *Dialogue between a Brownist and a
Schismatick,* 1642. [Hazlitt, iii. 65.]

FRANKLIN, or FRANCKLING (WILLIAM), bookseller in Norwich; In
the Market-place, 1646–55. He was the publisher of a political pamphlet
entitled *Vox Norwici; or, The City of Norwich,* 1646 [E. 358 (4)], and also
of a sermon by John Carter, pastor of Great St. Peters, entitled *The Nail
and the Wheel,* 1647, 4°. [B.M. 4473. aa. 9.]

FREEMAN (G.), bookseller (?) in London, 1666. Hazlitt, ii. 43, gives the
following: *The Prophecie of Thomas Becket, Archbishop of Canterbury
. . . . London, Printed for G. Freeman,* 1666. 4°.

FRERE (DANIEL), bookseller in London; Bull [or Red Bull] Little Britain,
1634–49. Took up his freedom July 7th, 1634. [Arber, iii. 687.] In 1637,
under the name of Fryer, he was assessed in the Churchwardens' Accounts
of St. Botolph's Without Aldersgate, 17s. 4d. towards the restoration of the
church. Frere was a publisher of facetiæ. He died on May 16th, 1649.
[Smyth's *Obituary,* p. 27.] His will was proved on May 24th, 1649.
From this it appears that he had a son Henry. [P.C.C. 72. Fairfax.]

FUSSELL (NICHOLAS), bookseller in London; the Ball, Pauls Churchyard.
1627–50. Took up his freedom May 3rd, 1624. [Arber iii. 685.] In 1627 he
married Judith, the daughter of Lawrence Camp, draper, the match being a

runaway one. A curious lawsuit resulted. [*Chan. Proc.*, Charles I, F. 34, 58.] At this time he was in partnership with Humphrey Moseley; the partnership was apparently dissolved in 1635. His subsequent address is unknown, that given above being recorded by Mr. Sayle in the Cambridge Catalogue (p. 1101). As a member of the Livery of the Company of Stationers he paid a sum of £3 to the poll tax on August 5th, 1641. [*Domestic State Papers*, Charles I, vol. 483 (11).]

FYFIELD, or FIFIELD (ALEXANDER), printer and typefounder in London, 1635–44. Took up his freedom July 20th, 1635. [Arber, iii. 687.] He was one of the four typefounders allowed by the Star Chamber Decree of 1637. Nothing is known of his foundry. Like other typefounders he also carried on the business of a printer, and was one of those who printed the "Directory" for public worship issued by the Assembly of Divines in 1644.

GALTON (GIFFORD), (?) bookseller in London; Kings Armes in the Poultrey, 1646. His name is found on the following political pamphlets: *The Burden of England, Scotland and Ireland; or, The Watchman's Alarum* .... *1646.* [E. 351 (1)]; *Truth Vindicated from the unjust accusations of the Independent Society, in the City of Norwich* .... *By S. T.* .... 1646. [E. 351 (4).]

GAMAGE (NICHOLAS), bookseller in London, (1) On London Bridge neere the Gate, 1646; (2) Three Bibles on London Bridge, next the Gate, 1648. From a deed of assignment dated January 10th, 1645, it appears that Nicholas Gamage was the son of Thomas Gamage, of Walden, in Essex. He had a brother John and a sister Mary. The earliest book found with his name is *The World's Prospect* .... by John Emersone, 1646. [E. 1183 (2).] He also published Thomas Decker's *English Villanies* [Ninth Edition], 1648. This is probably the same house, afterwards occupied by C. Tyus and T. Passinger, *q.v.*

GAMMON (RICHARD), bookseller in London; Over against Excester [*i.e.*, Exeter] house in the Strand, 1661–62. His imprint has been found in the following books: Brett (Arthur), *Patientia Victrix; or the Book of Job in Lyrick Verse*, 1661; Hemings (W.), *Fatal contract, a French comedy*, 1661; Davenport (Robert), *King John and Matilda. A Tragedy*, 1662.

GARFIELD (JOHN), printer (?) & bookseller in London ; The Rolling Press for Pictures, near the Royal Exchange in Cornhill, over against Pope's Head Alley, 1656–1659. On the title-page of George Thornley's *Daphnis and Chloe*, 1657. [B.M. E. 1652 (2)], is a plate of Garfield's press, labelled "The Printing Press for Pictures," showing three men at work, one employed with hands and feet in pulling the levers, one inking, and one removing the prints. The books sold by Garfield were printed for him by others.

GARRETT (WILLIAM), bookseller in London; Foster Lane, over against Goldsmiths' Hall, at the sign of the White Bear, 1622'-74. Took up his freedom March 5th, 1621. [Arber, iii. 685.] Dealt largely in school books, but in March, 165⅔, he took over from W. Humble, *q.v.*, all his copyrights in Speed's works. His address is given in a letter sent by T. Milbourne to the Secretary of State. [*Domestic State Papers*, Charles II, 182 (69).] He may have been the Mr. William Garrett described as "my loveinge freind" in the will of John Bill, the King's Printer, who died in 1630. [Plomer, *Wills*, p. 52.] He died between June 17th, 1674, and January 16th, 167⅔.

GARTHWAITE (ROGER), (?) bookseller in London. His name occurs in the imprint to the following : *A Royal letter from the King of France to the King of England* .... First printed in Paris by Peter de Boys and now reprinted in London for Roger Garthwaite. [E. 137 (30).]

GARTHWAITE (TIMOTHY), bookseller in London, (1) George in Little Britain, 1650; (2) King's Head in St. Paul's Churchyard, 1664 ; (3) Golden Lion in St. Bartholomew's Hospital, 1668 (1650–69). Associated for a short time with J. Allestree, *q.v.* Dealt chiefly in theological literature. His death took place on November 18th, 1669. [Smyth's *Obituary*, p. 84.] His will was proved in the Prerogative Court of Canterbury on the 24th of the same month, by which he left the profits of his £80 share in the stock of the Company of Stationers to his wife Mary, who was the daughter of Geo. Latham, *q.v.* He left no son, and was succeeded in the business by his widow. [P.C.C. 140 Coke.] The inventory of his effects is printed in the *Bibliographical Register*. [Autumn, 1905, pp. 20–22.]

GARWAY (JOHN), bookseller in London ; White-Lion near Py-Corner, 1660. Associated with John Andrews, *q.v.*, in the publication of John Reading's *Christmas Revived*, 1660.

GASCOIGNE (ROBERT), bookseller at Oxford, 1665. His name is found on Sir Balthazar Gerbier's *Subsidium Peregrinantibus*, 1665. [B.M. 1049, a. 25 (1).]

GAYE (WILLIAM), bookseller in London, (1) Hosier Lane, at the sign of the Axe; (2) Goldsmiths' Alley (21 June 1642). Publisher of political tracts. [Hazlitt, iii. 36, 310.]

GELLIBRAND (SAMUEL), bookseller in London, (1) The Brazen Serpent in Paul's Church Yard, 1643; (2) The Ball in St. Paul's Churchyard, 1650–66, 1669–75; (3) St. James Clerkenwell, 1666–68 (1637–75). Son of Henry Gellibrand, of London, Dr. of Physic, deceased, apprenticed to Henry Fetherstone, *q.v.*, from Midsummer, 1630. Took up his freedom June 26th, 1637. [Arber, iii. 688.] First book entry, July 18th, 1637. Became a well known bookseller, dealing chiefly in theological books, and was one of those who subscribed to Luke Fawne's *Beacon set on Fire*. There is an interesting reference to Samuel Gellibrand in the will of Walter Floyd, apparently a soldier, who died in 1645, and directed his executor to pay a sum of Five Pounds "to Mr. Samuel Gellibrand at the Brasen Serpent in St. Paul's Churchyard for Capt. Golledge." [P.C.C. 102, Rivers.] He is also mentioned in the marriage license of Henry Gellibrand in 1666, where his address was given as St. James' Clerkenwell. Samuel Gellibrand died between August 5th and November 10th, 1675. By his will it appears that he had three sons, John, Edward, and Henry, the latter pre-deceasing him. To his wife he left his stock of books bound and unbound, and also all his part in the English stock. One of the witnesses was Moses Pitt, who afterwards became a noted bookseller. [P.C.C. 110, Dycer.]

GIBBES, *see* Gibs.

GIBBS, *see* Gibs.

GIBS, GIBBES, or GIBBS (GEORGE), bookseller in London; Flower de Luce in Popes-Head-Alley, 1646. Only known from the imprint to L. Owen's *Unmasking of all Popish Monks*, 1646. [B.M. E. 339 (15).] Possibly a son of George Gibbs the elder, who was publishing at this address from 1613 to 1633. [Arber, v. 237; Sayle, 839.]

H

GIBS, GIBBES, or GIBBS (ROBERT), bookseller in London ; Golden Ball
in Chancery Lane, 1650–60.   Dealt principally in political tracts.   His
name is found on *A Seasonable Exhortation of sundry Ministers*, 1660.
[Ames' *Collection of Title-pages*, 2947.]   Robert Gibs was perhaps another
son of George Gibbs senior, noticed in the preceding entry.

GIBSON (ANTHONY), bookseller (?) in London, 1642.   His name occurs
in the imprint to . a pamphlet entitled *Some wiser then some*, 1642.
[E. 86 (30).]

GIBSON (JOHN), bookseller (?) in London, 1642.   There were several
stationers of the name of Gibson in London before 1640. [Arber, v. 237.]
John Gibson is only known from the imprint to a pamphlet entitled *Humble
remonstrance . . . . of many . . . . prisoners*, 1642. [Hazlitt, 1, 342.]

GILBERT (JOHN), (?) bookseller in London ; neer Temple Bar, 1641–8.
His name will be found on the following pamphlets : (1) *Foure Wonderfull,
Bloudy, and Dangerous Plots discovered*, 1642. [E. 147 (1)]; (2) *Articles
exhibited against the King*, 1648. [E. 536 (21).]

GILBERTSON, *alias* DERRICKE (WILLIAM), bookseller in London, (1)
Bible in Giltspur Street, without Newgate ; (2) Bible, near Newgate Street,
1640–1665.   In partnership with Francis Coles, John Wright, and
T. Vere, in the publication of ballads.   In April, 1655, he acquired
from Edward Wright a large number of copyrights of miscellaneous
literature, amongst which may be noted *The Tragicall History of King
Leire and his 3 daughters; A Play called The Shoomakers Holiday or the
Gentle Craft; Scoggins Jests; The Crown Garland of Golden Roses, both
parts*. [Stationers' Register, Liber E, pp. 339–42.]   Gilbertson died between
March 29th, 1665, and April 15th, 1665.   His will was proved in the
Prerogative Court. [P.C.C. 38, Hyde.]   From this it appears that he was a
native of Guildford, in Surrey, where he owned some property, and where
he desired to be buried.   He nominated Francis Coles, Thomas Vere, and
Robert White his pall bearers.   On April 18th, 1666, his copyrights were
assigned to Robert White. [Register, Liber F, p. 314.]

GILES (J.), *see* Gyles (J.).

GLEN (JAMES), printer and bookseller, Edinburgh; In the Parliament Yard, 1656–87. A James Glen appears among the debtors in Lithgow's Inventory, 1662. Probably one of the booksellers who in 1671 acquired the printing-house of the Society of Stationers. A partner of A. Anderson in the privilege and appointment of King's printer, 1671. His name as printer, alone and in partnership, appears in books from 1667 to 1681. In 1687 he was ordered to be imprisoned for causing to be reprinted *The Rout of Romish Rites.* [H. G. Aldis, *List of Books printed in Scotland,* 1905, p. 113.]

GODBID (WILLIAM), printer in London; Over against the Anchor Inn in Little Britain, 1656–77. Apprenticed to Richard Cotes, who at his death left him a legacy of forty shillings. A notable feature of Godbid's work was the printing of music. In 1657 and 1659 he printed John Gamble's *Ayres and Dialogues,* in 1658 Henry Lawes' *Ayres and Dialogues,* and in 1669 the same author's *Treasury of Music*; in 1658, 1667, and 1669 John Hilton's collection of catches under the title of *Catch that Catch can.* Amongst his other work as a printer was Richard Lovelace's *Lucasta,* 1659, and Sir Aston Cokain's *Plays and Poems.* In the survey of the press made in July, 1668, he was returned as having three presses, five workmen, and two apprentices. [Plomer, *Short History,* p. 226.]

GODWIN, or GOODWIN (JOSEPH), printer and bookseller in Oxford, 1637–67. His imprint is found in the following work: *Christophori Scheibleri Antehac in academia Gissena professoris .... Metaphysica .... editio ultima,* 1637. [F. Madan, *Oxford Press,* pp. 201, 308.] He was also the publisher of the later edition of 1665.

GOLDING (E   ), (?) bookseller in London, 1647. Only known from the imprint to the following pamphlet: *A True and Full Relation of the late Sea-Fight .... London, Printed for E. Golding,* 1647 (May 10th). [E. 386 (12).] He may have been a relative of John or Percival Golding mentioned in Mr. Arber's *Transcript,* iii. 684; v. xcii. His address has not been found.

GOODMAN'S FIELDS PRESS, London, 1645. A secret press, supposed to have belonged to William Larner, the Independent bookseller, was seized by Joseph Hunscot, the searcher for the Stationers' Company, in a house in Goodman's Fields, Whitechapel, some time between July and December, 1645. It is believed to have been the same press from which the Martin Mar-Priest tracts had appeared earlier in the year, and to have been hurriedly removed from Bishopsgate Street to avoid seizure. The following books are known to have been printed at it: (1) *The Copy of a Letter from Lieutenant Colonell John Lilburne, to a friend.* [August 9th, 1645.] 4°.; (2) *England's Birth-right justified against all Arbitrary Usurpation, etc.* [October 10th, 1645.] 4°. [*Library*, N.S., October, 1904, *Secret Printing during the Civil War*, pp. 374–403.]

GOODWIN, *see* Godwin.

GOULD (THOMAS), bookseller in London; The Church in Chancery Lane, 1635-59. Took up his freedom May 6th, 1633. [Arber, iii. 687.] His name is found on a broadside entitled *A Perfect List of the Lords* [Hazlitt, ii. 712], and other political pamphlets.

GRANTHAM (WILLIAM), bookseller in London, (1) Black Bear in St. Paul's Churchyard; (2) Bear in St. Paul's Church Yard, near the little North door. 1646-75. In partnership for a time with Nathaniel Webb, who, some time between 1655 and 1660, set up for himself at the King's Head in St. Paul's Churchyard. T. Gerey's *Meditations upon God*, 1658, contains after the "Contents" a four-page list of books sold by Grantham and Webb in 1658. It consists entirely of theological works, and was re-issued without alteration and without date two years later, at the end of a sermon by the same preacher called *A Mirrour for Anabaptists.* The last entry to Grantham in the *Term Catalogues* is Michaelmas, 1675.

GRAVES (WILLIAM), bookseller in Cambridge; Regent Walk, 1631(?)–65. His name is found on Richard Watson's *Sermon touching Schism*, 1642, *Liber Job Graeco carmine redditus per J. D. Editio altera* .... 1653. [Bowes' *Cambridge Books*, p. 28, No. 75; p. 34, No. 99.] A William Graves paid church rate from 1631 to 163⅔ for Great St. Maries. [Foster's *Churchwardens' Accounts*.]

GRAY (JAMES), bookseller in Edinburgh; At the upper side of the Great Kirk Stile, 1647. Known only from the imprint to D. Dickson's *Brief Exposition of* .... *Matthew.* No. 1271 in Mr. Aldis's *List of Books Printed in Scotland.*

GREEN (BENJAMIN), bookseller in London; Three Leg Court in Fleet Street, over against the White Friars, 1632–46. Took up his freedom June 9th, 1628. [Arber, iii. 686.] In partnership with Moses Bell, *q.v.* On October 27th, 1632, they entered in the Registers a broadside called *A Yearly Continuation of the Lord Maiours and Sherriffs of London.* [Arber, iv. 287.] Benj. Green's name is found on another broadside beginning *To the Right Honourable Thomas Adams* . . . . [B.M. 669. f. 10, 74.] •

GREEN (CHARLES), bookseller in London, (1) White Lion, St. Paul's Churchyard; (2) Gun in Ivy Lane. 1631–48. Took up his freedom June 30th, 1631. [Arber, iii. 686.] Publisher of plays and romances. On November 13th, 1633, he entered in the Stationers' Registers Thomas Morton's *New Englands Canaan.* This is a remarkable instance of the registration of copyright long before publication, as no copies of the book have been found with an earlier date than 1637, when it was printed at Amsterdam by Frederick Stam. Some copies are found with Greene's name, but without date, while internal evidence goes to prove that the book could not have been printed in 1633. [Publications of the Prince Society, Boston, Mass., 1883, edited by Ch. F. Adams, junr.] Charles Green was afterwards associated with Peter Whaley. He is probably the Charles Greene to whom Peter Parker, *q.v.*, left a bequest of a ring in 1648.

GREEN (GEORGE), senior, bookseller in London, 1621–42. Took up his freedom April 9th, 1621. [Arber, iii. 685.] There was also a George Green, junior, *q.v.* One of them was associated with John Jackson and F. Smith, in 1642, in publishing a broadside entitled *A Catalogue of sundry knights* . . . . [Hazlitt, ii. 359.] Their addresses have not been found.

GREEN (GEORGE), junior, bookseller in London, 1637–42. Took up his freedom February 6th, 1637. [Arber, iii. 688.] There was also a George Green, senior.

GREENE (THOMAS), bookseller in London, 1643. Only known from the imprint to a pamphlet entitled *A Chaleng sent from Prince Rupert and the Lord Grandison, to Sir William Belford* . . . . *London, Printed for Thomas Greene,* 1643. [B.M. 21 b. 10 (34).] A Thomas Greene, son of Robert Greene, of Brotherton, co. York, was apprenticed to William Jaggard on October 25th, 1602, for eight years. [Arber, ii. 267], but there is no record of his having taken up his freedom.

GREENSMITH (JOHN), bookseller in London, 1641-2. Took up his freedom January 19th, 1635. [Arber, iii. 687.] Chiefly a publisher of political pamphlets and broadsides. In 164½ he was examined before a Committee of the House of Commons in connection with the Hertfordshire Petition, and confessed that Martin Eldred, of Jesus College, Cambridge, and Thomas Harbert brought a copy of the petition to him and he paid them half-a-crown for it. He also confessed to having published various other pamphlets, *Good newes from Ireland, Bloudy Newes from Ireland,* and the *Cambridge petition,* which were composed by the same authors, and for each of which he gave the same sum. These pamphlets were printed by Bernard Alsop, *q.v.* [*House of Commons Journal,* January 25th, 164½.] Greensmith was sent to the Gatehouse for this offence. His address has not been found.

GRIFFIN (ANNE), printer in London; Old Bailey, St. Sepulchre's parish, 1634-43. Widow of Edward Griffin I, printer, 1613-21. She continued to carry on the business, and in 1638 her son, Edward Griffin II, was in partnership with her. Anne Griffin apppeared as a witness against Archbishop Laud in January, 164⅔, and is described in her depositions as a widow, forty-eight years of age. She deposed to reprinting, in 1637, Thomas Becon's *Displaying of the Popish Masse,* for which she was reprimanded by Laud, who threatened to put down her printing house. [*Domestic State Papers,* Charles I, vol. 500, No. 6.]

GRIFFIN (EDWARD) II, printer in London; Old Bailey, St. Sepulchre's parish, 1638-52. Son of Edward and Anne Griffin, 1613-38. Took up his freedom January 18th, 163⅞. This was an old-established printing house, originally founded in 1590 by John Jackson, Ninian Newton, Edmond Bollifant and Arnold Hatfield. Edward Griffin I began to print here in 1613. He died in 1621, and was succeeded by his widow Anne, who took John Haviland into partnership, and the press for some years was run by a syndicate consisting of John Haviland, Robert Young and Miles Flesher, who controlled several printing houses in London. [Arber, iii. 700-704.] On October 26th, 1638, Edward Griffin the second and his mother jointly entered in the register Dr. Sibbes' *Seven Sermons on Psalm 68* [Arber, iv. 442], and eventually Edward Griffin II succeeded to the business, which he continued to carry on until his death in 1652, when he in turn was succeeded by his widow Sarah Griffin.

GRIFFIN (SARAH), printer in London; Old Bailey St. Sepulchre's parish, 1653-73. Widow of Edward Griffin II, *q.v.* Succeeded to the business on the death of her husband in 1652. The last entry to her in the *Term Catalogues* is under date February 7th (Hilary), 1673. [Arber's *Term Catalogues*, vol. 1, 129.]

GRISMAND, *see* Grismond (J.).

GRISMOND (JOHN) II, printer in London; Ivy Lane, 1639 (?)-1666 (?). This was not the type founder mentioned in the Star Chamber Decree of 1637, for he died in 1638, his will being proved on the last day of December in that year. [P.C.C. 169, Lee.] He left no son. This John Grismond may have been the son of his brother, William Grismond, mentioned in the will. John Grismond II is first met with in the list of printers who were bound over in 1649 not to print seditious books. [*Calendar of State Papers*, 1649-50, pp. 522, 523.] In 1664, he was arrested at the instance of the Company of Stationers for illegally printing law books (*see* Fletcher, M.). The John Grismond who, in 1654, was entered as a scholar at Merchant Taylors' School, may have been a son of John Grismond II. [Reed, *Old English Letter Foundries*, 1887, p. 166, n.].

GROVE (FRANCIS), bookseller in London, (1) On Snow Hill, at the sign of the Windmill, neere vnto St. Sepulchre's Church, 1629; (2) Upper end of Snow Hill neere the Sarazen's Head, without Newgate, 1640. 1623-61. Took up his freedom June 30th, 1623. [Arber, iii. 685.] Dealt chiefly in ballads and the lighter literature of the period. The above addresses are taken from (1) R. Tarlton's *Newes out of Purgatory*, 1630, (2) *Pleasant history of Cawood the Rook*, 1640.

GROVE (JOHN), bookseller (?) in London; Betwixt St. Katharine's Stairs and the Mill, next door to the sign of the Ship, 1658. Only known from the imprint to a scarce pamphlet entitled *Wine, Ale, Beer and Tobacco*, 1658.

GUSTAVUS (CHARLES), bookseller in London, 1657-60. Chiefly a dealer in broadsides. His address has not been found. His name occurs on a broadside entitled *The Gang or the Nine Worthies and Champions*. [Lutt. Coll. II, 85.]

GUY (WILLIAM), bookseller in London, 1642. Only known from the imprint to the following pamphlet, *Votes and Declarations of both Houses of Parliament concerning the taking away . . . . the power of the Clergy . . . . Printed for Francis Leach and William Guy*, 1642. [Hazlitt, ii. 449.]

GYLES (JOHN), bookseller in London, (1) David's Inn, Holborn, 1642; (2) Furnivall's Inn, 1648 (1642–48). His name has been found on the following: (1) *The True Petition . . . . of the Kingdome of Scotland*, 1642. A broadside. [Bibl. Lind. Catal. of Broadsides, No. 28]; (2) *Works of . . . . Judge Jenkins*, 1648. [Harl, 5921 (341).]

HALES (THOMAS), bookseller in London, 1641. Took up his freedom June 5th, 1626. [Arber, iii. 686.] *To the Right Honourable the House of Peers . . . . the humble Petition of many thousands . . . . inhabiting within the cities of London and Westminster*, 1641. A broadside. [Lutt. Coll., 3, 66.] His address has not been found.

HALL (HENRY), printer at Oxford, 1642–79 (?). Apprentice to William Turner, *q.v.*, and upon the death of the latter, in 1643, purchased his "presses, letters, and utensils." Hall was elected printer to the University in Turner's place on November 21st, 1644. [Madan, *Chart of Oxford Printing*, p. 29.] He was the printer of the famous Oxford news-sheet, *Mercurius Aulicus*. In October, 1649, he was bound over in a sum of £300 not to print seditious or unlicensed books or pamphlets. [*Calendar of State Papers*, 1649–50, p. 524.] Hall married Dorothy Bowring not later than 1644, and had six children born between 1645 and 1653, in St. John the Baptist's parish, Oxford.

HALL (RICHARD), bookseller in London; Westminster Hall at the sign of the Golden Ball, 1661–62. Associated with Thomas Bassett, *q.v.*, in the publication of the *Life and Death of Thomas Cawton*, 1662. He was also the publisher of a tragedy called *Andronicus* in the previous year.

HALL (WILLIAM), bookseller in Colchester, 1663. *The Arithmetical Questions*, by John Duke or Le Duke, were advertised in the *Mercurius Publicus* of June 25th, 1663, to be sold by this bookseller. His name is also found on another book of local interest, John Le Duke's *Tables for the ready casting up of the price of Colchester Bays*, 1663.

HALL (WILLIAM), printer at Oxford, 1656–72. Briefly noticed by Mr. Madan in his *Chart of Oxford Printing*, p. 30. Probably related to Henry Hall, *q.v.* In 1662 he was University printer, with Henry Hall.

HAMMOND (JOHN), printer in London; Over against S. Andrews Church in Holborne, 1642–51. In partnership with M. Rhodes, *q.v.* Hammond was the printer of the news-sheet, *The Kingdoms weekly Post*, 1643, and a curious piece of Americana entitled *Of the Conversion of Five Thousand and Nine Hundred East Indians . . . . By means of M. Ro. Junius . . . . related by . . . . M. C. Sibellius . . . . Translated . . . . by H. Jessei . . . . with a Postscript of the Gospels good success also amongst the West Indians in New England. London. Printed by John Hammond, and are to be sold at his house over [i.e. over] against S. Andrewes Church in Holborne; and in Pope's-Head-Alley by H. Allen. 1650.* [E. 614 (6).]

HAMMOND (THOMAS), bookseller (?) in London, 1662. Only known from the imprint to the following, *Trade Revived, Or a way proposed to restore the . . . . trade of this our English Nation . . . . London, Printed by T. Leach for Tho. Hammond . . . . 1662.* [Hazlitt, ii. 287.]

HANCOCK (JOHN), bookseller in London, (1) Bible in Birchen Lane; (2) Pope's Head neer the Exchange; (3) In Cornhill at the entrance unto Pope's Head Alley. 1643–66. Took up his freedom October 1st, 1638. [Arber, iii. 688.] Dealt largely in political broadsides, but amongst his publications was an edition of Gildas' *Description of Great Britain*, 1652.

HANKEN (JER.), bookseller (?) in London, 1660. Only known from the imprint to the following pamphlet, *An exact accompt of the receipts and disbursements expended by the Committee of Safety*, 1660. [Hazlitt, ii. 107.]

HANSON (THOMAS), bookseller (?) in London, 1643. Only known from the imprint to the following, *The Humble Petition Of divers of the knights, gentry and other Inhabitants of the County of Berkes . . . . London. Printed for Thomas Hanson Anno Dom. 1643.* [B.M. C. 21, b. 10 (6).]

HARDESTY (JOHN), bookseller in London, (1) In the Strand, nigh Worcester House; (2) Black-Spread-Eagle in Duck Lane. 1646–48. Took up his freedom August 4th, 1634. [Arber, iii. 687.] Amongst his publications was Richard Boothby's *Brief discovery or description of the . . . .*

Island of Madagascar, London, 1646. Smyth in his *Obituary* (p. 46), under date April 26th, 1658, records, "Thos. Hardesty, bookseller in Duck Lane, a poore man, willingly leaping out of his window into the street 3 stories high, broke his neck and so died." As Smyth sometimes made mistakes in the spelling of names, he was probably referring to John Hardesty.

HARDY (HENRY), bookseller (?) in London, 1660. Only known from the imprint to a broadside entitled *A serious manifesto and declaration of the Anabaptist and other Congregational Churches.* [Bibl. Lind. *Cat. of B.*, No. 84.]

HARE (ADAM), (?) printer in London ; Red Cross Street, 1649–50. His name occurs in a list of printers and stationers who were bound over by the Council of State not to print seditious literature. [See *Calendar of State Papers*, 1649–50, p. 524.]

HARFORD (ELIZABETH), bookseller in London ; Bible and States Arms, Little Britain, 1666. Probably the widow of Ralph Harford, *q.v.* She is mentioned in the Hearth Tax Roll for the half-year ending Lady Day, 1666, as a bookseller in Little Britain, and was assessed for four hearths. [P.R.O. Lay Subsidy $\frac{252}{32}$.]

HARFORD (RALPH), bookseller in London, (1) Queenes-head-alley in Paternoster Row at the guilt Bible; (2) The Bible in Queens Head Alley in Paternoster Row, 1641 ; (3) The Bible and States Arms, Little Britain, 1651 (1629–51). Took up his freedom January 14th, 1627. [Arber, iv. 30.] Publisher of sermons, political tracts and miscellaneous literature.

HARINGMAN (HENRY), *see* Herringman.

HARNOM (J.), (?) bookseller in London, 1642. His name is found on the following pamphlet, *Sad and fearfull newes from Beverley*, 1642. [B.M. E. 108 (8).]

HARPER (RICHARD), bookseller in London ; Bible and Harp in Smithfield, 1633–52. Took up his freedom May 6th, 1633. [Arber, iii. 687.] First book entry May 22nd, 1633. [Arber, iv. 296.] Dealt chiefly in ballads, broadsides, political tracts and sermons.

HARPER (THOMAS), printer in London; Little Britain, 1614–56. The
son of William Harper, of Woolraston, co. Salop, minister. Apprentice to
Melchisedeck Bradwood, September 29th, 1604. [Arber, iii. 549.] Took
up his freedom October 29th, 1611. First book entry July 14th, 1614,
at which time he appears to have been in partnership with his brother
William. [*Ibid.*] In 1634 he bought the printing business of George
Wood and William Lee, which had previously belonged to Thomas
Snodham, who in his turn had succeeded Thomas East or Este. Wood
brought several actions against Harper in the Court of Requests and the
Court of Chancery, in all of which he was non-suited. In 1639 Harper
was in partnership with Richard Hodgkinson. [Sayle, 866.] During the
early years of the Rebellion he was more than once in trouble for printing
pamphlets against the Parliament. [*Commons Journals*, ii. 168.] He died
March 22nd, 16⅜⅞. [Smyth's *Obituary*, p. 41.] Many notable books came
from his press, amongst them George Ruggle's *Ignoramus*, 1630; John
Weever's *Ancient Funeral Monuments*, 1631; Camden's *Annales*, 1635,
and Camden's *Remaines*, 1636. He also printed music for John Playford.

HARRIS (JOHN), printer and bookseller, London and Oxford, 1647–69.
Mr. W. H. Allnutt in his papers on the English Provincial Presses, after
noticing the presses of Newcastle and Gateshead, refers to a statement
made by Lord Holles in his *Memoirs*, that the Parliamentary Army was in
1647 accompanied by a printing press. He also notices a statement made
by Mr. C H. Firth, who in 1891 edited the Clarke Papers for the Camden
Society, to the effect that, "The printer of these pamphlets seems to have
been a certain John Harris, who himself wrote several pamphlets under the
name of Sirrahniho." [*Bibliographica*, vol. 2, pp. 292–3.] This seems to
be confirmed by the two following imprints: (1) *Declaration of Master
William Lenthall, Speaker of the House of Commons* .... Oxford, printed
by J. Harris and H. Hills, living in Pennifarthing Street, 1647. [B.M. 103,
a. 39.] (2) *The humble address of the agitators 14ᵗʰ Augt 1647.* London,
for J. Harris, Printer to His Excellency Sir Thomas Fairfax. There was
also a John Harris carrying on the trade of a bookseller at Addle Hill off
Thames Street in 1649, who may have been the same person whose name is
found on a pamphlet entitled *The Accuser sham'd* [E. 624 (2)], while Hazlitt
in his Collections, and Notes (ii. p. 530), notices another book issued in 1669
by a John Harris, of which, however, no copy has been traced.

HARRISON (   ), Mrs., bookseller in London; Lamb, St. Paul's Churchyard, 1654. Widow of John Harrison, *q.v.*, 1641–53. Her name is mentioned in an advertisement of a lost horse in the *Perfect Account* of September 27th, 1654. [E. 812 (15).]

HARRISON (JOHN), bookseller in London; [Lamb or Holy Lamb (?)] St. Paul's Churchyard, 1641–53. Dealer in miscellaneous literature. Published amongst other things John Dennis's *Secrets of Angling*, 1652. [B.M. C. 31. d. 43.] Believed to have died before 1653.

HARRISON (JOHN), junr., bookseller in London; Holy Lamb East End of Pauls, 1654–56. Probably son of the preceding. His name is found on Robert Turner's *Microkosmus*, 1654.

HARRISON (MARTHA), bookseller in London; Lamb. East end of Paul's, 1649–57. Probably widow of John Harrison, *q.v.*, and mother of John Harrison, junr., *q.v.* On July 13th, 1649, a warrant was issued by the Council of State for the apprehension of Martha Harrison and Francis Heldersham, *q.v.*, for printing and publishing a seditious libel called *Pragmaticus.* [*Calendar of State Papers*, 1649–50, p. 541. *See also* Ellis, W.] A list of ten books published by her, including Mascal's *Government of Cattle;* Wentworth's *Miscellanea;* an edition of the fourth book of Cornelius Agrippa in English, as well as medical and astrological works, is given at the end of R. Turner's translation of L. Cambachius, *Sal, Lumen & Spiritus Mundi*, 1657. [B.M. 8630. a. 21.]

HARRISON (MILES), bookseller at Kendal in 1660. His name will be found on the following pamphlet: Brownsward (W.), *The Quaker Jesuit*, 1660. [E. 1013 (4).]

HARRISON (THOMAS), bookseller in London, 1643. Only known from the imprint to a pamphlet entitled *The Priviledges of Parliament . . . . London Printed for Thomas Harrison*, 1643. [B.M. 1093. b. 118.] His address has not been found.

HARROWER (JAMES), bookseller in Edinburgh, 1600 (?)–54. "In vol. 67, May 10, 1654, is registered the testament dative of James Harrower bookseller, burges of Edinburgh, 'quha deceist in the moneth of Fe. 1ᵐ vjᶜ

[... ?] ziers'; and in vol. 68, August 4, 1654, that of Jeonet Patersone, his relict spous, 'quha deceist in the moneth of December. 1651. ziers.'" [Bann. Misc. ii. 274; H. G. Aldis, *List of Books*, p. 114.]

HARSELL (RICHARD), bookseller in Bristol, 1643. Mr. Allnutt, in his papers on the English Provincial Presses, referring to Bristol notes the following: *Disloyalty of language Questioned and Censured. Or, a sermon Preached . . . . by Rich. Towgood, B.D., one of His Majesties Chaplains, and Vicar of Saint Nicholas Church in Bristoll. Jan 17. 1642 . . . . Bristoll, Printed for Richard Harsell, and are to be sold by him in Bristoll.* 1643. Sm. 8°. A copy in Trin. Coll., Dublin. [*Bibliographica*, vol. ii. p. 287.] His name is found again on *Certain observations upon the New League & Covenant*, 1643. [B.M. 8142. bb. 6.]

HART (JONA), bookseller in London, 1664. Only known from the imprint to Velthusius' (Lambert) *Renati Des Cartes Meditationes . . . . Londini: Excudebat J. F. pro Jona Hart.* 1664. [Ames Collection, 3192.]

HART (SAMUEL), bookseller in Edinburgh, 1621–43. Son of Andro Hart, bookseller. Baptised January 7th, 1599. Died about 1643. [H. G. Aldis, *List of Books*, p. 114.]

HART (Widow), printer and bookseller at Edinburgh. (?) On the North side of the gate, a little beneath the Crosse, 1621–42. Jonet Kene, second wife of Andro Hart. Opposed the passing of Young's appointment as King's printer in 1632. Died May 3rd, 1642. [H. G. Aldis, *List of Books*, p. 114.]

HARWARD, or HAWARD (HUMPHREY), bookseller in London; George on Ludgate Hill over against Bell-Savage, 1647–8. Publisher of political pamphlets, notably a series issued in 1648 by the Dissenters, of which the following was the most important: *Reasons presented by the Dissenting Brethren against certain propositions concerning Presbyteriall Government . . . .* London, Printed by T. R. and E. M. for Humphrey Harward . . . . 1648, 4°.

HATFIELD (RICHARD), bookseller (?) in London, 1647. Only known from the imprint to the following pamphlet: *A Declaration from the Right Honourable, the Lord Major, Aldermen, and Commons of the City of London, Presented to His Excellensy* [sic] *Sir Thomas Fairfax . . . .* Imprinted at London for Richard Hatfield, 1647. [B.M. E. 401 (11).]

HAYWARD (HUMPHREY), *see* Harward.

HAYES (JOHN), printer in London; Little Wood Street, 1658–66. Possibly a descendant of Lawrence Hayes, who was publishing up to 1637. [Arber, v. 241.] He was one of the eleven printers who in 1660 or 1661 drew up a petition for the incorporation of printers into a body distinct from the Company of Stationers. [Plomer, *Short History*, p. 200.] In 1662 Sir R. L'Estrange seized several books at the office of this printer, a list of which is extant. John Hayes was ruined by the Great Fire of 1666. [*Ibid.*, 202 and 225.]

HAYWARD (BERNARD), (?) bookseller in Manchester, 1643. Only known from the imprint to a pamphlet entitled *Manchester's Joy for Derbie's overthrow* .... Printed for Bernard Hayward, 1643.

HEAD (RICHARD), author and bookseller; The Heart and Bible in Little Britain, 1666–7. Born in Ireland about 1637. His father is believed to have been John Head, B.A., New Inn Hall, 1628, who became a nobleman's chaplain and was killed in Ireland by the rebels in 1641. Richard and his mother, after many sufferings, reached England, and Winstanley says that after studying for a short time at Oxford at the same hall as that from which his father had graduated, Richard Head was apprenticed to a Latin bookseller in London, and that he afterwards married and set up for himself. He gives no dates, but makes these events occur before the publication of Head's first work, the play of *Hic et Ubique*, which was written in Ireland and printed in London in 1663, that is before he was twenty-two years of age. There is no confirmation of this story. The earliest date at which Richard Head's name is found in the imprint of a book is the year 1666, when he issued Saml. Hieron's *Fair Play on both sides*. 4°. [B.M. 1077, h. 71 (4).] In the same year Richard Head and Francis Kirkman jointly issued a book of jests entitled *Poor Robin's Jests*, of which a copy is noted by Hazlitt. In the Luttrell Collection is a broadside dated 1667 entitled *The Citizens Joy for the re-building of London*, which was also one of Head's publications. His career as a bookseller was a short one, as he was a great gambler and was ruined by losses at play. He is said to have been drowned in 1686 when crossing to the Isle of Wight. Head is chiefly remembered as the author of *The*

English Rogue, in which a thief's career is set forth. The work became popular, and Francis Kirkman issued several additions to it, until its author began to doubt whether he would ever make an end of pestering the world with them. [Head (R), *Proteus Redivivus : Epistle Dedicatory.*]

HEARNE, HERNE, or HERON (RICHARD), printer in London; neer Smith-Field, 1632-46. Probably one of Adam Islip's apprentices, for that printer at his death in 1639 left Richard Hearne his "printing presses, letters and implements used for printing," besides a sum of £100. [P.C.C. 151, Harvey.] Hearne had taken up his freedom February 6th, 1632, and his first book entry in the Registers of the Company was T. Heywood's *Pleasant Dialogues*, entered on August 29th, 1635. [Arber, iii. 687 ; iv. 347.]

HEATH (THOMAS), bookseller in London ; Russell Street, neere the Piazza of the Covent Garden, 1651-54. Issued an edition of Sidney's *Arcadia*, 1651; Ed. Chamberlayne's *Rise & Fall of . . . . the Count Olivares*, 1652, and a few plays.

HEATHCOAT, or HEATHCOTE (NATHANIEL), bookseller in London ; Gilded Acorn in St. Paul's Churchyard, 1656. Only known from the imprint to the following pamphlet: Stephens (Nath.), *Plain and easie calculation*, 1656. [Harl. 5965 (158).]

HEATHCOTE, *see* Heathcoat.

HEBB (ANDREW), bookseller in London; Bell in St. Paul's Churchyard, 1625-48. Took up his freedom June 22nd, 1621. [Arber, iii. 685.] On May 6th, 1625, all the copyrights and parts belonging to Thomas Adams were transferred to Andrew Hebb. Andrew Hebb died October 28th, 1648, "of a dropsie." [Smyth's *Obituary*, p. 26.]

HEDGES (ROBERT), *see* Hodges.

HELDER (THOMAS), bookseller in London ; Angel in Little Britain, 1666-85. In 1667 he issued an edition of a very popular book of humour called *Wits Recreations*, or *Recreations for Ingenious Headpieces*, but he is chiefly remembered as one of the booksellers whose name appeared on the 1669 title-page of *Paradise Lost*. His name is first met with in the Hearth Tax Roll for the half-year ending Lady Day, 1666, where he is returned as having three hearths. [P.R.O. Lay Subsidy, $\frac{252}{33}$.]

HELDERSHAM (FRANCIS), bookseller (?) in London, 1649. Only known from a warrant granted by the Council of State on July 13th, 1649, to Serjeant Dendy to apprehend Francis Heldersham and Martha Harrison, for printing and publishing a seditious libel called *Pragmaticus*. The actual printing was done by William Ellis, *q.v.* [*Calendar of State Papers*, 1649–50, p. 541.]

HERNE, *see* Hearne (R.).

HERON, *see* Hearne (R.).

HERRICK, or HEYRICK (SAMUEL), bookseller in London; Gray's Inn Gate in Holborn, 1662–7. Mentioned in an advertisement in *Mercurius Publicus*, March 27th, 1662. His name occurs on John Dover's play, *The Roman Generall; or the Distressed Ladies* .... 1667. [B.M. 644, d. 80.]

HERRINGMAN (HENRY), bookseller in London; Blue Anchor in the Lower Walk of the New Exchange, 1653–93. Next to Humphrey Moseley, the most important bookseller in the period covered by this dictionary. He was the son of John Herringman, of Kessalton [*i.e.*, Carshalton], in Surrey, yeoman, and was apprenticed to Abell Roper, bookseller of Fleet Street, for eight years from August 1st, 1644. [Register of Apprenticeships, Stationers' Hall.] His first book entry, which curiously enough follows one by his great contemporary Moseley, was Sir Kenelm Digby's *Short Treatise of Adhearing to God, written by Albert the Great*, entered on September 19th, 1653, and he followed this on October 12th in the same year with Lord Broghall's *Parthenissa, a Romance*. At the time of Moseley's death in 1661, Herringman possessed copyrights of books by Sir Kenelm Digby and James Howell, and many of Sir R. Davenant's pre-Restoration operas. He was Dryden's publisher, and in 1663 acquired the copyright of Cowley's poems, and in the following year the copyright of Waller's poems, which he obtained no doubt by purchase from Moseley's widow. Herringman was also an extensive publisher of plays and all the lighter literature of the Commonwealth and Restoration periods. His shop was the chief literary lounging place in London, and is frequently referred to in Pepys' *Diary*. Herringman also held a share in the King's

Printing House, and in 1682 was defendant in a suit brought in the Court of Chancery by the trustees of Charles Bill, one of the children of John Bill II. [Chan. Proc., P.R.O., Mitford, 298, 69.] Mr. Arber, in his reprint of the *Term Catalogues* [vol. ii. p. 642] says that Herringman was apparently the first London wholesale publisher in the modern sense of the words. He turned over his retail business at the Blue Anchor to F. Saunders and J. Knight, and devoted himself to the production of the Fourth Folio Shakespeare, Chaucer's works, and other large publishing ventures. His last entry in the *Term Catalogues* was in Trinity, 1693, shortly after which he appears to have retired to his native place, Carshalton, in Surrey. Here he died on January 15th, 170⅔, and was buried in Carshalton Church, where a monument was erected to his memory. [Manning, *History of Surrey*, vol. ii. p. 516.] By his will, which was dated the day before his death, he left to his "kinsman" John Herringman all his copies and parts of copies when he attained the age of twenty-three, the profits meanwhile to go to his widow. To the Company of Stationers he left a sum of £20 to purchase a piece of plate. [P.C.C. 40, Ash.]

HEWER (THOMAS), bookseller in London; Old Bailey, 1638–53 (?) Took up his freedom October 1st, 1638. [Arber, iii. 688.] Associated with W. Moulton in 1642. His name is found on a pamphlet entitled *A subsidie granted to the King*, 1653. A "T. Hewer" is described as a printer in the imprint to Sylvanus Morgan's *Armilogia*, 1666. This may be the same as the above.

HEYRICK, *see* Herrick.

HICKMAN (JOHN), (?) bookseller in London, 1648. Took up his freedom April 1st, 1639. [Arber, iii. 688.] Published Borialis Guard's *Jovial Tinker*, 1648. [Hazlitt, i. 446.] His address has not been found.

HIERONS, or HIRONES (JEREMIAH), (?) bookseller in London; Bottle, Near the Great North Door of St. Pauls, 1656. Entered in the Registers on June 19th, 1656, a book or pamphlet entitled *The Unparaleled Thiefe, or an exact relation of the notable exploits Acted by that matchless Robber Richard Hannum.* [Stationers' Registers, Liber F, p. 473.]

I

HIGGINS (CHRISTOPHER), printer at Leith, 1652–54 (?), and Edinburgh ; in Harts-Close over against the Trone-Church, 1655–60. Succeeded Evan Tyler, and printed for the Government. According to Watson, "Tyler made over his part of the forfeited gift [of King's printer] to some stationers at London, who sent down upon us Christopher Higgins and some English servants with him." This was about 1652, and the tracts printed at Leith in 1652–4 were probably printed by Higgins, but his name does not appear till 1655, when he was printing at Edinburgh. Though Higgins printed in his own name, Watson's statement is probably correct, and he was succeeded by a Society of Stationers in 1660, in which year he seems to have either died or retired. [H. G. Aldis, *List of Books*, p. 114.]

HILL (FRANCIS), bookseller in London ; Little Britain, 1644. Only known from Smyth's entry as to his death on September 9th, 1644. [*Obituary*, p. 21.]

HILL (JOHN), bookseller at Edinburgh, 1652. Little is known of this bookseller beyond the date of his death, 1652. Amongst the items in his inventory was a debt to "Androw Crook, Inglischman." [H. G. Aldis, *List of Books*, p. 114.]

HILLS (HENRY), printer in Oxford and London. Oxford : Pennyfarthing Street, 1647. London : (1) sign of Sir John Oldcastle in Fleet yard next door to the Rose & Crown ; (2) At the sign of Sir John Old-Castle in Py-Corner ; (3) Over against St. Thomas's Hospitall in Southwark. 1641–88. Son of a rope-maker in Maidstone. Sent to London when very young and acted first as postillion to Harrison the regicide, who transferred him to John Lilburne, by whom he was apprenticed to Simmons & Payne, printers. In 1642 he ran away and joined the army, and was present at the battle of Edge Hill. In 1648 he was a Leveller and subsequently an Independent, and offered to print Cromwell's *Remonstrance*. He was subsequently made printer to the Rebel Army, *see* Harris (J.). In 1649, in company with Thomas Brewster and Giles Calvert, he was appointed "printer" to the Council of State. After 1653 he held the position alone. He was also appointed one of the "printers" to the Parliament in

conjunction with John Field, *q.v.*, a post he held until the Restoration.
He was still living in 1684, when a broadside was issued entitled *A View
of part of the many traiterous, disloyal, and turn-about actions of H. H.
senior, sometimes printer to Cromwell, to the Commonwealth, to the
Anabaptists Congregation, to Cromwells Army, Committee of Safety, etc.*
[B.M. 816, m. 2 (60); Solly, E. ; Henry Hills, the pirate printer ; *Antiquary*,
vol. ii. April, 1885, pp. 151–154.] Amongst his publications was *Ill-
Newes from New England. By John Clark*, 1652.

HIRONES, *see* Hierons.

HODGES (ROBERT), bookseller in London, 1649. Only known from the
imprint to W. Prynne's *Loyall vindication of the liberties of England*, 1649.
He may have been a descendant of George Hodges, who was publishing
between 1621 and 1632. [Arber, v. 242.]

HODGKINSON (RICHARD), printer in London ; Thames Street, near
Baynard's Castle, 1624–68. Took up his freedom April 8th, 1616.
[Arber, iii. 684.] In Sir John Lambe's notes he is said to have been
the son of a printer, possibly Thomas Hodgkinson, who is mentioned in
the Registers between 1580 and 1597. Some time in 1635, Richard
Hodgkinson was in trouble with the Star Chamber and his press and
letters had been seized, but on the recommendation of the Commissioners
they were restored to him. This, however, had not taken place at the time
when Lambe made these notes. [Acts of the Court of High Commission,
Domestic State Papers, Charles I, vol. 324, f. 307b.] On March 21st,
1637, another entry in the State Papers shows that he had purchased type
from Arthur Nicholls the type-founder, and some dispute as to payment
resulted. [*Domestic State Papers*, Charles I, vol. 350, 53, 53 (1).] In the
same year he was in trouble for printing Doctor John Cowell's *Interpreter*,
but this did not prevent his being chosen as one of the twenty printers
appointed under the Act. He was the printer of the first volume of
Sir W. Dugdale's *Monasticon*, which, next to the Polyglott Bible, must be
considered a " magnus opus " of the Commonwealth period. He was still
a master printer in 1668, but as no return of his office is given with the
rest, he would have appeared to have died or retired from business about
that time.

HOLDEN (JOHN), bookseller in London, (1) Blue Anchor in the New Exchange; (2) The Anchor in the New Exchange. 1650–1. Apparently the predecessor of Henry Herringman at this address. Publisher of Abraham Cowley's *Guardian*, 1650, and Sir W. Davenant's *Gondibert*, 1651. A list of thirteen miscellaneous books sold by him in 1651 occupies one leaf following the dedicatory epistle to L. Lessius' *Sir W. Rawleighs Ghost*.

HOLEMAN (WILLIAM), bookseller (?) in London; near the Hermitage-stairs, next to the Black-Swan in Wapping, 1666. Only known from the imprint to a pamphlet entitled, Horne (Henry), *Perfect and Compleat Bel-man*, 1666. [Douce Coll.]

HOLMER (THOMAS), printer in London, 1641. In the *Commons Journals* (vol. ii., p. 160), under date May 27th, 1641, is an order that Thomas Holmer, who was committed to the Gatehouse for printing an Elegy upon the Earl of Strafford, which was considered to be scandalous, should be admitted to bail. No master printer of this name is known, and Holmer was probably a journeyman. There are two broadsides in the British Museum of this date with the imprint, *Printed in the year 1641*. The first, entitled *The Earl of Strafford his Ellegaick Poem as it was pen'd by his owne hand a little before his death*, and the second *Verses lately written by Thomas Earle of Strafford*. [C. 20, f. 2 (6) (7).] It was perhaps the first of these that was referred to in the order.

HOMER (T   .), bookseller (?) in London, 1642. Associated with J. Jackson and G. Tomlinson. He was the publisher of numerous political pamphlets, and may be identical with the preceding. His address has not been found.

HOOD (HENRY), bookseller in London; St. Dunstan's Churchyard, 1636–54. Took up his freedom July 1st, 1635. [Arber, iii. 687.] Believed to have married the widow of Richard More or Moore, who carried on business at this address until his death in 1631. On May 12th, 1641, John More or Moore, the son of Richard, received from his mother the assignment of his father's copies, and the same day assigned them to Henry Hood. [Stationers' Registers, 1641.]

HOPE (WILLIAM), bookseller in London, (1) Glove in Cornhill, 1636;
(2) Unicorn near the Royal Exchange in Cornhill, 1639-40; (3) the Blew
Anchor at the back-side of the Roiall Exchange, 1657; (4) Blue Anchor
Old Exchange; (5) Near the Exchange, 1657; At the Anchor over against
St. Bartholomew's Church, near the Royal Exchange, 1665 (1634-65).
Took up his freedom October 4th, 1630. First book entry April 14th,
1636. [Arber, iii. 686; iv. 360.] In partnership for a time with Edward
Farnham. Bought books of Robert Bryson, of Edinburgh, q.v. A list of
31 books "printed or sold" by this bookseller in 1653 occurs on sig. 17
of *The Holy Lives of God's Prophets*, 1654 (1653). [B.M. E. 1493 (1).]

HOPKINSON (JONATHAN), bookseller in London; Without Aldgate, 1647.
Only known from the entry in Smyth's *Obituary*, p. 24: "Aug 31. 1647
Jonathan Hopkinson, bookseller w[th]out Algate, died."

HORNE (ROBERT), bookseller in London, (1) Turk's Head near the Royal
Exchange, 1661; (2) Angel, in Pope's Head Alley, 1664; (3) In the first
court entering into Gresham College, next Bishopsgate, 1669; (4) At the
South Entrance to the Royal Exchange, Cornhill. 1660-85. Amongst his
publications was *A Brief Description of the Province of Carolina, on the
coasts of Floreda . . . . Together with a most accurate map of the whole
Province. London, Printed for Robert Horne, in the first Court of Gresham
College, neer Bishopsgate-street. 1666.* [B.M. 10412, c. 16.]

HORNISH (JAMES), bookseller (?) in London, 1647-48. Publisher of
political pamphlets. His address has not been found.

HORSEMAN (THOMAS), bookseller in London, (1) between York House
& the New Exchange; (2) Three Kings in the Strand. 1664-5. Publisher
of Sir W. Killigrew's *Three Plays*, 1665.

HORTEN (SAMUEL), (?) bookseller in London (?) 1641. His name is found
on a pamphlet entitled, *A True Coppie of divers papers . . . .* [E. 180 (21).]

HORTON (GEORGE), bookseller in London, (1) Royal Exchange in Cornhill;
(2) Near the three crowns in Barbican; (3) Figg-Tree-Court in Barbican;
(4) Lower end of Red Cross Street over against St. Giles Church, neer
Cripplegate. 1647-60. Publisher of political pamphlets and news-sheets.

HOWELL (JOHN), bookseller (?) in London, 1642. Only known from the imprint to a political pamphlet entitled *Delightful news for all loyal subjects*, 1642. 4 leaves. His address has not been found.

HOWES (SAMUEL), bookseller in London, (1) Popes Head Alley; (2) Golden Ball in Cornhill near the Poultry. 1644–54. Son of Robert Howes, stationer, apprenticed to his father January 21st, 164⅔. [Stationers' Register of Apprenticeships.] Partner with John Blague, *q.v.* They published jointly H. Whitfield's *Strength out of Weakness*, 1652, and Phillip Barrough's *Method of Physick*, 1652.

HUCKLESCOTT (THOMAS), bookseller in London; George in Little Britain, 1653. Only known from the imprint to Sir William Denny's *Pellicanicidium, or the Christian Adviser against self murder . . . .* London, Printed for Thomas Hucklescott and are to be sold at the sign of the George, in Little Britain, 1653. [B.M. E. 1233.]

HUGHES (ROBERT), bookseller or printer in Dublin, 1648–51. Robert Hughes was admitted to the franchise of the City of Dublin in October, 1648, when he was described as a "stationer." In the same year he published a catalogue of the manuscripts in the library of James Ware, the imprint to which reads : " Dublinii. Excudebat Robertus Hughes. M.DC.XLVIII." In April, 1650, Hughes was appointed to collect the 'Keyadge' of Dublin city, and to account for it to the Mayor and Auditors at a commission of two shillings in the £, and in the January following, 1651, was jointly appointed with another person to collect the 'threepenny customs' at a commission of one shilling in the £. Each time his name is mentioned he is described as a 'stationer.' [Information supplied by E. R. McC. Dix.]

HUMBLE (WILLIAM), bookseller in London; The White Horse (?) in Pope's Head Alley, 1646–59. Probably a descendant of George Humble, who sold books at the White Horse in Pope's Head Alley. Publisher of John Speed's works, which he assigned over to William Garrett, *q.v.*, in March, 165⅞.

HUNDGATE (JO), (?) bookseller in London (?), 1642. This name is found on political pamphlets in 1642. No address is given.

HUNSCOT (JOSEPH), bookseller in London; Stationers Hall, 1624–60. Son of John Hunscot, of Wardenton, co. Oxon. Apprentice to Thomas Ensor for eight years from March, 1604. [Arber, ii. 275.] Took up his freedom March 23rd, 1612. [Arber, iii. 683.] First book entry January 9th, 1624. Appointed Beadle to the Company of Stationers. Was for some time printer to the Long Parliament, in which he was succeeded by Edward Husband. Joseph Hunscot was very active in seeking out secret presses, and in 1645 he unearthed one such press at Goodman's Fields in the East end of London. In 1649 he was appointed to assist the Masters and Wardens of the Company in carrying out the Act of that year, and seized a press belonging to Edward and John Crouch and was allowed to retain it as a reward for his services. He was still living in 1660, when he appointed a deputy to carry the Company's banner on horseback at the entry of Charles II into the City, and was allowed 20s. for his fee. [Timperley, p. 529; *Library*, October, 1904, pp. 385 *et seq.*]

HUNT (JOHN), (?) bookseller in London (?), 1642. His name is found on a political pamphlet entitled *Most Joyful Newes by Sea and Land*, 1642. [E. 126 (11).] No address is given.

HUNT (THOMAS), bookseller in Exeter; St. Peter's Churchyard, 1640–48. Probably the son of Christopher Hunt, of Exeter, who was publishing between 1593 and 1606. His name is found on a broadside in verse entitled *Stand up to your belief.* [Lutt. Coll. ii. 209.] A contemporary news-sheet, *Mercurius Civicus*, for October 1st, 1645, states that a press had lately been brought to Exeter and that Thomas Fuller's *Good Thoughts in Bad Times* was printed at it for "malignant Hunt." Mr. Allnutt in his papers on English Provincial Presses notices some other books on sale by Thomas Hunt, notably Robert Herrick's *Hesperides*, 1648. [*Bibliographica*, vol. ii. p. 289.]

HUNT (WILLIAM), bookseller and printer in London; Pye-Corner, 1647–60. His name is first met with on the petition of the Clothiers and Weavers presented to the House of Commons in 1647. [B.M. 669, f. 11 (2).] In 1651 he added printing to his bookselling business, and jointly with Edward Griffin printed an edition of Amos Komenski's *Janua Linguarum Reserata* in 1652. His most important work was Randle Cotgrave's

French and English Dictionary, of which he printed two editions in folio, those of 1650 and 1660.   In order to make the edition of 1660 as complete as possible he sent out interleaved copies of the previous edition to scholars inviting corrections and additions.

HUNTER (JOSEPH), (?) bookseller in London, 1648.   His name is found on a political pamphlet entitled, *King's . . . . Declaration for Peace*, 1648. [E. 465 (3).]   No address is given.

HUNTINGDON (THOMAS), bookseller in London; The Stars in Duck Lane, 1648–50.   Publisher of school books and miscellaneous literature. In partnership with T. Slater, *q.v.*

HURLOCK (GEORGE), bookseller in London; neere St. Magnus Corner, Thames Street, 1634–46.   Took up his freedom May 12th, 1624, and is believed to have succeeded to the business of John Tap.   Dealt in works on navigation.   In 1633 a fire destroyed a large number of houses on the north side of London Bridge, but apparently this house escaped.   His name occurs in 1641 in a list of those stationers who had paid the poll tax. [*Domestic State Papers*, Charles I, vol. 483 (11).]

HUSBAND (EDWARD), printer (?) and bookseller in London; The Golden Dragon, near the Inner Temple, 1641–60.   Took up his freedom March 3rd, 1634 [Arber, iii. 687], at which time he was certainly not a printer. He appears to have been one of several stationers to whom the Long Parliament farmed out its printing.   In the *Calendar of Domestic State Papers*, Charles I, Addenda (March, 1625, to January, 1649), pp. 626–7, the statement is made that he was the publisher of the *Diurnal Occurrences of this great and happy Parliament*, 1641, and of a companion volume entitled *Speeches & Passages in this great and happy parliament*, 1641, but the imprints state that these works were printed for William Cooke, of Furnival's Inn.   There is no mention of Husband either as printer or publisher, and the only foundation for the statement appears to be a MS. note bound in with the Burney copy of the *Diurnal*, which does not quote any authority for its assertion.   As early as August 1st, 1642, the *Commons Journals* record an order made for payment to "Usbands & Francke of their account for printing divers parcels by order of this House," but this proves nothing more than that they were given the order, and Husband certainly gave the printing to others. In 1646 he published a *Collection of Orders, Ordinances and Declarations of Parliament . . . . from Mar 9th 1642 . . . . until December 1646.* Again in 1650 the Council of State ordered him to collect all the ordinances down to the Act for the trial of the King, examine them, and "have them printed," as well as all the Acts from the trial of the late King to that date. [*Calendar of State Papers, Domestic*, 1650, p. 157.] On May 5th, 1660, he was again selected, this time with T. Newcombe, as printer to the Council of State, but he disappears at the Restoration.

HUTCHINSON (WILLIAM), bookseller in Durham, 1655. Only known from the following: *Fourteen Queries and ten absurdities about the extent of Christ's Death . . . . London: Printed by Henry Hills for William Hutchinson bookseller in Durham, 1655.* [E. 1492 (4).]

HUTTON (GEORGE), bookseller in London; Turnstile in Holborn, 1636–41. Publisher of R. Braithwaite's *Lives of . . . . the Roman Emperors,* 1636, and Glapthorne's *Tragedy of Albertus Wallenstein,* 1639. [Hazlitt, H. 492; Sayle, p. 1150.]

HUTTON (HENRY), bookseller (?) in London, 1642. Only known from the imprint to a political tract entitled *A Wonderful & Strange Miracle or God's Just Vengeance against the Cavaliers . . . . London Printed for Henry Hutton,* 1642.

HYETT (NATHANIEL), bookseller at Winchcombe, Gloucestershire, 1653. Only known from the imprint to some copies of a pamphlet entitled *The Disputation at Winchcombe Nov. 9. MDCLIII . . . .* Oxford, printed by L. L. and are to be sold at Winchcombe by Nathaniel Hyett. [Hyett and Bazeley, *Bibliographer's Manual of Gloucestershire Literature,* 1896, p. 380.]

IBBITSON (ROBERT), printer in London, (1) Smithfield near the Queen's-Head-Tavern; (2) Near Hosier Lane; (3) Kings Head in the Old Bayley (?). 1646–61. Printed much of the literature of the Commonwealth period, and was joint printer with John Clowes and others of the news-sheet called *Perfect Occurrences* (1647–49). In 1653 his name was

put forward for the office of printer to the Council of State, but the appointment was given to Hills and Field. There are many references to him in
the State Papers and Journals of Parliament. The third address given
above is possibly that of M. Wright, *q.v.*

INMAN (MATTHEW), printer in London; Addle hill. Thames St., 1660-
63 (?). Printed for James Crump and James Magnes. Dead before 1664,
when he was succeeded by his widow.

INMAN (   ), widow, printer in London; Addlehill Thames Street,
1664. Succeeded her husband, Matthew Inman.

IRELAND (RICHARD), bookseller at Cambridge, 1634-52. His name
appears in a list of the privileged persons in the University of Cambridge,
circa 1624. [Bowes, *Cambridge University Printers*, p. 336.] Paid church
rate in Great St. Maries from 162⅔ to 163⅓, and was churchwarden for the ·
year 1635-6. Amongst his publications were two editions of Thos.
Randolph's *Jealous Lover*, those of 1634 and 1640.

ISLIP (SUSAN), printer in London; (?) Smithfield, 1641-61. Widow of
Adam Islip, who died in 1639, leaving his printing presses, etc., to Richard
Hearne or Herne, *q.v.* Hearne appears to have died about 1646, when
probably Susan Islip succeeded to the business.

JACKSON (EDWARD), bookseller in London, 1643. Took up his freedom
December 20th, 1633. [Arber, iii. 687.] Dealt in political pamphlets.

JACKSON (JOHN), bookseller in London; Without Temple Bar, 1634-40.
Took up his freedom December 20th, 1633. [Arber, iii. 687.] Associated
with G. Green, T. Homer, and F. Smith, *q.v.*

JACKSON (T   ), bookseller in London; Starre in Duck Lane,
1623-48. Took up his freedom June 9th, 1623. [Arber, iii. 685.] Amongst
his publications was Christian Ravius' *General Grammar for the Ebrew,
Samaritan, Calde, Syriac, Arabic and Ethiopic tongues*, 1648. He was
apparently succeeded by Thomas Huntingdon, *q.v.*, at this address.

JENKINS (THOMAS), bookseller in London; Next the Eagle and Child, Giltspur Street, 1656. Only known from the imprint to a pamphlet entitled *Englands Golden Legacy* . . . . *Written by Laurence Price.* *London* . . . . 1656.

JENNER (THOMAS), bookseller, printseller and engraver in London, (1) At the White beare in Cornewell [*i.e.*, Cornhill]; (2) At the White Beare neare the exchange; (3) South Entrance to the Royall Exchange. 1623–66. Dealer in all kinds of illustrated books and pamphlets, maps and prints. He was himself an engraver, amongst his work being portraits of Oliver Cromwell and Queen Christina of Sweden, an etching of a ship called "The Sovereign of the Seas," and presumably a set of plates for a work dealing with the twelve months.

JOHNSON (EDWARD), bookseller in London, 1642–3. Publisher of political pamphlets. [Hazlitt, *Handbook*, 526, 638.] His address has not been found.

JOHNSON (JAMES), bookseller in London, 1660 (?)–1663 (?). Publisher of political broadsides and pamphlets. His address has not been found.

JOHNSON (JOHN), bookseller in London, 1642–7. Publisher of political pamphlets. His address has not been found.

JOHNSON (MARMADUKE), bookseller and printer in London, 1660. Publisher of political pamphlets. Subsequently went to Cambridge, Massachusetts, as a printer, where he worked in the same building as Samuel Green. He died in 1675. [Plomer, *Short History*, p. 219.] He was the author of a work entitled *Ludgate what it is not, what it was,* which was entered in the Registers by Thomas Johnson, *q.v.* It was reprinted by Strype in his *Survey of London & Westminster,* 1755.

JOHNSON (SALOMON), bookseller in London, 1641. Only known from the imprint to a pamphlet entitled *The Generous usurer Mr. Nevell.* [Hazlitt, *Handbook,* 415.]

JOHNSON (THOMAS), printer in London, (1) Key or Golden Key, St. Paul's Churchyard, 1661–4; (2) White Cock, Rood Lane, Margaret Pattens (St. Dunstans in the East), 1660–6 (1642–77). In the survey taken in 1668 he is returned as having two presses and three workmen.

[Plomer, *Short History*, p. 226.] In April, 1666, he was imprisoned in Ludgate for printing a book that offended the censor, and was bound over in £500 to be of good behaviour. [*Domestic State Papers*, Charles II, 155, 70.] In 1659 he entered in the registers a work entitled *Ludgate what it is not, what it was, Or a full discovery and description of the nature and quality, orders and government of that Prison. By Mr. Johnson Typograph a late prisoner there.* [Stationers' Registers, Liber F, p. 156.] This was written by Marmaduke Johnson, printer. A list of books printed and sold by Thomas Johnson in 1658 occupies sigs. E e 5–8 in T. Polwhele's *Treatise of Self Denial*, 1658. [E 1733.] It consists of 36 works on various subjects, arranged in sizes, the titles being set out in full.

JOHNSON (W   ), bookseller in London, 1642. Publisher of political pamphlets. His address has not been found.

JONES (   ), bookseller at Worcester, 1663. Mentioned in an advertisement of patent medicines in *The Intelligencer* and *Newes* of that year.

JONES (JOHN), bookseller in London, (1) Near to the, Pump in Little Britain; (2) Royal Exchange in Cornhill. 1658–65. Publisher of political pamphlets and broadsides. Died August 9th, 1665. [Smyth's *Obituary*, p. 64.]

JONES (RICHARD), bookseller in London; Jermins Yard, Aldersgate Street, 1666. Mentioned in the Hearth Tax Roll for the half-year ending Lady Day, 1666. [P.R.O. Lay Subsidy $\frac{252}{32}$.]

JORDAN (TOBIAS), bookseller in Gloucester, 1644–64. Sheriff of Gloucester in 1644 and Mayor in 1659. [Bibl. Glouc., pp. liii, clvi.] His name is found on a broadside entitled *A Perfect and most useful table to compute the year of our Lord*, 1656, which was to be sold in London at the shop of Master Michell in Westminster Hall. [B.M. 669, f. 20 (32).] On September 13th, 1664, a warrant was issued to certain Aldermen of Gloucester to search his house for seditious books and papers. [*Domestic State Papers*, Charles II, vol. 102, 51.]

JOYCE (GEORGE), bookseller in London; Westminster Hall, 1662. Advertisement of patent medicine in the *Kingdoms Intelligencer* for that year.

JUNIUS (JAMES), *see* Young (James).

KELS (R.), (?) bookseller in London, 1653. Only known from the imprint to a broadside entitled *Lillies Banquet, or the star gazer's feast. London: Printed for R. Kels,* 1653.

KEMBE (ANDREW), bookseller in London, (1) By St. Margaret's Hill in long Southwarke, 1636; (2) St. Margaret's Hill in Southwark, 1642; (3) St. Margarets Hill, near the Talbot in Southwark. 1635–64. Took up his freedom June 7th, 1631. [Arber, iii. 686.] Under the year 1653, May 17th, Smyth records the death of "Mr. Kemm bookseller in Duck Lane." [*Obituary*, p. 34.] No books with a Duck Lane imprint and bearing Andrew Kembe's name have been found, but if the entry relates to him then the above list of imprints must be revised, and those books dated after 1653 must be held to have been published by his successor, possibly a son. A list of eight books published by Andrew Kembe in 1664 is given at the end of *Palladine of England,* 1664. [B.M. 12450, d. 7.]

KEMM (   ), bookseller in London; Duck Lane, 1653. Smyth in his *Obituary*, p. 34, under date May 17th, 1653, has the following entry : "Mr. Kemm, bookseller in Duck Lane, died." This may refer to Andrew Kembe.

KENDAL (G.), bookseller (?) in London; near the Old Bayly, 1663. Only known from the imprint to a pamphlet entitled *Merry Newes from Epsom Wells,* 1663. [Hazlitt, iii. 242.]

KEYNTON (MATTHEW), bookseller in London; Fountain in St. Pauls Churchyard, 1656. Only known from the imprint to a pamphlet entitled : Stephens (Nath.) *Plain and Easie calculation,* 1659. [Harl. 5965 (158).]

KINGSTON, or KYNGSTON (FELIX), printer in London, (1) Over against the sign of the checker, Paternoster Row, 1603 [Sayle, p. 604]; (2) In Pater-Noster-Row, at the Signe of the Gilded Cock, 1644. 1597–1651. Son of John Kingston, printer, 1553–84. Originally a member of the Company of Grocers, from which he was transferred to the Company of Stationers and admitted a freeman June 25th, 1597. [Arber, ii. 718.] According to Sir John Lambe's notes he succeeded his father in 1615, in

which year he had two presses. [Arber, iii. 699.] In 1618, in company
with Matthew Lownes and Bartholomew Downes, Felix Kingston was
appointed by Privy Seal one of the King's Printers in Ireland. He also
held a share in the Latin stock, in which he was one of the second rank,
but only paid £35 out of the £50 due from him, and subsequently with-
drew from the venture. [*Library*, July, 1907, p. 290 *et seq.*] Master of the
Company of Stationers, 1635-6. One of the twenty printers appointed
under the Act of 1637. Mr. Sayle states that he used five devices before
1640. At the time of his death he must have been one of the oldest
printers in London. For a list of books printed by him the reader is
referred to Gray's *Index to Haslitt*, p. 425. In the will of John Reeve, of
Teddington, co. Middlesex, husbandman, proved on December 24th,
1621, several bequests are made to a Felix Kingston and other persons
of the name of Kingston, but there is no evidence that they refer to the
printer. [P.C.C. 89 Savile.] The second imprint given above occurs in
Richard Bernard's *Thesaurus Biblicus seu Promptuarium Sacrum*, 1644.

KIRBY (GEORGE), (?) bookseller in London, 1642. Only known from the
imprint to a pamphlet entitled *Organs Funeral*, 1642.

KIRKMAN (FRANCIS), bookseller in London, (1) John Fletcher's Head,
over against the Angel-Inn, on the back side of St. Clements, without
Temple Bar, 1661-2; (2) Princes Arms, Chancery Lane, 1662, 1666-
8(?); (3) Under St. Ethelborough's Church in Bishopsgate Street, 1669;
(4) Ship, Thames Street, over against the Custom House, 1671; (5) Over
against the Robin Hood, Fenchurch Street, near Aldgate, 1674; (6) Next
door to the Princes Arms, St. Paul's Churchyard, 1678. 1657-78.
Francis Kirkman was the eldest son of Francis Kirkman, citizen and
blacksmith of London. In the "Preface to the Reader," in the Second
Part of the *English Rogue*, printed in 1668, he gives some interesting
particulars of his life. He was first apprenticed to a scrivener, but in 1656
set up as a bookseller, but "having knaves to deal with" he abandoned
bookselling and confined himself to his business as a scrivener. He then
lived in the East of London, possibly in Ratcliff, where his father was then
living. After the Restoration he moved into the West End, probably to
the house known as the John Fletcher's Head, and again set up as a
scrivener and bookseller. From his boyhood he had been a collector of

plays, and had written in 1657 a dedicatory epistle to an edition of Marlowe's *Lust's Dominion*. Kirkman was now drawn into the printing of play-books, of which, however, he declares he only printed three, which were his own copies, but his partners (*i.e.*, Nathaniel Brooke, of the Angel in Cornhill, Thomas Johnson, of the Golden Key in St. Paul's Churchyard, and Henry Marsh, of the Princes Arms in Chancery Lane, with whom he was then in business) printed the best plays then extant, though they were other men's copies. The owner of these copyrights issued a warrant, and one of Kirkman's partners, in order to avoid trouble, sold Kirkman his share, and a day or two afterwards sent the searchers to his house where they seized 1,400 play-books. At that time owing to a family bereavement, the death of his father, which took place between August, 1661, and May, 1662, he was unable to attend to business and never recovered any of the books. Being now left in good circumstances, Kirkman decided to give up business, and was induced to trust the partner who had before deceived him with the sale of his stock, but could never get any considerable return for his books. This person, who was un-doubtedly Henry Marsh, died of the plague in 1665 considerably indebted to Kirkman, who, in order to recover his money, secured the estate. This accounts for the second imprint of the Princes Arms in Chancery Lane, where once more in 1666 Kirkman set up in business as a bookseller. In 1661 he had printed a catalogue of all the English plays then printed, 690 in number, and this he now issued again, augmented to 806 items. Kirkman was accused by his contemporaries of asking exorbitant prices for his plays and issuing corrupt texts, but Mr. Greg finds no confirmation of this. His name appears for the last time in the *Term Catalogue* of Easter, 1678. [W. W. Greg, *List of English Plays*; D.N.B.; Arber, *Term Catalogue*, i. 310, 554.]

KIRTON (JOSEPH), (?) bookseller in London; King's Arms, St. Paul's Churchward, 1667. Smyth, in his *Obituary*, has this entry (p. 76): "Octr. 1667. This month Joseph Kirton sometime a bookseller at ye Kings Arms in Paul's Churchyard died; buried in St. Faith's."

KIRTON (JOSHUA), bookseller in London, (1) Foster Lane, next to Gold-smith's Hall, 1644; (2) White Horse in Paul's Churchyard, 1638-46; (3) Golden-Spread-Eagle, St. Pauls Churchyard, 1649 (1638-59). Took up his freedom November 7th, 1636. [Arber, iii. 688.] Originally in partnership with Thomas Warren. Shared with Humphrey Robinson, Richard Thrale and Samuel Thompson the copyrights of T. Whitaker, *q.v.*, consisting of 109 copies. Was one of the six stationers who in 1652 published a list of Popish books under the title of *A Beacon set on Fire.*

KNIGHT (THOMAS), bookseller in London; Holy Lamb Paul's Church-yard, 1629–60. Took up his freedom August 26th, 1627. [Arber, iii. 686.] Succeeded Clement Knight at this address. [Sayle, 591.]

KYNGSTON, *see* Kingston, F.

LAMBERD (WILLIAM), bookseller in London, 1641. Mentioned in a list of stationers dated August 5th, 1641, as paying five shillings as his propor-tion of the Poll Tax. [*Domestic State Papers,* Charles I, vol. 483. 11.] His address has not been found.

LAMBERT (JOHN), printer in London; Pilkington Court, Aldersgate Street, 1666. Mentioned in the Hearth Tax Roll for the half-year ending Lady Day, 1666. [P.R.O. Lay Subsidy $\frac{252}{32}$.]

LAMBERT (RICHARD), bookseller in York; The Crown Minster Yard, 1660–68. Publisher of Robert Wittie's *Scarborough Spaw,* 1660, 1667. Mentioned in an advertisement of patent medicines in the news-sheets of the year 1663.

LAMBERT (THOMAS), bookseller in London, (1) Horse-shooe, neare the Hospitall gate in Smithfield; (2) neere the Red Crosse in Little Britain. 1633–43. Publisher of ballads, broadsides, and other ephemeral literature. His first imprint is found on the title-page of a pamphlet entitled *A True Discourse of the Two infamous upstart Prophets Richard Farnham .... and John Bull,* 1636. [B.M. G. 20167.]

LAMBETH (THOMAS), stationer in London; Scroope's Court over agaynst yᵉ church in Holborne, 1661. Mentioned in the parish register of St. Andrew's, Holborn, 1661.

LANE (PHIL), (?) bookseller in London. Gray's Inn Gate, 1643. Appears to have been in partnership with Matthew Walbanck at the above address. Their names are found on a pamphlet entitled: *The Proceedings of the Commissioners ....* 1643. [E. 247 (28).]

LANGFORD (TOBY), bookseller in Gloucester, 1646. Mentioned in Hyett and Bazeley's *Manual of Gloucestershire Literature*, vol. i, p. 258, as publisher of Giles Workman's *Private men no pulpit men*, 1646.

LARKIN (GEORGE), bookseller and printer in London; Two Swans without Bishopsgate, 1666-90. Publisher of John Bunyan's *Grace Abounding*, 1666, 8°. Afterwards became a printer. [Gray's *Index to Haslitt*, p. 435.]

LARNER (WILLIAM), bookseller in London, (1) Golden Anchor, neere Paul's Chain, 1641; (2) The Bible in East Cheap, 1642; (3) Blackmoor in Bishopsgate Street, 1650; (4) Blackmoor near Fleet Bridge, 1652 (1641-59). A noted Puritan and Independent bookseller. In 1642 he published a kind of history of Lilburne's sufferings, which he entitled the *Christian Man's Trial*. He served in the Parliamentary army, but was invalided home and resumed his trade as a bookseller at the sign of the Blackamoor in Bishopsgate Street. He assisted Henry Robinson, Robert and Richard Overton, and John Lilburne to print books secretly, and is believed to have taken an active part in the working of the Coleman Street Press, 1643 (?)-4⅜; the Martin Mar Priest Press, 1645-46; the Goodman's Fields Press, 1645, and a press in Bishopsgate Street, 1646. Larner's premises were searched on several occasions, and he was at last thrown into prison, where he remained for many months. No more is heard of him after 1659. [Plomer, *Secret Printing during the Civil War*; *Library*, October, 1904, p. 374 *et seq.*]

LATHAM (CHRISTOPHER), bookseller in London. 1641-2. Took up his freedom January 18th, 1636. [Arber, iii. 687.] Edward Griffin printed for him. In 1642 he was associated with T. Creake in publishing several political pamphlets. His name disappears after July, 1642.

LATHAM (GEORGE), bookseller in London, (1) Brazen Serpent, St. Paul's Churchyard; (2) Bishop's Head, St. Paul's Church Yard. 1622-58. Took up up his freedom January 31st, 1620, and the same day took over several copyrights from the widow of George Bishop. [Arber, iii. 664, 685.] On November 6th, 1628, he received another assignment from Humphrey Lownes, but these he reassigned to Robert Young on December 6th, 1630. Latham was master of the Company of Stationers in 1650. His death

K

took place on April 21st, 1658 [Smyth's *Obituary*, p. 46], and his will was proved on May 10th following. From this it appears that he had a son George, who was at one time in partnership with him, but who had set up for himself; his daughter Ann married Edward Curle, and another daughter, Mary, was the wife of Timothy Garthwaite, *q.v.* [P.C.C. 244, Wotton.]

LATHAM (J   ), bookseller (?) in London; Mitre, St. Paul's Churchyard, 1661. Only known from the imprint to the Marquis of Argyle's *Instructions to a son*, 1661.

LAURENSON (G.), (?) bookseller in London, 1649. His name occurs in the imprint to a pamphlet entitled *The King of Scots his message and Remonstrance*, 1649. [E. 562 (8).]

LAWSON (THOMAS), bookseller in Edinburgh, 1645. Died May 11th, 1645. Inventory states: "His haill librarie and books withine his booth, being sold and roupeit, are estimat to the sowme of j^m ix^c and ffowrtie marks." [H. G. Aldis, *List of Books*, p. 116.]

LEACH (FRANCIS), printer in London; Faulcon in Shoe-Lane, Fleet Street, 1641–57. Took up his freedom June 30th, 1631. [Arber, iii. 686.] Printer of the news-sheet called *A Continuation of certain special and remarkable passages from both Houses of Parliament*. Administration of his effects was granted to his widow Joane, on July 8th, 1658. [*Admon. Act Book*, 1658.]

LEACH (JOHN), bookseller in Dublin; Castle Street, 1666. Only known from the imprint to: Bladen (Thos.), *Praxis Francisci Clarke* . . . . 1666. [B.M. 5063. aa. 1.]

LEACH (THOMAS), printer in London; Falcon in Shoe-Lane, Fleet Street, 1658–69. Possibly a son of Francis Leach, *q.v.* Some time in 1662 he was arrested at the instance of Sir John Birkenhead for printing seditious literature "with a base stollen edition of poor Hudibras." [*Domestic State Papers*, Charles II, vol. 49 (19); vol. 67 (30) and (161); vol. 89 (87).] In the Survey taken on July 29th, 1668, he is returned as having "one press and no more, provided by Mr. Graydon, and 1 workman." [Plomer, *Short History*, p. 227.]

LEAKE (WILLIAM), bookseller in London, (1) Crown in Fleet Street, between the two Temple gates; (2) In Chancery Lane, near the Rolls. 1635–81. Son of William Leake, stationer (1592–1634). Took up his freedom July 22nd, 1623. On June 1st, 1635, Widow Leake assigned over to him all his father's copyrights, and in 1638 he obtained from Robert Mead and Christopher Meredith the copyrights that had once belonged to Richard Hawkins. [Arber, iv. 340, 420.] Both these assignments contained several plays. The following issues contain lists of books : Beaumont and Fletcher's *Maid's Tragedy*, 1650, 53 entries; Shakespeare's *Merchant of Venice*, 1652, 16 entries; *The Fort Royal of Holy Scriptures* . . . . *by J. H.* . . . . 1652, number not stated; Beaumont and Fletcher's *King and No King* (sig. L 4 verso) and Shakespeare's *Othello* (sig. M 4 verso) both issued in 1655, 46 entries; James Shirley, *The Wedding* (sig. A 1 verso) 52 entries; James Shirley, *Grateful Servant* [1660?], 53 entries; Beaumont and Fletcher's *Philaster* [1660?], 60 entries. William Leake died in 1681, and his will is in the P.C.C. (184 North). [W. W. Greg, *List of English Plays*, Appendix.]

LEE, or LEY (WILLIAM), bookseller in London, (1) Paul's Chain, 1640–46; (2) Fleet Street, neere Sergeant's Inne, at the signe of the Golden Buck, 1621–52; (3) Turk's Head in Fleet Street next to the Miter and Phoenix [over against Fetter Lane], 1627–65; (4) Lombard Street, 1659 (1623–65). Three stationers of the name of Lee or Ley took up their freedom between 1601 and 1640, *i.e.*, William Lee, son of Frauncis Lee of Southwark, apprentice to Edward Venge for eight years from March, 1603 [Arber, ii. 270]; William Lee, made free October 2nd, 1620 [*ibid.*, iii. 685]; and William Lee, made free October 2nd, 1637 [*ibid.*, iii. 688]. A William Lee, of Lombard Street, was Master of the Company of Stationers in 1659. [Arber, v. lxv.] One of these men was associated with Richard Rogers in publishing a catalogue of plays in 1656 in an edition of Goffe's *Careless Shepherdess*. [W. W. Greg, *List of Plays*. Appendix II.]

LEE (WILLIAM), junior, bookseller in London; in Chancery Lane, a little above Crown Court, next the Bell, 1658. Probably the stationer whose freedom is recorded on October 2nd, 1637.

LEGATE (JOHN), printer in Cambridge and London ; Little Wood Street,
1620–58. Son of John Legate, printer at Cambridge (1588–1620).
Admitted Freeman of the Stationers' Company, September 6th, 1619.
[Arber, iv. 45.] Appointed printer to the University of Cambridge by
Grace, July 5th, 1650, in succession to Roger Daniel, *q.v.* His patent was
cancelled for neglect October 10th, 1655, after which he appears to have
come to London and settled in Little Wood Street. Smyth in his
Obituary, p. 49, has this entry, "Novr. 4th 1658, Mr. Legat in Little
Wood Street, printer, once printer at Cambridge, since distempered in
his senses, died." [R. Bowes, *Biographical Notes on the University
Printers*, p. 306.]

LEIGH (JOSEPH), bookseller in London ; Upper end of Bassinghall Street,
near the Naggs-Head-Tavern, 1662–5. Publisher of broadsides and
medical tracts. [Bibl. Lind., 95 ; Hazlitt, iii. 28.]

LEWIS (STEPHEN) and (THOMAS), booksellers in London ; Shoe-Lane, at
the signe of the book-binders, 1657–8. Their names are found in the
following work : H. Bold's *Wit a sporting in a pleasant grove of new
fancies*, 1657.

LEY (WILLIAM), *see* Lee (W.).

LEYBORNE, or LEYBOURN (ROBERT), bookseller and printer in
London, (1) Star, Cornhill ; (2) Monkswell Street in Lambes Chappel neer
Criplegate. 1645–61. Began as a bookseller and publisher of political
pamphlets. Printer of the news-sheet called the *Moderate Intelligencer*,
1647–8. In partnership with William Leyborne, or Leybourn, and printed
numerous scientific and mathematical books.

LEYBORNE, or LEYBOURN (WILLIAM), bookseller, printer, and mathe-
matician in London ; Monkswell Street Cripplegate, 1645–65. Possibly a
brother of Robert Leyborne, with whom he was in partnership as a
printer from about 1651, and carried on the business until the year 1665.
Together they printed books on mathematics, and it is as a mathema-
tician that William Leyborne is best remembered. He was the author of
several works on the subject, notably one entitled *Panarithmologia, being a*

Mirror Breviate Treasure Mate for merchants .... a work that was long popular and better known as the *Ready Reckoner or Trader's sure Guide.* The year of William Leyborne's death is uncertain, but it is believed to have occurred about 1700.

LEYBOURN, *see* Leyborne.

LIACH (F.), (?) printer in London, 1657. *See* Hazlitt, 4th series, p. 138. Probably a misprint for Leach, F., *q.v.*

LICHFIELD (ANNE), bookseller in Oxford, 1657–69. Widow of Leonard Lichfield, senr., was for a time in business with her son, Leonard Lichfield, junr.

LICHFIELD, or LITCHFIELD (LEONARD), printer in Oxford; Butcher Row [Queen's Street], 1635–57. Son of John Lichfield, and succeeded his father as University printer in 1635. He was a staunch Royalist, and was described in Puritan tracts as the "malignant printer." About 1643–4, he was churchwarden of St. Martin's (Carfax) Church. His printing office was destroyed in the great fire that broke out on October 6th, 1644. His imprint was frequently forged for books printed in London. Amongst the curiosities of his press is an imperfect copy of part of the Epistle of Barnabas in Greek and Latin belonging to an edition printed in 1642. The remainder of the edition was entirely destroyed in the fire, and this copy owes its preservation to the fact that it was wrongly imposed and is supposed to have been taken home by the printer or compositor. [Madan, *Chart of Oxford Printing*, p. 40.] Lichfield died in 1657.

LICHFIELD (LEONARD), junr., bookseller in Oxford. Son of Leonard Lichfield, senr. On the death of his father in 1657 he and his mother, Anne Lichfield, were appointed University printers.

LILLIECRAP, or LILLIECROP (PETER), printer in London, (1) Crooked Billet on Addle Hill; (2) The Five Bells near the church in Clerkenwell Close. 1647–72. Son of Peter Lillicrap, of Queatheack, co. Cornwall. Apprentice to Miles Fletcher, or Flesher, for seven years from April 5th, 1647. At the outbreak of the Civil War he made a discovery of arms, hidden by a Parliament man, and gave information to the High Sheriff of Cornwall, by whom they were seized. Lilliecrap afterwards served in the

Royalist army and was wounded and taken prisoner four times. On the expiration of his apprenticeship he set up for himself as a printer, but was watched with suspicion by the Parliamentary party, and the May before Cromwell died his press was seized by the official printer, Henry Hills, and he was sent a prisoner to the Tower for printing Walter Gostello's *Coming of God in Mercy and Vengeance.* He was in trouble again in 1663 for printing *Farewell Sermons* and other seditious literature, but was discharged from custody after a few weeks. Lilliecrap succeeded Daniel Maxwell as printer of the news-sheet *Mercurius Publicus.* At the survey of the press made in July, 1668, he was returned as employing one press, one apprentice, one compositor and one pressman. [Plomer, *Short History,* p. 227 ; *Domestic State Papers,* Charles II, vol. 77 (37) ; 78 (37–40).]

LINCOLN (STEPHEN), bookseller in Leicester, 1663. Gave information against Nathan Brookes, of London, for dispersing a book entitled the *Year of Prodigies.* [*Domestic State Papers,* Charles II, vol. 43 (9).]

LINDESAY (JAMES), printer in Edinburgh; "On the south side of the Cow-gate a little above the College winde," 1643–9. Appointed printer to Edinburgh University. Will registered December 13th, 1649. Probably died or was incapacitated about 1646, as in that year the heirs of R. Bryson printed the University Theses. Lithgow succeeded him as printer to the University on July 5th, 1648.

LINDSEY (GEORGE), bookseller in London; Over against London Stone, 1642–8. Associated with F. Coles. Published the following amongst other political pamphlets : L. (W.), Esquire's *Courts of Justice corrected and amended,* 1642. [B.M. E. 108 (31)]; *Roundhead uncovered,* 1642. [B.M. E. 108 (9)]; *Tub-preachers overturned,* 1647. [B.M. E. 384 (7).]

LITCHFIELD, *see* Lichfield.

LITHGOW (GIDEON), printer in Edinburgh, 1645–62. In 1645 named cautioner in the confirmation of will of R. Bryson, *q.v.* Appointed printer to Edinburgh University July 5th, 1648, in succession to J. Lindesay. Wife, Isobel Harring, probably widow of R. Bryson. Died in December, 1662. Some of his ornaments formerly in possession of Hart and J. Bryson, and afterwards used by A. Anderson. [H. G. Aldis, *List of Books,* pp. 116, 117.]

LITTLEBURY (ROBERT), bookseller in London; Unicorn in Little Britain, 1652–67. One of the overseers to the will of W. Dugard. Mentioned in the Hearth Tax Roll for the half-year ending Lady Day, 1666. [P.R.O. Lay Subsidy, $\frac{252}{32}$.]

LLOYD (HENRY), printer in London, 1662–8. In the return made of the London printers in July, 1668, he is briefly stated to have one press. He printed for William Dugard an edition of Sidney's *Arcadia* in 1662, which was published by George Calvert. His address has not been found.

LLOYD (LODOWICKE), bookseller in London, (1) Next to the Castle Tavern in Cornhill; (2) The Castle in Cornhill, 1655–74. Presumably a son of Llodowicke Lloyd the poet. He is first met with as a bookseller in partnership with Henry Cripps, of Pope's Head Alley, in the publication of Henry Vaughan the Silurist's *Silex Scintillans or Sacred Poems* in 1655. They were also associated in other ventures. Amongst Lloyd's other publications may be mentioned the *Poems* of Matthew Stevenson issued in 1665, and the works of Jacob Boehme. Catalogues of books printed for him will be found at the end of John Norton's *Abel being Dead yet speaketh*, 1658. [E. 937 (6)]; and Samuel Pordage's *Mundorum Explicatio*, 1661. [B.M. 1077, d. 35.] Lloyd's name appears in the *Term Catalogues* for the last time in Easter, 1674. [Arber, *T.C.*, i. 175.] His address is somewhat of a puzzle. In the same book it will be found in the two forms given above, one on the title-page and the other on the "Catalogue of Books" at the end. Humphrey Blunden, *q.v.*, also gave his address as the Castle in Cornhill.

LOCK (T.), printer (?) in London; Sea-cole Lane. 1655–60. Printer for the Rosicrucians. [Gray's *Index to Haslitt*, p. 458; Ames' *Collection of Title-pages*, No. 2862.]

LONDON (WILLIAM), bookseller at Newcastle upon Tyne, Bridge Foot, 1653–60. Chiefly remembered for his *Catalogue of the most vendible books in England*, published first in 1657, with a supplement down to June 1st, 1658, and a further supplement in 1660 down to Easter term of that year, issued under the title, *A Catalogue of New Books By Way of Supplement to the Former. Being such as have been Printed from that time till Easter Term.* 1660. In this he held out the expectation of another issue of the catalogue in the following year, but nothing is known of any further supplement. In this catalogue the books were arranged in classes, Divinity coming first, and being followed by History, Physick, etc. In each class the works were arranged alphabetically under the authors. This catalogue has been absurdly attributed to William Juxon, Bishop of London, and later to Thomas Guy the bookseller. [Growoll (A.), *English Booktrade Bibliography*, p. 48.] London also printed several books against the Quakers, which were printed for him by Stephen Bulkley at York.

LOWNDES (RICHARD), bookseller in London, (1) Adjoyning to Ludgate [on Ludgate Hill]; (2) White Lyon in St. Paul's Churchyard; (3) White Lyon, Duck Lane near West Smithfield. [Arber, *Term Catalogues*, i. 557.] 1640–75. Took up his freedom September 26th, 1639 [Arber, iii. 688.] Dealt in miscellaneous literature. Amongst his publications was Francis Quarles' *Barnabas and Boanerges*. 1644.

LUGGAR, or LUGGARD (WILLIAM), bookseller in London, (1) Blind Knight, Holborn; (2) Upon Holborn Bridge; (3) Postern by the Tower. 1599–1658. Apprentice with Henry Carr. Took up his freedom July 21st, 1597. Publisher of mathematical and nautical books. In partnership with William Fisher, *q.v.* Died in 1658. [Smyth's *Obituary*, p. 47.]

LUNNE (ROBERT), bookseller in London; Next the Old Crane, Lambeth Hill [at the end of old Fish Street], 1641–6. Took up his freedom June 15th, 1627. [Arber, iii. 686.] Publisher of George Chapman's play, *Bussy D'Amboise*, 1641, 1646.

MABB (RALPH), bookseller in London; Greyhound St. Paul's Churchyard, 1610–42. Son of John Mabb, goldsmith of London. Apprentice to William Leake for eight years from Christmas, 1603. Took up his freedom January 16th, 1610. [Arber, ii. 269; iii. 683.] Amongst his publications may be mentioned the first edition of John Gwillim's *Display of Heraldrie*, and a play called *The Spanish Bawd*, by James Mabbe.

MABB (THOMAS), printer in London, (1) Ivy Lane; (2) St. Pauls Wharf, next doore to the signe of the Ship [neer the Thames], 1650–65. Thomas Mabb is first found in partnership with A. Coles, the earliest book in which their joint imprint is found being Alexander Ross's translation from John

+ c. c. R.

Wallebius, entitled *The Abridgment of Christian Divinitie*, an octavo printed in 1650. Their office was furnished with a large assortment of type in all sizes, which will bear favourable comparison with that in use in other London printing offices at that time. The partnership appears to have been dissolved some time after August 12th in the following year, and Thomas Mabb is afterwards found printing alone. He was employed by many of the London booksellers, amongst others Henry Atkinson, J. Playfere, W. Sheares, J. Starkey, E. Thomas, and M. Young. In 1663 he is found printing books in conjunction with Richard Hodgkinson. Thomas Mabb was one of the chief witnesses against his brother printer, John Twyn, of Cloth Fair, who was executed at Tyburn for printing a book against the Government, and he afterwards printed an official account of the trial. Amongst other books that came from his press may be noticed Richard Kilburne's *Brief Survey of the County of Kent*, 1657; R. Fletcher's translation of *Martials Epigrams*, 1656; Jo. V. Belcamp's *Consilium & Votum Pro Ordinanda & Stabilienda Hibernia*, 1651, a folio of 38 pages, containing proposals for the settlement of Ireland in the interests of the Adventurers; and John Tatham's *London Tryumphs*, 1658 and 1661, being the author's account of the pageant in connection with the Lord Mayor's annual procession. Mabb probably fell a victim to the Plague of 1665, as no more is heard of him after that date.

MABORNE (F.), *see* Mawborne (F.).

MACOCKE (JOHN), printer in London; Addle or Addling Hill [Thames Street], 1645–92. First entry in the Registers April 5th, 1645. In 1660 he was appointed printer to the Parliament in conjunction with John Streator, and also held the post of printer to the House of Lords with Francis Tyton. He was associated with T. Newcombe in printing *Mercurius Publicus* and the *Parliamentary Intelligencer*. In 1664 he was in trouble for printing law books. [P.R.O. Chan. Proc. before 1714, Reynardson, B. 31, Stationers' Company *v.* Flesher.] On June 4th, 1666, he commenced a news-sheet called the *Current Intelligence*. When the survey of the press was made in 1668 he was found to have three presses, three apprentices and ten workmen; it was, in fact, one of the largest printing houses in London. Macocke was Master of the Stationers' Company in 1680, to which at his death he left a silver cup. [Timperley, p. 575.]

MAGNES (JAMES), bookseller in London; Russell Street near the Piazza in Covent Garden, 1660–79. Publisher of plays and novels, succeeded in 1679 by M. Magnes, probably his widow. [Arber, *Term Catalogues*, i. p. 557.]

MALPAS (JOAN), bookseller (?) at Sturbridge [*i.e.*, Stourbridge] in Worcestershire, 1661. Found in the imprint to the following pamphlet : *Monarchiæ Encomium est sceptrum sive solium Justitia Stabilitum, or A congratulation of the King's Coronation .... By Tho. Malpas, Preacher of the Gospel at Pedmore in Worcester-shire. London, Printed by T. Leach, and are to be sold by .... Joan Malpas in Sturbridge in Worcester-shire*, 1661.

MAN (EDWARD), bookseller in London; Swan in St. Paul's Church-Yard, 1665. Successor to S. Man, *q.v.*, at this address. His name is found on the following book : *The Princesse Cloria or, the Royal Romance .... The Second Edition. London : Printed for Edward Man at the sign of the Swan in St. Pauls Church-yard.* 1665, a re-issue of the unsold copies previously published by William Brooke in 1661.

MAN (SAMUEL), bookseller in London, (1) Swan in Paul's Church yard; (2) Ivy Lane. 1616–74. Apprentice to William Welby. Warden of the Company of Stationers 1643, 1644, and Master in the years 1646, 1654 and 1658. He died in April, 1674, at the age of eighty-seven. [Smyth's *Obituary*, p. 101.] His will was dated December 28th, 1672, and mentions three sons, Thomas, James, and Edward. He left a sum of £320 in the English stock to his wife Anne, and appointed Samuel Gellibrand, *q.v.*, the overseer of his will. [P.C.C. 49. Bunce.]

MARRIOT (JOHN), bookseller in London; [White] Flower de Luce, Fleet Street [St. Dunstan's Churchyard], 1616–57. Published the works of Breton, Donne, Drayton, Massinger, Quarles, and Wither. His son, Richard Marriot, *q.v.*, was for some time in partnership with him, and eventually succeeded to the business.

MARRIOT (RICHARD), bookseller in London; Under St. Dunstan's Church in Fleet Street [White Flower de Luce], 1645–79. In partnership with his father, John Marriot, *q.v.*, for some years. On May 3rd, 1651, his father assigned over to him a large number of copyrights. Amongst his most noted publications was the first edition of Isaak Walton's *Complete Angler*, 1653, printed for him by T. Maxey.

MARSH (HENRY), bookseller in London, (1) Princes Armes at the lower end of Chancery Lane, neer the Inner Temple Gate in Fleet Street; (2) Over against the golden Lyon tavern in Princes Street; (3) Swan Alley, Ludgate Hill. 1641–65. Took up his freedom October 5th, 1635. [Arber, iii. 687.] Associated with Francis Kirkman in publishing plays. He died before the end of the year 1665, and by his will dated September 10th left everything to his mother, Susan Tyton, widow, of St. Andrew's, Holborn. His brother, Michael Marsh, administered the will, but Kirkman took over the business. A list of books on sale by Marsh in 1661 occupies the last three pages of Montelion's *Don Juan Lamberto*, 1661, 4°. Amongst the folios was Ed. Grimstone's edition of *Polybius*; amongst the quartos, Walker's *History of Independency*; and amongst the octavos, Quarles' last poems. [B.M. E. 1048 (6); P.C.C. 100. Hyde.]

MARSHALL (JOHN), bookseller in London; Hand and Pen in Corn-hill over against the Royall Exchange, 1646. William Bentley, *q.v.*, printed for him Dr. Peter Chamberlen's *Voice in Rhama* .... *London*, 1647. [E. 1181. (8).]

MARTIN (EDWARD), bookseller in Norwich; Upper Half Moone in the Market Place, 1646. His name is found on a pamphlet entitled *Hue and Cry after Vox Populi*, 1646. [E. 355. (13).]

MARTIN, or MARTYN (JOHN), bookseller in London; Bell in St. Paul's Churchyard, 1649–80. Partner with James Allestry, *q.v.*, and succeeded him as publisher to the Royal Society. The last entry to him in the *Term Catalogues* is in May, 1680. [Arber, *T.C.*, i., p. 398.]

MARTIN (R   ), bookseller in London; At the Venice in the Old Bayly, 1641. His name is found on the following work: *Antipathie betweene the French and Spaniard Englished by Robert Gentilys*, 1641.

MARTIN MAR-PRIEST PRESS. The writings of Richard Overton against the Presbyterians, under the pseudonym of Martin Mar-Priest, were printed at a secret press in Bishopsgate Street, supposed to have belonged to William Larner, between April 8th, 1645, and January, 164⁶⁄₇. [*Library*, October, 1904, p. 382.]

MASON (EDWARD), (?) printer in London, 1660. Found in the imprint to a pamphlet entitled *Sir Arthur Hesilrigs lamentation & Confession*, 1660. [E. 1016 (4).] The name is probably a pseudonym.

MATHEWES (JOHN), (?) bookseller in London, (?) 1647. Hazlitt, iii. p. 37, records the following: *A True Abstract of a list, In which is set down the severall entertainments allowed by His Majesty to the Officers and other souldiers of his Army . . . . London, Printed for John Mathewes* [about 1647].

MATTHEWS (THOMAS), bookseller in London, (1) ad insigne Galli Gallinacei in cœmeterio Paulino juxta portam Borealem minorem ; (2) At the Cock in St. Pauls Church-Yard ; (3) White Horse in St. Paul's Church yard, 1651–7. Published amongst other things in 1652 an edition of Ant. Buscher's *Ethicæ Ciceron.*, of which the first edition was printed at Hamburg in 1610. [Schweiger, *Handbuch der classichen Bibliographie*, 1832, p. 252.] The title-page of Matthews' edition is preserved amongst the Ames Collection (No. 2254), but no copy of the book has been seen.

MAWBORNE, or MAWBURNE (FRANCIS), bookseller in York, 1662–6. This bookseller was doubtless in business some years before his name appears in the imprint to the Visitation sermon printed for him by Stephen Bulkley, the York printer, in 1663. In 1666 Mawburne and Bulkley were arrested, the one for printing seditious papers, and the other for selling foreign printed Bibles and seditious papers. Mawburne petitioned Lord Arlington for release from custody, and one John Mascall wrote a letter to Secretary Williamson, dated October 15th, on behalf of the prisoners, in which he described the bookseller as "quiet but weak in business," who "would not wilfully disperse any unlicensed book or pamphlet." On giving bond for his good behaviour Mawburne was released after a few weeks' imprisonment. [*Domestic State Papers*, Charles II, vol. 175 (28) ; *Library*, January, 1907.]

MAXEY (THOMAS), printer in London ; Bennet Paul's Wharf, Thames Street, 1637–1657. Took up his freedom October 2nd, 1637. [Arber, iii. 688.] First book entry June 23rd, 1640. Amongst the famous books that passed through his press was Izaak Walton's *Complete Angler*, 1653, which he printed for R. Marriot. Maxey also printed for William Weekly, bookseller of Ipswich, *q.v.* His name is found in the Churchwardens' books of St. Bennet from 1655. His will was dated January 2nd, 165⁹⁄₇, and proved on the 20th of the same month. He left his estate to his wife Anne, who succeeded him in the business. A son Jonathan is also mentioned, and legacies were left to his servants [*i.e.* apprentices] David Maxey, Thomas Putnam, William Godfrey. [P.C.C. 3. Ruthen.]

MAXEY (ANNE), printer in London; Bennet Paul's Wharf, 1657. Widow of Thomas Maxey. Printed several works for William Weekly, bookseller at Ipswich.

MAXWELL (ANNE), printer in London; Thames St. near Baynards Castle, 1665–75. Widow of David Maxwell. In the survey made on July 29th, 1668, she is returned as having two presses, no apprentices, three compositors and three pressmen. [Plomer, *Short History*, p. 227.]

MAXWELL (DAVID), printer in London; Thames Street, near Baynard's Castle, 1659–65. His name appears in the Churchwardens' books of St. Bennet, Paul's Wharf, from 1658–63. Published a newspaper called *Mercurius Veridicus* on June 12th, 1660, but when only two numbers were issued it was stopped by order of the House of Commons. Maxwell died about 1665, when the business passed to his widow, Anne Maxwell.

MAYNARD (JOHN), bookseller in London; George in Fleet Street, 1641. Took up his freedom July 20th, 1635. [Arber, iii. 687.] Associated with Timothy Wilkins in the publication of the writings of John Wilkins, Bishop of Chester. [Hazlitt, ii. 494, 644.]

MEAD (ROBERT), bookseller (?) in London; (?) Crane in St. Paul's Churchyard. [Ch. Meredith's house], 1617–56. Son of Thomas Mead, of Weston, co. Somerset, husbandman. Apprentice to John Standish for nine years from Michaelmas, 1599. Took up his freedom October 3rd, 1608. [Arber, iii. 683.] Warden of the Company of Stationers, 1638, 1642; Master of the Company, 1644, 1645, 1649. In company with Christopher Meredith took over all the copyrights of Richard Hawkins, but they transferred them to William Leake a few months later. [Arber, iv. 420, 452.] No book has been found bearing Mead's name in the imprint.

MEARNE (SAMUEL), bookseller and bookbinder in London; Little Britain, 1655–83. The first heard of Samuel Mearne is in 1655, when in company with Cornelius Bee, *q.v.*, and W. Minshew, he was granted a pass to go to Holland [*Domestic State Papers*, 1655, p. 598]. In 1659 he entered a book in the Registers of the Stationers' Company entitled *Meditations in Three Centuries*, by the Rev. Henry Tabb, so that he was clearly in business as a bookseller at this time. He was appointed a searcher under the Company of Stationers at the Restoration, and an interesting series of papers dealing with this part of his work will be found in the Hist. MSS. Commn. Report 9 [Appendix, p. 72 *et seq.*] Mearne also held a share in the King's Printing Office. [*Library*, N.S., October, 1901, p. 373.] At the desire of Charles II he purchased the collection of pamphlets made by the bookseller George Thomason, but does not appear to have been paid for them, and they were subsequently sold by his successors to King George III. It is, however, chiefly as a bookbinder that Samuel Mearne is remembered. In 1660 he received a patent as bookbinder to Charles II for life at an annual fee of £6 per annum, and several of his accounts for binding books are preserved among the Wardrobe accounts at the Public Record Office. From these it appears that he generally bound his books in red or black Turkey leather. He executed some very choice bindings, the best known being those described as the "cottage" design. Samuel Mearne died in 1683, and his will is in the Prerogative Court of Canterbury. [C. Davenport, *Samuel Mearne, Binder to K. Charles II.* Publications of the Caxton Club. Chicago, 1906.]

MEIGHEN (MERCY), bookseller in London, (?) Under St. Clements Church [Strand], 1642–54. Widow of Richard Meighen. In partnership with G. Bedell. In 1650 Thomas Collins was taken as third partner. The retirement or death of M. Meighen in 1654 caused some confusion. Gabriel Bedell's name is found in connection with R. Marriot and T. Garthwaite, and the imprint J. Crook, G. Bedell & Partners is held to refer to this house, which before the end of the year became Gabriel Bedell & T. Collins.

MEIGHEN (RICHARD), bookseller in London; Under St. Clements Church [Strand], 1615–41. Is found in partnership with Ephraim Dawson, W. Lee, and D. Pakeman in the publication of law books early in 1641, but he died before the close of this or early in the succeeding year, administration of his goods being granted to his widow, Mercy Meighen, on March 21st, 164½.

MELVILL (DAVID), bookseller in Aberdeen, 1622–43. Buried February 8th, 1643. Son, Robert Melvill. All his books that have been found were printed for him by E. Raban. [H. G. Aldis, *List of Books*, p. 117.]

MEREDITH (CHRISTOPHER), bookseller in London; Crane in St. Paul's Churchyard, 1629–53. Took up his freedom October 4th, 1624. [Arber, iii. 686.] Was associated at one time and another with Edward Brewster, Robert Mead, and Philemon Stevens. Dealt chiefly, if not wholly, in theological books. He died on May 19th, 1653. [Smyth's *Obituary*, p. 34.] His will, dated January 24th, 1652, was proved on September 1st, 1653. He left no son, and bequeathed his copyrights to his brother-in-law, Andrew Kembe, *q.v.* His two houses in St. Paul's Churchyard, the one he occupied (The Crane), and the one occupied by Francis Egglesfield (The Marigold), which he had purchased of Thomas Man, were left to the Company of Stationers (1) To provide an annual sum of £10 to be lent to poor freemen of the Company; (2) To provide bibles for his tenants of the manor of Kempsey, co. Worcester, and school books for the use of the school there. Meredith also owned the house in Paternoster Row called The Chequer. Philemon Stephens, John Legate, and Andrew Kembe were named as executors in the event of the death of the executors nominated [P.C.C. 229. Brent.]

MERREALL (ALEXANDER), bookseller in London; White Hart and Bear in Bread Street, 1662. Mentioned in an advertisement of the Welsh bible in octavo, in *Mercurius Publicus*, February 6th, 166½.

MICHAEL, *see* Mitchel (M.).

MILBORNE, or MILBOURNE (ROBERT), bookseller in London, (1) At the Great South Door of Pauls, 1623–6. [Sayle, 930]; (2) The Greyhound, Paul's Churchyard, 1628–35. [Sayle, 930]; (3) Unicorn, near Fleet Bridge, 1636–9; (4) Holy Lambe in Little Britain, 1641; (5) Britains Burse (?) [New Exchange, Strand]. 1618–41. Took up his freedom March

1st, 1617. [Arber, iii. 684.] He died at the end of 1642 or the beginning of 1643, as on February 23rd in the latter year thirty-four of his copyrights were transferred to Thomas Dainty, and by him re-assigned to the widow of Ch. Meredith. [Stationers' Registers, Liber D.]

MILBOURNE (THOMAS), printer in London; Jewin Street [Aldersgate Street], 1659–67. Took up his freedom July 7th, 1634. [Arber, iii. 687.] Was in trouble in 1666 for printing *The Catholic Apology*. [*Domestic State Papers*, Charles II, vol. 182 (68, 69).] He made overtures for printing the weekly *Gazette*, and undertook that a new fount of type should be cast for it. In the survey taken on July 29th, 1668, he was returned as having two presses, no apprentices and two workmen.

MILLER (ABRAHAM), printer in London; Blackfriars, 1646–53. Eldest son of George Miller. He succeeded to the business on the death of his father in 1646. Printed, amongst others, for E. Dod, Nath. Ekins, William Lee and Christopher Meredith.

MILLER (GEORGE), printer in London; Blackfriars, 1601–46. Son of George Miller, of Kettering, co. Northampton, schoolmaster. Apprentice to Richard Field, successor to Thomas Vautrollier, for seven years from Michaelmas, 1604. [Arber, ii. 281.] Field at his death left him a bequest of twenty shillings to purchase a ring. [Plomer, *Wills*, p. 51.] George Miller and Richard Badger afterwards purchased the business. [Arber, iii. 703.] George Miller died before October 8th, 1646, on which day his will, dated July 20th preceding, was proved in the Prerogative Court of Canterbury. [P.C.C. 147. Twisse.] In it occurs this passage : "*Item* I give to my sonne Abraham the lease of my house in the Blackfriars with the letter and presses copies and all other utensils belonginge to the printinge house to enter all these immediately after my decease." Miller had four other sons, William, John, Symon, and George, all of whom except John are found as booksellers. The will also mentions a daughter Martha, a brother William, and sisters Elizabeth Coe, Ellen Brewster, Elizabeth Archer, and Sarah Foster, the residue being left to his wife Anne. Amongst the witnesses was John Clarke, probably the bookseller of that name.

MILLER (GEORGE), junior, printer in London, 1665. His imprint is found in John Webster's *The White Devil*, 1665. [B.M. 644 f. 76.] He was probably the son of George Miller, printer at Blackfriars.

MILLER (JAMES), bookseller at Edinburgh, (1) In the Cowgate, at the sign of S. John the Divine, at the foot of the Colledge-wynd', 1665; (2) On the North side of the street against the Crosse, at the sign of S. John the Divine, 1671. (1665–72). One of the six booksellers who in 1671 appealed against A. Anderson. Will registered August 2nd, 1672. [H. G. Aldis, *List of Books*, p. 117.]

MILLER (SIMON), bookseller in London; Star in St. Paul's Churchyard, 1653–84. Son of George Miller. Apprenticed April 24th, 1645, to Andrew Crooke. Four books published by him are advertised at the end of Parivale's *Historie of the Iron Age*, 1659.

MILLER (WILLIAM), bookseller in London; Gilded Acron [acorn] in St. Paul's Churchyard, near the little north door, 1661–98. Believed to be the son William mentioned in the will of George Miller, printer at Black-friars, who died in 1646. William Miller was an important bookseller throughout the reign of Charles II and James II. [Arber, *Term Catalogues*, vols. i. and ii.]

MILLESON (JOHN), bookseller in Cambridge; Over against Great St. Maries, 1642. Only known from the imprint to a pamphlet entitled *A Protestants account of his orthodox holding in matters of religion*, 1642. [Bowes, *Cambridge Books*, p. 29, no. 79.]

MILLION (JOHN), bookseller in London; Man in the Moon, in the Little Old Bayly, 1666. Only known from the imprint to Elkanah Settle's *Mare Clausum: Or a Ransack for the Dutch*, 1666, printed by Peter Lilliecrap, *q.v.* He appears to have been succeeded by Henry Million, possibly a son. [Arber, *Term Catalogues*, i., pp. 57, etc.]

MILLS (RICHARD), bookseller in London; Pestel and Mortar without Temple Bar, 1665–74. Last entry in *Term Catalogues*, Easter, 1674. [Arber, *Term Catalogues*, i. 171.]

L

MILNER (PETER) (?) bookseller in Warrington, Lancashire, *c.* 1641. In the will of James Milner, of Warrington, co. Lancashire, stationer, proved on the 18th April, 1639, occurs the following passage: "To Peter Milner my servant the half of the books in my shop in Warrington and all such patternes, workloomes, and colers wch I use to paint and drawe worke withall." [*Transactions* of the Historic Society of Lancashire and Cheshire, Vol. 37, pp. 67–115; *Booksellers and Stationers in Warrington, 1639–1657.* By W. H. Rylands, F.S.A.]

MILWARD (WILLIAM), bookseller in London; Without Westminster Hall Gate, 1656. Only known from the imprint to F. Duke's *Fulness & Freeness of God's Grace,* 1656.

MINSHALL (W.), *see* Minshew (W.).

MINSHEW (WILLIAM), bookseller (? in Chester), 1655. In company with Cornelius Bee, and Saml. Mearne, he was granted a pass to go to Holland in 1655. The name may be a misreading for William Minshall, who took up his freedom July 7th, 1634. [Arber, iii. 687.] There were booksellers of the name of Minshull in Chester some years later.

MITCHEL, or MICHAEL (MILES), bookseller in London, (1) Within the Gate [*i.e.*, Westminster Hall Gate]; (2) At the first shop in Westminster Hall, 1656–63. He was London agent for T. Jordan, of Gloucester, *q.v.*

MOND (DUNCAN), stationer at Edinburgh, *c.* 1650. "Duncan Mond, stationer in Edinburgh, had a gift of King's printer conferr'd on him, which entirely cut off Tyler." [Watson, 10.] Mr. H. G. Aldis does not confirm this statement, though he quotes it, neither has he apparently come across a single work that bears it out. [H. G. Aldis, *List of Books,* p. 117.]

MOONE (RICHARD), bookseller in London; Seven Stars in St. Paul's Churchyard neer the great north doore, 1653–5. Issued books in conjunction with John Allen, *q.v.* His mark, consisting of a play upon his name, will be found amongst the Bagford fragments. [Harl. 5963 (75).] There was also a Richard Moon or Moone, bookseller in Bristol, who may be identical with the above.

MOONE, or MOON (RICHARD), bookseller in Bristol; Winn Street, 1661-3. In 1663 he was imprisoned for selling seditious literature. Letters were found on his premises from Thomas Brewster and S. M., probably Simon Miller, with whom he admitted having dealings, as well as with Eliz. Calvert, and other London booksellers. [*Domestic State Papers*, Charles II, vol. 81, No. 73, 73 i., ii., iii.] He may be identical with the Richard Moone, bookseller in London, 1653-5.

MOORE (JOSEPH), bookseller in London; Little Britain, 1657-67. Only known from the imprint to a pamphlet entitled *Killing is Murder* .... London. Printed for Joseph Moor .... 1657. [Hazlitt, ii. 150.] There are several stationers of the name of Moore mentioned in the *Transcripts* [Arber, v. 254.]

MOORE (SUSANNA), bookseller in Bristol, 1667. Is mentioned in an information laid by the Mayor of Bristol as having received certain books relating to the Fire of London from Elizabeth Calvert. [*Domestic State Papers*, Charles II, vol. 209 (75).]

MORDEN (WILLIAM), bookseller in Cambridge, 1652-79. Buried March 9th, 167⅞, in St. Michael's Parish [Venn's *St. Michael Registers*, p. 127; Bowes' *Catalogue of Cambridge Books*.]

MORE (JOHN), Assigns of [*i.e.*, Miles Fletcher, John Haviland, and Robert Young], 1629-61. On January 19th, 15 James I [1618], letters patent were granted to John More or Moore, Esquire, for the sole printing of all books of the Common Law, Statutes, as well as Rastell's and Poulton's Abridgements, for a term of forty years, on the expiration of the patent previously held by Thomas Wight and Bonham Norton, which expired on March 10th, 162⅞. Whether or not More himself actually printed is uncertain, but he provided a stock of type. On May 1st, 1629, he assigned over all his printing rights to Miles Fletcher and his partners John Haviland and Robert Young, for an annual payment of £60 and a third of the profits. John More died on August 17th, 1638, leaving this annuity to his daughter Martha, the wife of Richard Atkyns, *q.v.* This legacy was the subject of a law suit which ended disastrously for Fletcher, who, after the death of his partners, had made a verbal assignment of his rights to the Company of Stationers for a cash payment of £200, but subsequently refused to carry it out, alleging that by a decree made in the Court of Chancery the patent was vested in Richard Atkyns. [P.R.O. Chancery Proceedings. Before 1715. Reynardson, Bund. 31, 126.]

MORGAN (JOHN), bookseller in London; Old Bayly, 1642. Only known from the imprint to John Taylor's *Heads of all fashions .... London, Printed for John Morgan, to be sold in the Old-baily, 1642.* [Hazlitt, H. 601.]

MORGAN (JOHN), printer (?) in London, 1660. Hazlitt, ii. (107), records *The Royal Pilgrimage .... By an Eye-witness. London, Printed by John Morgan,* 1660.

MORGAN (THOMAS), bookseller (?) in London, 1660. Only known from the imprint to a pamphlet entitled *Short Representation performed before the Lord General Monk,* 1660.

MORGAN (W   ), bookseller (?) in London; Near the Blue Boar Ludgate Street, 1661. In Mr. G. J. Gray's Index to Hazlitt there is a reference under this name, but it appears to be a misprint.

MORISON (JOHN), bookseller in Glasgow, 1659–62. One of the debtors in Lithgow's inventory, 1662. [H. G. Aldis, *List of Books*, p. 117.]

MORTLOCK (HENRY), bookseller in London, (1) Phœnix in St. Paul's Churchyard; (2) White Hart in Westminster Hall. 1660–1702. Chiefly a publisher of theological literature.

MOSELEY (ANNE), bookseller in London; Prince's Arms, Paul's Churchyard, 1661–4. Widow of Humphrey Moseley.

• MOSELEY (HUMPHREY), bookseller in London; Princes Arms St. Paul's Churchyard, 1630–61. Conjectured to be a son of Samuel Moseley, a Staffordshire man, who was a stationer in London. [Arber, ii. 249; iii. 683.] Took up his freedom May 7th, 1627. [*ibid.*, iii. 686.] His first book entry May 29th, 1630. He became the chief publisher of the finer literature of his age. He published the first collected edition of Milton's Poems, as well as the works of Cartwright, Crashaw, D'Avenant, Denham,

Donne, Fanshaw, Howell, Vaughan, and Waller. He died January 31st, 1660–61, and was buried in St. Gregory's. By his will he appointed his wife Anne and his only daughter Anne his executors, and bequeathed £10 for a bowl to the Stationers' Company. [D.N.B.] An interesting list of books sold by him in 1640, with dates of publication and prices attached, is amongst the *State Papers*, Charles I, vol. 478, no. 16. This consists of 76 items, the greater part being plays, and the average price was sixpence apiece. Printed lists of his publications were issued with many of his books, of which the following have been noted: Sir Aston Cokain's *Dianea*, 1654 (B.M. 12470, bb. 8), containing a list of 180 works, and Richard Brome's *Five New Playes*, 1653 (B.M. E. 1423), which has an added sheet containing 135 items.

MOTTERSHEAD (EDWARD), printer; St. Bennet, Paul's Wharf [near Doctors Commons], 1641–65. Took up his freedom January 20th, 1640. [Arber, iii. 688.] In the Churchwardens' Books of St. Bennet, Paul's Wharf, he is described as cousin germane to Thomas Mottershead of that parish. In partnership with T. Ratcliffe, *q.v.* In 1664 he was arrested at the instance of the Company of Stationers for illegally printing law books. [*Chan. Proc. Before 1714*, Reynardson, bundle 31, Stationers' Co. *v.* Flesher.]

MOULE (GREGORY), bookseller in London; Three Bibles in the Poultry, under St. Mildreds Church, 1649–51. In partnership with T. Brewster in the publication of theological, political, and miscellaneous literature. Moule's name is lost sight of at the end of 1651.

MOULTON (CHARLES), bookseller (?) in London, 1663. Only known from the imprint to: Carleton (Mary), *Historicall Narrative*, 1663. [Hazlitt, iii. 30.]

MOULTON (W.), bookseller (?) in London, 1642. Only known from the imprint to a pamphlet entitled: *His Maiesties Letter, To the Lord Mayor and Aldermen of the Citie of London . . . . London: Printed for Tho. Hewer and W. Moulton*, 1642. His address has not been found.

MOXON (JAMES), printer in London; (?) Upper end of Hounsditch neere Bishop's Gate, 1647–50. Was evidently a relative, presumably a brother, of Joseph Moxon the typefounder. Their joint names occur in the imprint to a broadside entitled: *Victories obtained . . . . both by land and sea . . . . London, Printed by James Moxon and Joseph Moxon for Tho. Jenner . . . . 1647* [January 23rd.] [B.M. 669, f. 10 (112).]

MOXON (JOSEPH), printer and typefounder in London, (1) Upper end of Houndsditch neere Bishop's Gate; (2) Atlas, by St. Michiel's Church in Corn-hil; (3) Atlas on Ludgate Hill neer Fleet Bridge; (4) Atlas in Warwick Lane; (5) Atlas, Russell Street, Westminster; (6) Westminster Hall, right against the Parliament Stairs. 1647–94. Born at Wakefield, in Yorkshire, August 8th, 1627, and brought up to the trade of a mathematical instrument maker. In 1647 he and James Moxon, possibly a brother, were established in London as printers, for their joint names are found on a broadside entitled *Victories obtained . . . both by land and sea . . . . London. Printed by James Moxon and Joseph Moxon in 1647.* In 1654 Joseph Moxon was living at the sign of the Atlas in Cornhill, and in 1659 he added typefounding to his other callings. He issued his first specimen sheet in 1669. His foundry was fitted with a large assortment of type, mostly from Holland, and included a fount of Irish type. His work as a printer was poor, and he is best remembered for his useful treatise on printing and typefounding, which formed the second part of the *Mechanick Exercises,* and is still a standard work on both these subjects. The date of Joseph Moxon's death is unknown.

MYN, or MYNNE (FRANCES), bookseller in London; St. Paul, Little Britain, 1663–65. Son of Richard Myn, or Mynne. Smyth in his *Obituary,* p. 69, records under date of October 12th, 1665, "Fran. Myn bookseller in Little Britain, son of Richard Myn, buried ex peste."

MYN, or MYNNE (RICHARD), bookseller in London; St. Paul, Little Britain, 1628–50. Took up his freedom June 30th, 1623. [Arber, iii. 685.] Mentioned in a list of secondhand booksellers who, in 1628, were required to send catalogues of their books to the Archbishop of Canterbury. Succeeded by his son, Francis Myn, or Mynne.

NEALAND (REBECCA), bookseller in London; Crown in Duck Lane, 1644. Was perhaps the widow of Samuel Nealand, bookseller, who was in business at the same address from 1618 to 1632. [Arber, iii. 623.] In 1644 she republished a controversial pamphlet entitled *An Historicall Narration*

.... *concerning Gods election* .... which had been issued by Samuel Nealand in 1631 and called in at that time by order of the Archbishop of Canterbury, as containing "divers dangerous opinions." [E. 21 (10).] She is only known from the imprint to this book.

NEALAND (WILLIAM), bookseller in Cambridge, 1655-60. Several entries with his imprint occur in Bowes' *Cambridge Books* between these years. There was also a bookseller of the same name in London during the same period, who may be identical.

NEALAND (WILLIAM), bookseller in London; Crown in Duck Lane, 1649-62. Probably the same as the preceding.

NEDHAM, *see* Needham.

NEEDHAM, or NEDHAM (RALPH), bookseller in London; Bell, Little Britain, 1665-72. Mentioned in the Hearth Tax Roll for the half-year ending Lady Day, 1666. [P.R.O. Lay Subsidy $\frac{142}{29}$]. He died in July, 1672. [Smyth's *Obituary*, p. 96.]

NEILE (FRANCIS), printer in London; Aldersgate Street, 1644-54. Took up his freedom September 4th, 1626. [Arber, iii. 686.] Printer of *The Weekly Intelligencer* [1651-55]. In partnership with Matthew Simmons.

NEILL (JOHN), bookseller in Glasgow, 1642-5. Named as a debtor in inventories of J. Bryson (1642), and R. Bryson (1645). The David Neill in Glasgow mentioned in Lithgow's Inventory (1662) may be a successor. [H. G. Aldis, *List of Books*, p. 118.]

NEVILL (JOSEPH), bookseller in London; Plough, St. Pauls Church Yard, 1660-64. Publisher of R. Baxter's *Treatise of self denial, 1660.*

NEVILL (PHILIP), bookseller in London; Ivy Lane, 1638-42. Son of Philip Nevill, of Smalpace, co. Chester, yeoman. Apprentice to John Grismond I. for eight years from Midsummer, 1630, who at his death in 1638 left him a bequest. [P.C.C. 169, Lee.]

NEWBERY (THOMAS), bookseller in London, (1) Over against the
Conduit in Cornhil [near the Royal Exchange]; (2) Three Lions [or
Three Golden Lions [Cornhill]; (3) Sweeting's Rents, Cornhill, 1653–8.
Probably a descendant of Nathaniel Newbery, bookseller in Cornhill
between 1616–32.

NEWCOMBE, or NEWCOMB (THOMAS), printer in London, (1) Parish
of St. Bennet, Paul's Wharf, Thames Street; (2) The kings printing house
in the Savoy. 1649–81. Son of Thomas Newcomb of Dunchurch, co.
Warwick. Apprentice to Gregory Dexter for eight years from November
8th, 1641. [Register of Apprenticeships, Stationers' Hall.] At the expiration of his time in 1649 he married Ruth, the widow of John Raworth,
printer, and succeeded to the business. In the same year, on September
1st, the Council of State ordered his committal to Newgate for printing
Lilburne's *Outcry of the Young Men and Apprentices of London*, and he
remained a prisoner for three weeks. [*Domestic State Papers*, 1649–50,
vol. ii., Proc. of the Council of State.] After this he appears to have made
his peace with the Government. He printed John Milton's *Pro populo
Anglicano Defensio secunda* in 1654, and in the pamphlet entitled *The
London Printers Lamentation or the Press Opprest and overprest*, he was
bitterly assailed as the printer of much of the Commonwealth literature.
At the Restoration he continued in favour and was associated with
J. Macock in printing the public journals *Mercurius Publicus* and the
Parliamentary Intelligencer. He also held a sixth part in the King's
Printing House, and became the printer of the Oxford and London
Gazettes. In 1664 he was a Common Councillor of the City, and presented a book of homilies to the Church of St. Bennet, Paul's Wharf.
[Guildhall MSS., $\frac{877}{1}$.] In the survey taken on July 29th, 1668, he was
returned as having three presses and a proof press, one apprentice, seven
compositors and five pressmen, in other words, his was one of the largest
printing houses in London at that time. [*Domestic State Papers*, Charles II,
vol. 243, p. 181.] Some interesting notes about Newcombe at a later date
will be found in the Appendix to the 9th Report of the Hist. MSS. Commissioners. His death took place between December 22nd, 1681, and
January 11th, 168$\frac{1}{2}$, when his will was proved in the Prerogative Court of
Canterbury [7 Cottle.] His share in the King's Printing Office he left in
trust to pay annuities to ten poor and aged workmen printers or their

widows, the residue to go to his son Thomas. He bequeathed the Company of Stationers a piece of plate value £20, and left sums for the poor of Dunchurch, co. Warwick, and those of St. Bennet's, Paul's Wharf. Amongst others mentioned in the will were Henry Herringman, of St. Martin's-in-the-Fields, gent., and Henry Hills, St. Anne's, Blackfryar's, gent.

NEWMAN (DORMAN), bookseller in London, (1) King's Arms in the Poultery neer Grocer's Alley; (2) Surgeon's Arms Little Britain; (3) Ship and Anchor at the Bridge-Foot [near the Bridge Gate] on Southwark side. 1665–93. Another bookseller, the bulk of whose work lies outside the scope of this dictionary. His first imprint is found in Geo. Swinnock's *Christian Man's Calling*, 1665. The rest are given by Mr. Arber in the *Term Catalogues*.

NICHOLAS (AUGUSTINE), printer in London, 16$\frac{49}{50}$. On the 8th March, 1650, the attention of the House of Commons was drawn to a book entitled *The Doctrine of the Fourth Commandment*. Nicholas, who was examined about the matter, stated that he was servant to Gertrude Dawson, who printed the book for James Oakeford. It may be presumed, therefore, that Nicholas was a workman in her service. [*Commons Journals*, vol. 6, p. 378.]

NICHOLLS (JOHN), bookseller in London; Old Bailey, c. 1641. Possibly a brother of Thomas Nicholls.

NICHOLLS (THOMAS), bookseller in London; Bible, Pope's Head Alley, 1637–41. Died in 1641, his will being proved November 9th. In it he refers to his father and mother as still living and a brother John. He nominated his wife Susanna sole executrix, and Miles Flesher and William Hope, overseers. [P.C.C. 141, Evelyn.]

NICHOLSON (ANTHONY), bookseller at Cambridge, 1648–52. An Anthony Nicholson was christened in St. Michael's Church, Cambridge, on August 6th, 1601 (Venn, p. 4), and an Anthony Nicholson paid church rate at Great St. Mary's from 1624-5 to 1634-5. [Foster.] Three books issued by him are noticed in Bowes' *Cambridge Books*, pp. 33, 34.

NICHOLSON (JOHN), bookseller in London; Under St. Martins Church in Ludgate, 1640–2. Took up his freedom December 7th, 1635. [Arber, iii. 687.] Publisher of plays and political pamphlets.

NICHOLSON (ROBERT), bookseller in Cambridge, 1662-73. Published a Latin edition of the Book of Ecclesiastes, 1662. Possibly son, or brother, of Anthony Nicholson, *q.v.*

NICKOLSON, *see* Nicholson.

NICKSON (EDWARD), bookseller (?) in London, 1643. Only known from the imprint to a pamphlet entitled *The Actor's Remonstrance, or Complaint .... London, Printed for Edw. Nickson,* 1643. [E. 86 (8).]

NICOLLS, *see* Nicholls.

NICOLSON, *see* Nicholson.

NIDALE (JAMES), bookseller (?) in London, 1660. Only known from the imprint to a ballad entitled *The Parliament-Complement,* 1660. [Lutt. Coll. ii. 160.]

NORTON (ALICE), printer in London, 1641-2. Printer of political pamphlets and broadsides. It is not clear what relationship, if any, she bore to the other Nortons of this period.

NORTON (JOHN), printer in London, 1621-45. This is probably the John Norton who took up his freedom on July 8th, 1616. [Arber, iii. 684.] There were three stationers of this name at work in London during the first quarter of the 17th century, (1) John Norton, cousin of William Norton, and printer of Sir H. Saville's *Chrysostom,* who died in 1612; (2) John Norton, son of Mark Norton, citizen and grocer of London, apprentice to John Atkinson in 1598 and out of his time in 1605, of whom no more is heard, and (3) the subject of the present article, whose first book entry occurs in the registers on September 18th, 1621. [Arber, iv. 59.] He was in partnership with John Okes, who had succeeded to the business originally established by Thomas Judson in 1586, and in the hands successively of John Harrison the Younger, George and Lionel Snowden, and Nicholas Okes. The position of this printing house is unknown. [Arber, iii. 669 *et seq.*; *Library,* April, 1906, pp. 165, 166.] John Norton was for a time associated with Augustine Mathewes, who died in 1625

NORTON (LEONARD), bookseller in London, 1647. John Norton, the printer who died in 1612, left a legacy to his nephew, Leonard Norton [Plomer, *Wills*, p. 46], but whether he is to be identified with this bookseller is not known. His name appears in the imprint to a pamphlet entitled *Charge . . . . against Sir John Gayer Lord Mayor*, 1647.

NORTON (LUKE), printer in London, 1642–5. There were two stationers of this name, one of whom took up his freedom March 2nd, 1612, and the other June 1st, 1635. [Arber, iii. 683, 687.] This was probably the later man, who was in partnership with John Field, *q.v.*

NORTON (ROGER), printer in London, 1658. Smyth in his *Obituary*, p. 49, has the following entry: "Rog. Norton, printer, who married Nell Houlker, died very poore," November 27th, 1658. Whether this printer was any relation to Roger Norton of Blackfriars, *q.v.*, is not known.

NORTON (ROGER), printer in London; Blackfriars [(?) Hunsdon House], 1639–62. Son of Bonham Norton, King's Printer 1596–1635, and grandson of William Norton, of the King's Arms, St. Paul's Churchyard, 1561–93. Roger Norton took an active part in the proceedings between his father and Robert Barker the Second in the matter of the King's Printing House, and with his brother John broke into the premises by night and carried off the whole of the stock and printing materials. At the Restoration he petitioned to be appointed King's printer on the grounds that the decree made in the Court of Chancery was illegal, and that he had been of service to His Majesty during the late troubles, both by printing letters and papers and by sheltering those who came from abroad on His Majesty's service. His claim was not allowed. Roger Norton died April 1st, 1662, and his death is recorded by Smyth in his *Obituary* (p. 55): "Mr. Roger Norton printer in Blackffriers died, whose daughter my coz Dr Thos. Clutterbuck marrd." His will was proved April 7th, 1662, and by it he left to Susan his wife his house in Blackfriars excepting the workhouse [*i.e.*, the printing house] and the warehouse, which, with all his printing materials, copyrights and patents, he bequeathed to his son Roger Norton. He had another son, Ambrose, to whom he bequeathed certain lands in Somerset, and several daughters. The rest of his real estate, including lands in Stretton in Shropshire, he left to his wife Susan for life. [*Library*, October, 1901, pp. 353–57; P.C.C. 52, Laud.]

NORTON (ROGER) the Younger, printer in London; Kings printing office in Hebrew, Greek and Latin, (1) Blackfriars [(?) Hunsdon House]; (2) Clerkenwell Green; (3) Little Britain. 1662–86. Son of Roger Norton, printer, of Blackfriars, *q.v.*, and grandson of Bonham Norton. Succeeded to his father's business in 1662. His premises were burnt in the great fire, and he moved to Clerkenwell Green, and later, back to Little Britain, where he built a printing house. In the survey of the press taken in 1668, he is returned as having three presses, one apprentice, and seven workmen.

NOTT (WILLIAM), bookseller in London, (1) Ivy Lane; (2) White Horse in Paul's Churchyard; (3) Queens Arms in the Pell-Mell. 1660–84. Published a book of devotion called *Private forms of Prayer*, 1660, and Anne Wyndham's *Claustrum Regale Reseratum*, 1667. There was a W. Nott, bookseller in Oxford in 1665.

NOTT (W.), bookseller in Oxford, 1665. [Madan, *Chart of Oxford Printing*, p. 30.] He may be identical with the London bookseller, William Nott.

NOWELL (NATHANIEL), bookseller in London; Little Britain, 1664–7. Churchwarden of St. Botolph's without Aldersgate, 1664–5. Died March 9th, 166⅝. [Smyth's *Obituary*, p. 74.] His will was proved on March 26th, by which he left everything to his wife Joane. Samuel Mearne and Marmaduke Thompson were witnesses. [P.C.C. 49, Carr.]

NOWELL (WILLIAM), bookseller in Norwich, 1660–1. Published T. Brabourne's *God save the king*, 1660.

NUTHALL (JAMES), bookseller in London, (1) Over against the George, near Holborn Bridge, 1650; (2) In Fleet Street at the sign of the Hercules Pillars, 1651; (3) Minories, next door to the Dolphin, 1660. 1650–60. Publisher of mathematical, surgical and theological books. Amongst these were John Chatfield's *Trigonal Sector*, 1650 [E. 1381 (1)]; T. Vicary's *Surgions Directorie*, 1651 [E. 1265]; and Zachary Crofton's sermon, *The Pursuit of Peace*, 1660. [E. 1025 (19).]

OAKES (EDWARD), printer in London, 1663–8. Set up in business after the Act of 1663. In the survey taken on July 29th, 1668, he is returned as having two presses, no apprentices, and two workmen. [Plomer, *Short History*, p. 227.]

OAKES, or OKES (JOHN), printer in London; Little St. Bartholomews neare Smithfield, 1636–44. Son of Nicholas Okes (1606–39). Took up his freedom January 14th, 1627, and was for some years in partnership with his father. They had a large and old established business, originally founded by Thomas Judson in 1586. John Okes printed for Daniel Frere, Thomas Nabbes' tragedy of *The Unfortunate Mother*, 1640.

OAKES, or OKES (MARY), printer in London; Little St. Bartholomews [Smithfield], 1643-4. Probably the widow of John Okes.

OGILBY (JOHN), author, translator, and publisher in London; Whitefriars, 1600–76. John Ogilby was neither a bookseller nor a printer by trade, but from the facts that he was the promoter of some of the finest books issued during this period, and that he was his own publisher, and even organised lotteries for the sale of his books, he is entitled to notice. He began life as a dancing master, then became schoolmaster to the Earl of Strafford's children. During the troubles of the Civil War he lost everything, was shipwrecked on his way from Ireland, and arrived in London penniless. He proceeded to Cambridge on foot, and was there given Latin lessons by some of the scholars. He also is said to have learnt Greek about the same time. At the Restoration he was made Master of the Revels in Ireland. He was besides given the titles of "king's cosmographer" and "geographic printer." He died September 4th, 1676, and was buried in St. Bride's Church, Fleet Street. Ogilby spared no cost in the production of his books, which were printed by the best men, with the best type, and on the best paper procurable, with illustrations drawn and engraved by the first artists and engravers of the period. A magnificent example of the typography of the period is his translation of the Works of Virgil, printed by Thomas Roycroft in 1658. To facilitate the sale of his books Ogilby was allowed to establish a lottery in which all the prizes were his own works. A copy of the prospectus for one of these lotteries is amongst the Bagford fragments. During the last years of his life he devoted himself to the production of books of geography and topography. [D.N.B.]

OKES, *see* Oakes.

OLIVER (WILLIAM), bookseller in Norwich; Next door to the Castle and Lyon, 1663. Mentioned in an advertisement in *Mercurius Publicus* for the year 1663, and in the same year he published for John Winter, curate of East Dereham, in Norfolk, a sermon called 'Απλῶς και Καλως, *Honest plain dealing*, 1663. [226 g. 23 (9).]

OLTON, *see* OULTON.

OTWELL (JOHN), bookseller in London, 1642. His name occurs as the publisher of one of Pym's speeches in 1642. [E. 200 (65).]

OULTON or OLTON (RICHARD), printer in London; Near Christ-church [Newgate Street], 1633–43. Son of Elizabeth Alde or Allde by a former husband. Succeeded to the business of Edward Alde or Allde and used his device. In 1641 he was joined by G. Dexter, *q.v.*, and in the same year paid a sum of £3 as his share of the poll-tax. [*Domestic State Papers*, Charles I, vol. 483, 11.]

OVERTON (HENRY), bookseller in London, (1) White Horse without Newgate [Sayle, 1121]; (2) Entrance to Pope's Head Alley out of Lombard Street, 1629–48. Took up his freedom June 1st, 1629. [Arber, iii. 686.] Dealt chiefly if not wholly in theological literature, and was one of the syndicate including John Bellamy, A. and J. Crooke, D. Frere, J. Rothwell, R. Sergier, and R. Smith, who published the sermons of the Rev. J. Stoughton.

OVERTON (JOHN), bookseller in London; White Horse in Little Brittain, next door to Little St. Bartholomews Gate, 1667–1703. Published in 1667 an edition of Robert Fage's *Cosmography*.

OWSLEY (JOHN), printer in London; 1658–66. This printer was ruined by the fire of London in 1666. [Plomer, *Short History*, p. 225.] His imprint will be found in Robert Fage's *Description of the whole world*, 1658. [E. 1595 (3).]

OXLAD (FRANCIS), senior, bookseller in Oxford, 1665–67. [Madan, *Chart of Oxford Printing*, p. 30.] His name is found in 1665 on the following: Ryff (Peter), *Questiones Geometricæ*, 1665. [Ames Collection, 3236.]

OXLAD (FRANCIS), junior, bookseller in Oxford, 1667. [Madan, *Chart of Oxford Printing*, p. 30.]

PAGE (DIXY), bookseller in London, (1) Tower Street; (2) Anchor and Marriner in East Smithfield, near the King's slaughter house. 1664–8. In April, 1666, this bookseller, with Thos. Johnson the printer, *q.v.*, was imprisoned for dispersing seditious books, and was bound over in a sum of £500 to be of good behaviour. [*Domestic State Papers*, Charles II, vol. 155 (71).] His second address is from John Newton's *Scale of Interest*, 1668. [Harl. 5987, p. 56.]

PAGE (ROBERT), bookseller (?) in London; Barbican, Three Pigeon Alley [or Court], 1659. His name is found in the imprint to a pamphlet entitled *An ancient and true prophesie*, 1659. [E. 993 (23).]

PAINE (THOMAS), *see* Payne (T.).

PAKEMAN (DANIEL), bookseller in London; Rainbow Fleet Street, 1635–64. Chiefly a publisher of law books, some time in partnership with Ephraim Dawson, W. Lee and Richard Meighen. Died in September, 1664. [Smyth's *Obituary*, p. 61.]

PALMER (RICHARD), (?) bookseller in London, 1643. His name is found in the imprint to the following pamphlet: *Danger wherein the Kingdom of England now standeth, May 2, 1643*.

PALMER (THOMAS), bookseller in London; Crown in Westminster Hall, 1664–73. A "stationer" of this name, whose will was proved in the Prerogative Court of Canterbury [P.C.C. 50, Bath], died at Tewkesbury in Gloucestershire in March, 167 9/10, but he was probably a different person.

PALMER (WILLIAM), bookseller in London; Palm Tree in Fleet Street, 1660–61. Publisher for James Howell and Dr. Peter Heylyn. A list of books sold by him occurs at the end of Howell's *Parly of Beasts*, 1660.

PARIS (NATHANIEL), bookseller in London; The George in Little Britain, 1657–66. Took up his freedom October 3rd, 1639. Associated with T. Dring, *q.v.*, in publishing the Rev. John Gaule's *Sapientia Justificata*, 1657. Churchwarden of St. Botolph's without Aldersgate in the years 1665 and 1666.

PARKER (JOHN), bookseller in London, (1) The Ball, Paul's Churchyard, 1618 [Sayle, 934]; (2) The Three Pigeons, Paul's Churchyard, 1620–48 (?) 1617–48. Son of George Parker, of Honington, Warwickshire, yeoman. Took up his freedom March 1st, 1617. [Arber, iii. 684.] Parker was associated with Henry Fetherston until 1619, and in 1620 he took over the copyrights of W. Barrett which had previously belonged to Gabriel Cawood and W. Leake, amongst which were Shakespeare's *Venus and Adonis* and Lylly's *Euphues*. About this time he bought the shares of several of the adventurers in the Latin stock. Nominated overseer to the will of John Grismond, who died in 1638; Warden of the Company of Stationers, 1641, 1644, 1645; Master of the Company, 1647 and 1648. Died July 30th, 1648. [Smyth's *Obituary*, p. 26.] His will, an interesting document, was dated October 28th, 1647, and proved on August 16th, 1648. The following stationers received rings: Andrew Crooke, Charles Greene, Francis Egglesfield, Octavian Pullen, Richard and Thomas Whitaker, while Miles Fletcher was nominated one of the overseers. [P.C.C. 124, Essex.]

PARKER (PETER), bookseller in London, (1) At the end of Popes Head Alley next Lombard Street, 1665; (2) Under Creed Church, nr Aldgate, 1667. One of the publishers of the first edition of Milton's *Paradise Lost*, 1667. [Masson's *Life of Milton*, vol. vi, p. 516.]

PARKHURST (THOMAS), bookseller in London, (1) George in Little Britain, 1653–6; (2) Three Crowns at the lower end of Cheapside [near the Conduit or near Mercers Chapel]; (3) Golden Bible upon London Bridge, 1666–7. (1653–67). Dealt chiefly, if not entirely, in theological literature. A list of 25 publications on sale by him in 1657 is found at the end of the first part of S. Purchas's *Theatre of Political Flying Insects*, 1657. [B.M. 452, a. 37.] A much longer list, arranged under sizes, was issued with W. Secker's *Nonsuch Professor*, 1660.

PARRY (LEONARD), printer in London; Dogwell Court, Whitefriars, 1660–63. In partnership with Thomas Childe.

PARTRIDGE (JOHN), bookseller in London, (1) Purse Court in the Old Bailey, 1641; (2) Sun in St. Pauls Churchyard, 1644; (3) Cock in Ludgate Street, 1645; (4) Blackfriars, going into Carter Lane, 1648–9 (1623–49).

At the outbreak of the Civil War, Partridge added a trade in astrological books to his other branches of bookselling, and with H. Blunden, *q.v.*, became the publisher of the writings of William Lilly and John Booker. Thomas Brudnell did a good deal of printing for him, and after Partridge's death in 1649 brought an action against his executors to recover a sum of money which he claimed for printing certain books. [P.R.O. Chancery Proc. before 1714, Brudnell *v.* P. Stephens and L. Fawne.] The details of the account are set out in a schedule, and there is also an inventory of the stock of books owned by Partridge at his death. [*Library*, January, 1906, pp. 32–45.] Mr. Sayle states that Partridge used a device of "the sun in splendour." This was not a device, it was only an ornament, a portion of an old wooden block, just as likely to have belonged to the printer as to the publisher.

PASSENGER, *see* Passinger.

PASSINGER (THOMAS), bookseller in London ; Three Bibles on London Bridge, 1664–88. Son of Thomas Passinger, of Guildford, co. Surrey. Apprentice to Charles Tyas, or Tyus, bookseller at the Three Bibles on London Bridge for eight years from July 25th, 1657. [Register of Apprenticeships, Stationers' Hall, 1606–66.] On the death of Tyas in 1664, Passinger appears to have succeeded to the business, probably by marrying the widow. He died in 1688 and his will was proved in the Prerogative Court of Canterbury. He left to his kinsman, Thomas Passinger, all his copies and parts of copies and copperplates, as well as his share of books and ballads which he had in partnership with William Thackerye of Pye Corner. He left a bequest of forty shillings to the Company of Stationers and a book of the value of forty shillings to the public library at Guildford. [P.C.C. 82, Exton.]

PATERSON (MICHAEL), bookseller in Glasgow, 1659–62. One of the debtors mentioned in G. Lithgow's *Inventory*, 1662. [H. G. Aldis, *List of books*, p. 118.]

PATERSON (WILLIAM), bookseller in Edinburgh, 1662. One of the debtors mentioned in G. Lithgow's *Inventory*, 1662. [H. G. Aldis, *List of books*, p. 118.]

PAULETT, *see* Pawlett.

M

PAWLETT, or PAULETT (ROBERT), bookseller in London; Bible in Chancery Lane near the Inner Temple Gate, 1660–67. Publisher of political pamphlets. [Gray's Index to Hazlitt, p. 585.]

PAWLEY (ROBERT), bookseller in London; In Fleet Street, 1661–5. His name is found on the title-page of a book entitled *A Compendious Abridgement of all statutes*, 1661. [Ames Collection, 2992.] He was associated with Henry Twyford in publishing an edition of Hugo Grotius' *De Rebus Belgicis, rendered into English by T. M.*, April 21st, 1665. He may have been a descendant of Simon Pawley, the bookseller, of the earlier part of the century.

PAXTON (EDMUND), bookseller in London; Pauls Chain, over against the Castle-tavern. 1655. His name is found in the imprint to *England's Complete Law judge*, 1655. [E. 860 (3).] An *Edward* Paxton took up his freedom June 7th, 1630. [Arber, iii. 686.]

PAYBODY, or PAYBODIE (THOMAS), printer (?) & bookseller in London; Queens Head Alley, Paternoster Row, 1642–65. Smyth in his *Obituary*, p. 69, records, "15th Octr. 1665 Tho. Paybodie a printer buried *ex peste*." His name is found in the imprint to a pamphlet entitled *An Answer* .... *upon some* .... *observations* .... *against his* .... *majesty, 1642*, which also has on the title-page a block having the letters T.P. on it, which may have been Thomas Paybody's device. [E. 108 (39).]

PAYNE, or PAINE (THOMAS), printer in London; In Goold-Smiths Alley in Redcross Street [Cripplegate], 1630–50 (?). Took up his freedom March 3rd, 1628. [Arber, iii. 686.] During the Commonwealth he was employed by the Council of State, which on September 19th, 1650, ordered twenty pounds to be given to him "as a gratuity for his sufferings by printing a book for the cause of Parliament, written by Mr. Walker." The Mr. Walker referred to was doubtless Clement Walker, the author of the *History of Independency*, but it was clearly not that book for which the printer was paid, and no further light can be thrown on the passage. [*Domestic State Papers*, Interr. 10, pp. 27–30.]

PERRY (HUGH), bookseller in London; Neere Ivy Bridge in the Strand. 1626–45. Took up his freedom December 15th, 1626. [Arber, iii. 686.] His first book entry in the registers of the Company occurs on the 19th

July, 1627 [*ibid.*, iv. 181.] On the 10th February, 163¾, Thomas Archer assigned over to him several copyrights, in which were included Thomas Middleton's play, *The Roaring Girle* ; John Marston's play, *The Insatiate Countess*, and Timberlake's *Travels* [*ibid.*, iv. 248]. Some of these Perry afterwards assigned to Henry Taunton and Francis Coles [*ibid.*, iv. 327, 336.] Between 1642 and 1645 he issued several political pamphlets, after which he is lost sight of.

PIENNE (PETER DE), printer at Cork & Waterford, Ireland, 1644-54. Printed an edition of the *Eikon Basilike* in Cork in 1649. In 1652 he is found printing at Waterford *An Act for the settlement of Ireland*. In that year an order was made by the Council for the affairs of Ireland forbidding the Commissioners of the Revenue at Waterford to pay Peter de Pienne any salary from that time. [E. R. McC. Dix, *Irish Provincial Printing prior to 1701*. *Library*, October, 1901, pp. 344-5.]

PIERREPOINT (THOMAS), bookseller in London; Sun in St. Paul's Churchyard, 1651-8. Issued in 1655 in conjunction with George Calvert a folio edition of Sidney's *Arcadia*. [B.M., C. 39, h. 10.]

PILKINGTON (STEPHEN), bookseller in London; Next to the Red-lyon Inne in Fleet Street, 1647. His name occurs in the imprint to a pamphlet entitled *Trodden down strength*, 1647. [B.M. 1417. a. 13.]

PITT (MOSES), bookseller in London, (1) White Hart, Little Britain; (2) Angel, St. Paul's Churchyard, over against the little North door. 1666-81. Mentioned in the Hearth Tax Roll for the half-year ending Lady Day, 1666, as a bookseller in Little Britain. [P.R.O. Lay Subsidy $\frac{252}{32}$.] Published in 1667 a *Short Account of the life and death of Pope Alexander VII*. He became one of the most important booksellers of the second half of the seventeeth century. (*See* Arber, *Term Catalogues*.)

PITTS (JOSEPH), *see* Potts (J.).

PLACE (JOHN), bookseller in London, (1) Furnivall's Inn Gate; (2) Greyhound Yard, Holborn. 1645-86. Dealer in law books. Several of his children were baptized at St. Andrew's, Holborn.

PLACE (WILLIAM), bookseller in London; Gray's Inn Gate, 1657-77. Doubtless a relative of J. Place. Also dealt in law books.

PLAYFERE (JOHN), bookseller in London, (1) White Bear in the upper walk of the New Exchange [Strand]; (2) White Lion in the upper walk of the New Exchange. 1664–5. A list of books issued by him in 1665 precedes the *Three Plays* of Sir W. Killigrew and is inserted immediately before the title to *Selindra*.

PLAYFORD (JOHN), bookseller in London; Inner Temple near the church door, 1623–86? Younger son of John Playford, of Norwich, born in 1623. Dealt chiefly in music books. Temporarily in partnership with John Benson and Zachariah Watkins, 1664–5. His printers were Thomas Harper, 1648–52; William Godbid, 1658–78; Ann Godbid and her partner John Playford the younger, 1679–83; John Playford alone, 1684–5. He was the inventor of the "new ty'd notes." In 1672 he began engraving on copper plates. The D.N.B. records no less than seventeen collections of music books published by John Playford, who was succeeded by his son Henry. [D.N.B.]

POCOCK (SAMUEL), bookseller in Oxford, 1662. His name is found in the imprint to P. Du Trien's *Manuductio ad logicum*, 1662. [Ames Collection, 3072.]

POLLARD (ROBERT), bookseller in London; Ben Johnson's Head behind the Exchange, 1655–8. Associated with John Sweeting in the publication of plays.

POPE (WILLIAM), (?) bookseller in London; Neere Essex House, 1642. A political pamphlet entitled *To the Right Honourable the Lords assembled in Parliament* .... bears the imprint *London, Printed for William Pope, and are to be sold at his shop neere Essex House, 1642.* [E. 114 (9).]

POTS, or POTTS (JOSEPH), bookseller (?) in London; In the [great] Old Baily neer the Sessions-House, 1646. His name is found in the imprint to a broadside entitled *Life and Death of the .... Earle of Essex* [October 12th], 1646. [B.M. 669, f. 10 (93).] He was perhaps a descendant of Robert Potts, who was publishing from 1621–3. [Arber, v. 259.]

POUNCET, or POUNCE (JOHN), bookseller (?) in London, (1) Lower end of Budge Row neere Canning [*i.e.,* Cannon] Street; (2) Hand and Bible lower end of Budge Row neer Dowgate. 1646–7. His name is found in the imprints to the two following pamphlets: *Certain Queries touching the ordination of ministers. By. A. W., 1647*, 4°, and *Vox Populi, 1646*, 4°. [Hazlitt, i. 440.]

POWEL (EDWARD), bookseller in London; White Swan, Little Britain, 1660. Mentioned in the Hearth Tax Roll for the half-year ending Lady-Day, 1666, as a bookseller in Little Britain. [P.R.O. Lay Subsidy $\frac{252}{32}$.]

POWELL (THOMAS), bookseller in London; Bethlehem [*i.e.*, the precincts of Bethlehem Hospital], 1622–41. A stationer of this name took up his freedom March 1st, 1622. [Arber, iii. 685.] He is named in a list of secondhand booksellers who, in 1628, were ordered to send catalogues of their books to the Archbishop of Canterbury. In 1641 he figures as a publisher of political pamphlets.

PRICE (JOHN), bookseller (?) in London, 1642. His name occurs in the imprint to a pamphlet entitled *Copy of the Queens Letter, 1642*.

PRICE (NEHEMIAH), bookseller (?) in London, 1660. His name occurs in the imprint to W. Prynne's pamphlet *Title of Kings proved to be Jure Devino, 1660*.

PRIDMORE (ISAAC), bookseller in London, (1) The Falcon neer the New Exchange, 1656; (2) The Falcon beyond the New Exchange in the Strand; (3) At the Golden Falcon neere the New Exchange. 1656–9. His name is first met with on an eight-leaf pamphlet entitled *Death in a New Dress, or Sportive Funeral Elegies*, published in August, 1656. [E. 885 (11).] Dealer in plays and broadsides.

PULLEYN, or PULLEIN (OCTAVIAN), the Elder, bookseller in London, (1) The Rose in St. Paul's Churchyard, 1636–66; (2) neer the Pump in Little-Brittain, 1667. Took up his freedom December 14th, 1629. [Arber, iii. 686.] First book entry February 12th, 1636 [*ibid.*, iv. 354.] He is found in partnership with Geo. Thomason from 1639 until about 1643. They occupied one of the houses built by Reginald Wolfe on the site of the charnel house on the North side of the Cathedral between the Great North Door and the church of St. Faith's, known by the name of the Rose. Next to it on the East side was the Three Pigeons, occupied by

Humphrey Robinson, while on the West was the yard of the charnel house, possibly a paved open space near the Great North Door. These premises being destroyed in the fire, Octavian Pulleyn moved into Little Britain "neer the Pump," where he issued Samuel Woodford's *Paraphrase upon the Psalms of David*, 1667. [B.M. 6, a. 3.] Meanwhile Geo. Thomason had apparently set up for himself at the sign of the Rose and Crown in another part of the Churchyard. The date of Octavian Pulleyn's death is unknown.

PULLEYN, or PULLEIN (OCTAVIAN), the Younger, bookseller in London; The Bible in St. Pauls Church yard near the little North door, 1664-7 (?). Probably son of Octavian Pulleyn the Elder. Dealer in French literature in conjunction with John Dunmore. His name is found on a pamphlet entitled *Discours d'un bourgeois de Paris*, 1665. [Ames Collection, 3265.]

PURSLOWE (ELIZABETH), printer in London; East End of Christ Church, 1633-46. Widow of George Purslowe, printer, who died in 1632.

PURSLOWE (G.), printer in London, 1664. Possibly a son of George and Elizabeth Purslowe. His name is found on E. Ford's *History of Parismus*, 1665.

RABAN (EDWARD), printer at Edinburgh, St. Andrews, and Aberdeen, 1620-58; Edinburgh, at the Cowgate, at the signe of A.B.C., 1620; St. Andrews, (1) At the signe of the A.B.C., 1620-22; (2) In the South street of the Citie, 1620; (3) Dwellinge in the Kirke Wynde, 1622; Aberdeen, dwelling upon the Market-place, at the townes Armes, 1622-49. Had also a shop at the end of the Broadgate from 1643. An Englishman. Printer to St. Andrew's University. The first printer in Aberdeen. Succeeded by James Brown in 1650. Died November-December, 1658. Device, Aberdeen City Arms. [H. G. Aldis, *List of Books*, p. 119.]

RAMSAY (PATRICK), printer at Edinburgh, c. 1660-80. Watson, pp. 10-13, says that after the death of Christopher Higgins, the Society of Stationers appointed Ramsay to be overseer of that house, and that about 1680 he set up with John Reid. No book has been found bearing Ramsay's name. [H. G. Aldis, *List of Books*, p. 119.]

RAMZEY (JOHN), Printer at the Hague, 1659. Printed Sir W. Lower's plays, *The Amorous Fantasme*, 1659, and *The Noble Ingratitude*, 1659. It seems probable that he was an exile from Scotland.

RAND (SAMUEL), bookseller (?) in London; Barnards Inn, Holborn, 1642. His name is found on the imprint to H. Peacham's *Art of living in London*, 1642. [E. 145 (?0).] There was a bookseller of this name living at Holborn Bridge between 1611 and 1634. [Arber, v. 260.] This may be the same or a successor.

RAND, or RANDS (WILLIAM), bookseller (?) in London, 1659. Hazlitt (H. 169) records an edition of Will. Drummond's Poems, published by him in 1659.

RANDALL (JAMES), bookseller (?) in London, 1641. Mentioned in a list of stationers as one of the "better sort of freemen" who paid twenty shillings as his proportion of the poll tax. The return is dated August 5th, 1641. [*Domestic State Papers*, Charles I, 483 (11).]

RANDS, *see* Rand.

RANEW (NATHANIEL), bookseller in London; Angel in Jewin Street, 1663-7. In partnership with Jonathan Robinson. His name is found in the imprint to the Rev. J. Dyke's *Worthy Communicant*, 1667. [Ames Coll. 3306.] He also published an account of the burning of London, by Samuel Rolls.

RATCLIFFE (THOMAS), printer in London; St. Bennet Pauls Wharf, near Doctors Commons, 1646-67. Took up his freedom January 14th, 1628. [Arber, iii. 686.] About May, 1646, he joined partnership with Edward Mottershead. They had an extensive business, and their initials T.R. and E.M. are met with on the books and pamphlets of this period at every turn. In 1659 Ratcliffe petitioned the Vestry of St. Bennet's to be relieved from serving as a vestryman on the ground that he was above the age of threescore years. [Vestry Books of St. Bennets, Paul's Wharf; Guildhall MSS. $\frac{877}{1}$, p. 182.] The date of his death is unknown. In the survey taken on July 29th, 1668, a Thomas Ratcliffe is returned as having two presses, two apprentices, and seven workmen [Plomer, *Short History*, p. 226], but this and later references probably refer to a son. [G. J. Gray, Index to Hazlitt, p. 639; Hist. MSS., Comm. Report 9, App. p. 73ᵃ.]

RAWLINS (WILLIAM), bookseller (?) in London, 1659. His name occurs in the imprint to a pamphlet entitled *True Relation of the great fight* .... *near Northwich*, 1659.

RAWORTH (JOHN), printer in London; Parish of St. Bennet Paul's Wharf, 1638–45. Took up his freedom February 6th, 1632. In 1645 he is found borrowing a sum of £25 of the parish of St. Bennet's, for which he paid 5 per cent. interest. He died towards the end of July, 1645, his will being proved August 5th. [P.C.C. 104, Rivers.] In 1648 his widow married Thomas Newcombe.

RAWORTH (ROBERT), (?) bookseller in London; (?) Old Fish Street, near St. Mary Maudlin's Church, 1633–47. His name is found on the imprint to T. Heywood's *English Traveller*, 1633, and Hazlitt in his *Handbook* (p. 246) gives an edition of B. Guarini's *Il Pastor Fido* as published by Robert Raworth in 1647. A Robert Raworth was one of the witnesses to the will of John Raworth.

RAWORTH (RUTH), printer in London; Parish of St. Bennet Paul's Wharf, 1646–8. Widow of John Raworth. In 1648 she married Thos. Newcombe.

RAYNOR, REYNOR, or REINOR (JOHN), (?) bookseller in London, 1659. His name occurs on the imprint to the following pamphlet: *Bloody Almanack* .... *London, Printed for John Raynor*, 1659. [E. 993. (19).]

RAYNOR, REYNOR, or REINOR (T.), bookseller (?) in London, 1641. His name occurs on the imprint to the following pamphlet: *The Welch-man's Answer*, 1641. [Hazlitt, iii. 52.]

RAYNOR, REYNOR, or REINOR (WILLIAM), bookseller (?) in London, 1642. His name occurs on the imprints to the following political pamphlets entitled *Prince Charles His Letter to the Lady Marie His most Royall Sister* .... *London, Printed for William Raynor*, 1642. [Hazlitt, ii. 681]; *The Truest most joyfull Newes that ever came from Ireland*. [E. 136 (7).]

REA (FRANCIS), bookseller in Worcester, 1651–63. Son of Ann Rea, of Churchill, co. Worcester, apprentice to Francis Ash, *q.v.*, for seven years from January 6th, 1644. His name is found on the imprint to Andrew

Yarranton's *Improvement improved, By a Second edition of The great Improvement of Lands by Clover* .... *London, Printed by J. C. for Francis Rea, Bookseller in Worcester,* 1663. [B.M. 724, a. 21.]

REA (ROGER), bookseller (?) in London, (1) Golden Cross Cornhill ; (2) Gilded Cross, Westminster Street [near Gresham College]. 1660–67. Advertised in the *Kingdoms Intelligencer*, September 9th, 1661, an edition of Sir R. Stapylton's translation of Juvenal's *Mores Hominum*, published in 1660.

REDMAN, *see* Redmayne.

REDMAYNE, or REDMAN (JOHN), printer in London ; Lovell's Court Paternoster Row, 1659–88. One of the printers of the *Perfect Diurnal of every dayes Proceedings in Parliament*, which began on February 21st, 16⅗, and the *Publick Intelligencer* in 1660. At the survey taken on July 29th, 1668, he was returned as having two presses, one apprentice, four compositors, and two pressmen. [Plomer, *Short History*, p. 227.]

REDMAYNE (WILLIAM), bookseller (?) in London, 1648. Hazlitt, iii. 276, records an edition of John Allibond's *Rustica Academiæ Oxoniensis* .... *Londini, impensis G. Redmayne,* 1648.

REINOR, *see* Raynor.

REYBOLD, *see* Roybould.

REYNOLDS (JOHN), bookseller (?) in London, 1642. Only known from the imprint to a pamphlet entitled *Cornucopia ; or Roome for a Ram Head.* [Hazlitt, H. 520.]

REYNOLDS (ROWLAND), bookseller in London ; Sun and Bible, Postern Street, neere More-gate, 1667–84. Hazlitt records an edition of Abraham Cowley's *The Mistresse, or Several Copies of Love Verses,* as published by him in 1667. [Hazlitt, i. 105.]

REYNOR, *see* Raynor.

RHODES (MATTHEW), (?) printer in London; (?) Over against St. Andrews Church in Holborn, 1642. His name is found on the imprint to a pamphlet entitled *Declaration or Remonstrance of the Office of a Prince. London, Printed by John Hammond and Math. Rhodes*, 1642. [E. 108 (38).] A bookseller of this name was publishing between 1622 and 1633 [Arber, v. ciii.], but whether he is to be identified with the above is not known.

RICE (AUSTIN), bookseller in London, (1) At the Three Hearts, neer the West end of Pauls; (2) The Crown in St. Paul's Churchyard. 1657–61. Dealer in political pamphlets and broadsides. The addresses given above occur in the two following issues: (1) N. Billingsley's *Brachy-Martyrologie*, 1657. [Ames Coll. 2653]; (2) Edw. Dun, Presbyter, *The Execution of the Covenant, Burnt by the Common Hangman.* [A broadside.] 1661. [Lutt. Coll., 2, 78.]

RICHARDS (GODFRAY), bookseller (?) and author in London; Peacock in Cornhill near the Royal Exchange, 1663. His name is found on the imprint to *The first book of Architecture, By Andrea Palladio. Translated .... by Pr Le Muet .... London, Printed by J. M. and sold by G. Richards .... and by Simon Miller*, 1663. [Hazlitt, iii. 184.]

RICHARDSON (HUMPHREY), bookseller (?) in London, 1643. His name is found on the imprint to a pamphlet entitled *Most excellent and remarkable speech delivered by .... Queen Elizabeth .... London, Printed for Humphrey Richardson. Jan. 28. An Dom. 1643.* [E. 86 (29).]

RIDER (THOMAS), bookseller (?) in London, 1642. Publisher of political tracts and broadsides. [Hazlitt, ii. 449, 489, 558; iii. 36.] His address has not been found.

RIDLEY (BENJAMIN), bookseller (?) in Cambridge, 1647. His name appears on the imprint to a pamphlet entitled *Manifesto from .... Sir T. Fairfax, and the army .... June 27, 1647. Cambridge, Printed for Benjamin Kidley for the use of the Army, under his Excellencie Sir Thomas Fairfax, Anno Dom. 1647.* [E. 394 (15).]

RIDLEY (JOHN), bookseller in London; Castle in Fleet Street near Ram Alley, 1649–53. Originally in partnership with J. Martin, but the partnership was dissolved in 1651, when Martin moved to the Bell in St. Paul's Churchyard.

RISHTON (R.), bookseller (?) in London, 1648. Hazlitt, ii. 103, gives the imprint to a political pamphlet as *Printed for R. Rishton, 1648.* This may be a misreading for *Royston.*

ROBERTS (GEORGE), bookseller (?) in London, 1649. Publisher of political pamphlets. His address has not been found. [Hazlitt, ii. 412, 499.]

ROBERTS (TH[OMAS ?]), bookseller (?) in London, 1663. His name occurs on the imprint to Thomas Porter's *A Witty Combat, 1663.* [B.M. 643, c. 8.]

ROBINSON (HUMPHREY), bookseller in London: Three Pigeons, St. Paul's Churchyard, 1624–70. Took up his freedom June 30th, 1623. [Arber, iii. 685.] Became one of the largest and most important booksellers of this period. On March 7th, 1652, in partnership with R. Thrale, Joshua Kirton, and Samuel Thompson, he took over the copyrights of Thomas Whitaker, 109 in number. He was also connected with Humphrey Moseley in the publication of plays, and may be said to have had a share in the chief publications of the time. During the Commonwealth he was in correspondence with Jos. Williamson, afterwards Secretary of State, and this series of letters is amongst the State papers. They give an interesting insight into the many parts that a bookseller of those days was called upon to play [*Domestic State Papers*, 1655-8.] Humphrey Robinson was Master of the Stationers' Company in the years 1661 and 1667. Smyth in his *Obituary* (p. 89), has the following record of his death :—" Nov. 13th, 1670, Die Dominica, circa hora 6. post merid. obiit Hum. Robinson, Bibliopola Trium Columb. in Cœmiter. D. Pauli, reliquens unum fil. et unam filiam. Sepult. in ruinis Eccles. S. Fidei sub. ecclesiam Cathedr. D. Pauli die Lunæ 21 Nov., 1670." His will was dated November 10th, and proved on the 23rd, by which he bequeathed to his daughter Grace his two new built houses in St. Paul's Churchyard. His son, Humphrey Robinson, is described as a fellow of All Souls' College, Oxford. He left a bequest of £10 to the Company of Stationers to rebuild their hall. [P.C.C. 151, Penn.]

On the Hustings Rolls (331, 20) his premises are described as being in "paule crosse churchyard" between the tenement late Richard Bankworth's on the east and the tenement sometime Alice Bing's widow and the yard called the Charnell chappell yard on the West, the churchyard of Pauls on the South and the wall to the churchyard on the North. One of the two houses was in the occupation of Octavian Pulleyn, and was known by the sign of the Rose.

ROBINSON (JOHN), bookseller (?) in London, 1643. His name occurs on the imprint to the following pamphlet: *Widowes Lamentation, 1643.* [E. 88 (26).]

ROBINSON (JONATHAN), bookseller in London; Angel in Jewen Street, 1667–97. In partnership with Nathaniel Ranew.

ROBINSON (RICHARD), bookseller (?) in London, 1648. Issued political pamphlets in that year. [E. 474 (12); E. 475 (5).]

ROBINSON (THOMAS), bookseller in Oxford, 1640–63. Amongst his notable publications was Francis Osborne's *Advice to a Son*, the first part of which was printed in 1655, and the second in 1658. Died April 22nd, 1663. [Smyth's *Obituary*, p. 57.] His will was proved on May 25th. To his son George he left his house in Warwick Lane, London; to his son William certain leases in Oxford, held of Magdalen College; to his son Robert lands at Bladon, in Oxford. Richard Davis, bookseller, of Oxford, was nominated one of the overseers. [P.C.C. 72, Juxon.]

ROGERS (RICHARD), bookseller in London; Paul's Chain near Doctors Commons, 1656. Associated with William Ley in publishing plays.

ROOKES (MARK), bookseller (?) in London; Grub Street neer to the Flying Horse, 1641. Associated with J. Salmon in publishing the following political pamphlets relating to Ireland:—(1) *Bloody Newes from Ireland*, 1641 [E. 179, (9)]; (2) *Treacherous Plot of a confederacie in Ireland*, 1641 [E. 179, (15).]

· ROOKES, or ROOKS (THOMAS), bookseller in London, (1) Lamb, at the East End of St. Paul's Church, 1658–66; (2) Lamb and Ink Bottle, at the entrance into Gresham College, next Bishopsgate Street; (3) In Gresham

College, next the stairs entering upon the Exchange near Bishopsgate-Street, 1667; (4) Gresham College, next the stair or warehouse in Moor Fields, against the Cardinal's Cap, 1668. [1658–68?] Issued a catalogue of books that escaped the fire of London. A copy of this is preserved in the Bodleian. [*Bibliographica*, vol. iii, pp. 183–4.] Amongst other books which he published may be noticed Simon Latham's *Faulconry*, 1658. He made a speciality of writing inks, and hence the addition of the ink bottle to his sign. The last three imprints given above probably all refer to the same place.

ROPER (ABEL), bookseller in London, (1) Black Spread Eagle, over against St. Dunstan's Church, in Fleet St., 1641; (2) Sun in Fleet Street, 1650 (?)–1667. [1638–80.] Born at Atherston, co. Warwick. Took up his freedom April 3rd, 1637. [Arber, iii. 688.] In company with Thomas Collins, was appointed "printer" to the Council of State, *i.e.*, they were allowed to sublet the printing, and on April 24th, 1660, a sum of £88 was paid to them for printing proclamations. [*Calendar of State Papers*, 1659–60, p. 598.] Abel Roper died early in the year 1680, his will being proved on March 4th, 167$\frac{9}{80}$. He died without issue, and left the interest in his stock of books to his executors for the benefit of his nephew, Abel Roper. Henry Herringman was his cousin, and one of the executors to his will. [P.C.C. 40, Bath.]

ROSSETER (EDWARD), bookseller in Taunton, co. Somerset, 1658. Published a sermon preached by the Rev. John Norman, minister at Bridgewater, at an Ordination at Somerton, co. Somerset, entitled *Christ's Commission Officer. or The Preacher's Patent Cleared.* [Ames Coll., 2781.]

ROTHWELL (JOHN), the elder, bookseller in London; Sun in St. Paul's Churchyard, 1628–49. Dealt almost wholly in theological works. The first entry to him occurs in the Registers on 9th October, 1628. Rothwell served as Warden of the Company of Stationers in 1634 and 1638. Died early in 1649, his will being proved January 11th. He left four sons, John, William, Henry, and Andrew. [P.C.C. 15, Fairfax.]

ROTHWELL (JOHN), the younger, bookseller in London, (1) Sun in Paul's Church Yard; (2) Fountain and Bear in Goldsmith's Row, Cheapside. 1633–60. Son of John Rothwell the elder. Took up his freedom

January 12th, 1631. [Arber, iii. 686.] In 1657 he published a *Catalogue of approved divinity books*. He sometimes used a device showing a bear standing beside a fountain.

ROUNTHWAIT (RALPH), (?) bookseller in London, 1640–63. Smyth records his burial on June 8th, 1663 [*Obituary*, p. 58.] He was probably a descendant of the earlier Ralph Rounthwaite, 1618–26. [Arber, v. 262.] His address is unknown.

ROWLANDSON (THOMAS), bookseller in Gateshead, Yorks. [c. 1664.] His burial is recorded in the parish registers of St. Mary, Gateshead, on August 7th, 1664. [*Notes and Queries*, 10th Series, vol. 6, p. 443.]

ROYBOULD (WILLIAM), bookseller in London; Unicorn in Paul's Church-yard, 1651–60. A list of nineteen works published by him in 1652 occupies the verso of the last leaf of Francis Fulwood's *Churches and Ministry of England . . . . 1652.* [E. 671 (2).]

ROYCROFT (THOMAS), printer in London, (1) Bartholomew Close; (2) Printing House, Charterhouse Yard. 1651–77. Among English printers of the seventeenth century who did credit to their profession, Roycroft is conspicuous. He was the printer of the Polyglott Bible described by Mr. T. B. Reed in his *Old English Letter Foundries* as a lasting glory to the typography of the seventeenth century. The work, consisting of six folio volumes, was carried through in four years, and was the impression of English type, supplied by the four recognised typefounders. Roycroft was also the printer of the handsome editions of the classics published and edited by John Ogilby. On the accession of Charles II he was appointed the King's printer in the Oriental languages, and in partnership with George Sawbridge and others he held a share in the King's Printing House. Roycroft's printing house was totally destroyed in the Fire of London, and many valuable books perished with it. He became Master of the Stationers' Company in 1675. Roycroft died on August 10th, 1677, and was buried in the church of St. Bartholomew the Great. His will is in the Prerogative Court of Canterbury. [P.C.C. 86, Hale.]

ROYSTON (RICHARD), bookseller in London and Oxford; London, Angel in Ivy Lane, 1629–86; St. Bartholomew's Hospital, 1667. His first book entry occurs on January 28th, 162⅞. [Arber, iv. 208.] In 1631 he published T. Heywood's *Fair Maid of the West.* In 1645 he was accused of being a factor for scandalous books and papers against the Parliament, and thrown into prison. [Hist. MSS. Comm., 6th Rep., pp. 71-2.] The first edition of Εἰκὼν Βασιλικὴ was published by him in 1648. [Almack, *Bibliography of the King's Book, 1896.*] He was several times called before the Council of State for publishing unlicensed and scandalous books and pamphlets, and was with other booksellers and printers bound in sureties in 1649-50. [*Cal. of Domestic State Papers,* 1649-50, pp. 362, 524.] At the Restoration he was granted the monopoly of printing the works of Charles I, and was allowed a sum of £300 in consequence of his losses by the Fire of London in 1666. [*Cal. of Domestic State Papers,* 1666-7, p. 167.] He was Master of the Stationers' Company in 1673 and 1674. Royston died in 1686, aged 86. By his will, proved on November 16th, he desired to be buried in St. Paul's, but probably the Cathedral was not then finished, and his wishes could not be carried out, so he was buried in Christ Church, Newgate Street. He bequeathed all his copyrights to his grand-daughter Elizabeth Maior, daughter of Mary, the wife of Richard Chiswell, on the understanding that she married with her mother's consent, otherwise the copyrights were to pass to his grandsons, Royston Chiswell, Richard Chiswell, and John Chiswell. Another curious clause in connection with these copyrights was that the holder of them was to be a member of the Church of England. Whether these conditions were fulfilled is unknown, but Elizabeth, the daughter of Mary Chiswell, married Luke Meredith, her grandfather's apprentice. [Timperley, p. 569.] Royston left bequests to the following booksellers of Oxford: George West, Richard Davis, John Crosley and John Wilmot, which seems to bear out the statement that he had a bookseller's shop there. [Madan, *Chart of Oxford Printing,* p. 29.] He also bequeathed a piece of plate of the value of twenty pounds to the Company of Stationers. [P.C.C. 154, Lloyd.] *A Catalogue of some books printed for Richard Royston at the Angel in Ivie Lane, London, and some formerly printed at Oxford,* is found at the end of the second part of William Langley's sermon, *The persecuted Minister,* 1655 [1656.] [E. 860 (4), D.N.B.]

RUDDIARD (JOHN), bookseller (?) in London; Unicorn, Cornhill, under the Royal Exchange, 1662. His name is found in the imprint to the following broadside: *An exact and true relation of the landing of Her Majesty at Portsmouth, 1662.* [B.M., C. 20, f. 2 (50).]

RYDER, *see* Rider, Th.

SADLER (LAURENCE), bookseller in London; Golden Lion in Little
Britain, 1631–64. Possibly a son of the Lawrence Sadler found publishing
in 1599. [Arber, v. civ.] Smyth in his *Obituary*, p. 60, records " Augt. 2,
1664. Mr. Laur. Sadler, bookseller, died at ye Hague, of ye Plague."

SADLER (THEODORE), bookseller in London, (1) Bible, over against the
little North Door of St. Paul's Church, 1660; (2) Next door to the Golden
Dolphin, over against Exeter House in the Strand, 1663; (3) Little Britain,
1666 (1660–6.) Probably a relative of Laurence Sadler, *q.v.*, whom he
seems to have succeeded. At the outset of his career he was in partnership
with T. Davies at the Bible in St. Paul's Churchyard. He is mentioned in
the Hearth Tax Roll for the half-year ending Lady Day, 1666, as a bookseller in Little Britain. [P.R.O. Lay Subsidy, $\frac{252}{32}$]

SALMON (JAMES), bookseller (?) Grub Streete, neere to the Flying Horse,
1641. Associated with M. Rookes, *q.v.*, in publishing the following political
pamphlets relating to Ireland: (1) *Bloody Newes from Ireland*, 1641.
[E. 179 (9)]; (2) *Treacherous plot of a confederacie in Ireland*, 1641.
[E. 179 (15).]

SAMUEL (G   ), bookseller (?) in London, 1651. His name occurs in
the imprint to a pamphlet entitled *A Great Fight at Sea . . . . Imprinted
at London for G. Samuel*, 1651. [Hazlitt, ii. 550.]

SANDERS (JAMES), bookseller in Glasgow, 1625–42. Sold a bible to the
Cathedral authorities in 1625. One of the debtors in J. Bryson's inventory,
1642. [H. G. Aldis, *List of books*, p. 119.]

SANDERS (ROBERT), printer in Glasgow, 1661–96; "Printer to the Toun,"
1662; Printer to the City and University, 1672; One of His Majesties
printers, 1683. Succeeded Andrew Anderson as printer at Glasgow, and
during his thirty years' work produced a large amount of literature.
Nephew of William Sanders, Professor of Mathematics in St. Andrew's
University. On September 23rd, 1661, the town council of Glasgow
granted him an annual subsidy of forty pounds Scots. One of the debtors
in Lithgow's inventory, 1662. Prosecuted in 1671 by A. Anderson, and by
his heir in 1680 for infringement of their patent. About 1683 purchased

George Swintoun's share of the gift as king's printer. In 1684 was interdicted by the Privy Council from pirating Forbes' Aberdeen almanacs. Died July 12th, 1694. Succeeded by his son Robert. [H. G. Aldis, *List of Books*, p. 119.]

SANDERS (WILLIAM), bookseller (?) in London, 1663. His name occurs in the imprint to a pamphlet entitled *The Tryal of Captain Langston* .... *London, Printed for William Sanders, 1663*. [Hazlitt, iii. 146.]

SANDERSONNE (ROBERT), bookseller in Glasgow, 1654. One of the debtors in Andrew Wilson's inventory, 1654. [H. G. Aldis, *List of Books*, p. 120.]

SATTERTHWAITE (SAMUEL), bookseller in London, (1) Black Bull in Budge Row neare to Saint Antholin's Church; (2) Sun on Garlick Hill, 1642–9. Took up his freedom August 6th, 1639. [Arber, iii. 688.] His addresses are found on the imprints to the following books: (1) J. Cotton's *True Constitution* .... 1642; (2) Robert Gell's *Stella Nova* .... *a sermon*, 1649.

SAWBRIDGE (GEORGE), printer and bookseller in London, (1) Bible on Ludgate Hill; (2) At his house on Clerkenwell Green, 1667. (1647–81.) Appears to have commenced business in partnership with E. Brewster about 1653, in which year their names are found on one of Edward Calamy's sermons, *A Christians Duty and Safety in Evill Times*. [E. 1434 (3).] After the Restoration Sawbridge became a partner with Samuel Mearne, Richard Roycroft and others in the King's Printing House, and held shares in the chief publications of his day. Dunton, in his *Life & Errors*, refers to Sawbridge as "the greatest bookseller that had been in England for many years." He was treasurer to the Company of Stationers during the greater part of his life, and was Master of the Company in 1675. He died a wealthy man in 1681, and was succeeded by his son George. [Arber, *Term Catalogues*.]

SAYWELL (JOHN), bookseller in London, (1) The Starre in Little Britain, 1646; (2) The Greyhound in Little Britain. 1646–58. The first of the above signs is found mentioned in William Hussey's *Just provocation*, 1646. [E. 357 (6).] Saywell sometimes used as a device an engraved plate of a greyhound running.

SCOTT (RICHARD) bookseller in Carlisle, 1656–9. The following books were printed for him: T. Polwhele's *Treatise of Self Denial*, 1659; *The Agreement of the Associated Ministers and Churches of the Counties of Cumberland and Westmorland* .... 1656. [E. 498 (3).]

SCOTT (ROBERT), bookseller in London; Princes Arms, Little Britain, 1661–91. In partnership with William Wells, *q.v.*, whom he seems to have succeeded in 1673.

SEAMER (H   ), bookseller (?) in London; Near the Inner Temple, 1660. His name occurs on the imprint to a pamphlet entitled *Landing of His .... Majesty .... at Dover, 1660*. [Hazlitt, iii. 38.]

SEAT, *see* Scot.

SEILE (ANNA), bookseller in London; Fleet St. over against St. Dunstan's Church, 1661–7. Probably the widow of Henry Seile.

SEILE (HENRY), bookseller in London, (1) Tiger's Head, St. Paul's Church-yard, 1622–36. [Sayle, 992]; (2) Tiger's Head in Fleet Street, over against St. Dunstan's church, 1641–61. Took up his freedom April 13th, 1617. Arber, iii. 684.] First book entry August 3rd, 1619. [Arber, iii. 654.] Master of the Stationers' Company, 1657. Died about 1661, when the business passed to Anna Seile, probably his widow.

SEYMOUR (RICHARD), bookseller (?) in London (?) 1642. His name occurs on the imprint to a pamphlet entitled *A Joyful Message .... to Sir John Hotham .... Printed for Richard Seymour, Augt. 4th, 1642*. [E. 109 (1).]

SHAW (JOHN). *Discourse Concerning the Object of Religious Worship*, 1665. At the end a Catalogue of books sold by A. Swalle.

SHEARES (MARGARET), bookseller in London, 1664. Probably the widow of William Sheares. She published an edition of the *Remains of Sir W. Raleigh*, 1664. [Hazlitt, ii. 510.]

SHEARES or SHEARS (WILLIAM), bookseller in London, (1) Great South dore of Pauls, 1631; (2) Britains Bursse and neare York House, 1635–59; (3) Bible in Bedford St., Covent Garden, 1642–62; (4) Bible in Paul's Church Yard near Little North Door, 1655; (5) Westminster Hall, 1657.

[1625-62.] Took up his freedom June 9th, 1623. [Arber, iii. 685.] He appears to have had shops in various parts of London, and was the publisher of much of the best literature of the period, including Alexander Brome's *Cunning Lovers*, 1654; John Cleveland's *Poems*, 1659; Phineas Fletcher's *Sicelides*, 1631; Thomas May's version of Lucan's *Pharsalia*, 1651; Quarles' *Divine Fancies*, 1632. Sheares was suspected of having had a hand in printing *Leicester's Commonwealth*, a notorious satire on the House of Lords. [*Domestic State Papers*, Chas. I, vol. 484 (75).] He died September 21st, 1662. [Smyth's *Obituary*, p. 56.]

SHELMERDINE (RALPH), bookseller in Manchester, 1661-3. Son of William Shelmerdine, bookseller in Manchester. [Fishwick, *Lancashire Library*, p. 398, n.] His name occurs in the imprint to the Rev. R. Heyrick's *Sermon*, 1661. [E. 1088 (9).] Also mentioned as a bookseller in an advertisement of patent medicines in *The Intelligencer* and *Newes* of 1663.

SHEPERD, *see* Shepheard.

SHEPHEARD, or SHEPERD (HENRY), bookseller in London, (1) Bible, Chancery Lane [Sayle, 1149]; (2) Bible in Tower Street [on Tower Hill]. 1635-46. Took up his freedom September 15th, 1634. [Arber, iii. 687.] Publisher of plays and political tracts. Associated with W. Lee.

SHERLEY, *see* Shirley.

SHIRLEY, or SHERLEY (JOHN), bookseller in London; Golden Pelican in Little Britain, 1644-66. His name is found on the following among other books: W. Lilly's *Prophecy of the White King*, 1644, and Saml. Parker's *Tentamina Physico-Theologica*, 1665. [Ames Collection, 3267.] Smyth in his *Obituary* (p. 71), has this record, January 23rd, 166$\frac{4}{5}$, "Mr. John Shirley, bookseller in Little Britain, hora 10 *sub nocte*, died."

SHIRLEY, or SHERLEY (REBECCA), bookseller in London; Little Britain (? Golden Pelican), 1666. Probably the widow of John Shirley. Mentioned in the Hearth Tax Roll for the half-year ending Lady Day, 1666, as a bookseller in Little Britain [P.R.O. Lay Subsidy, $\frac{242}{52}$.]

SIMMONS (MARY), printer in London; Aldersgate St., 1656–67. Her name occurs in the Hearth Tax Roll for the six months ending Lady-Day 1666. She is returned as having thirteen hearths, a greater number than any other printer on the roll, so that her premises were large. She is probably identical with the Mistress Simmons mentioned as the "Custom House printer" in the return of printing houses made in 1668, and was perhaps the widow of Mathew Simmons. [P.R.O. Subsidy Roll, $\frac{252}{32}$; *Domestic State Papers*, Chas. II, vol. 243, no. 126.]

SIMMONS (MATHEW), bookseller and printer in London, (1) Golden Lyon in Duck-Lane, 1636; (2) Goldsmiths Alley [? Cripplegate]; (3) Next door to the Golden Lion, Aldersgate Street. 1636–54. Took up his freedom January 14th, 163½. [Arber, iii. 687.] Apparently he began as a bookseller, as the 1636 edition of Geo. Gilpin's *Beehive of the Romish church* was printed by M. Dawson and sold by Simmons at the Golden Lyon in Duck Lane. [B.M., 3935, a. 43.] In 1641 he was still in a small way of business, as in the return made on August 5th of those who had paid their proportion of Poll Tax, he is entered amongst those who paid the smallest amount. [*Domestic State Papers*, Charles I, vol. 483 (11).] He appears to have started a press some time after 1641, and quickly rose into favour, his press being largely employed by the Independents. He printed many of John Milton's writings, and amongst the orders of the Council of State are the following: *Sept. 4th, 1649. Mr. Frost to see that Mr. Simmons the Printer is satisfied for printing some books put out under the title of Discoverer. December 26th, 1651. Simmons the printer to attend Frost to give in bond, according to his bargain with Mr. Ledsom, not to sell or part with any of the reams or sheets of paper now in his hands, of the History of Independency.* Simmons was also the printer of the news-sheet entitled *A Briefe Relation of some affairs and transactions, Civill and Military begun Oct. 1., 1649.* He died May 19th, 1654. [Smyth's *Obituary*, p. 38.]

SIMMONS (NEVILL), bookseller in Kidderminster and London, (1) Three Crowns over against Holborn Conduit; (2) Prince's Arms, St. Paul's Churchyard; (3) Three Golden Cocks at the West End of Pauls. 1655–81. Chiefly remembered as publisher for Richard Baxter from 1655 to 1681. [G. Hester, *Nevill Simmons, bookseller and publisher*, 1893. 8°.]

SIMMONS (SAMUEL), printer in London; Next door to the Golden Lion in Aldersgate, 1666–76. Probably son or nephew of Mathew Simmons, *q.v.* Printer of John Milton's *Paradise Lost*, 1667, the copyright of which Milton sold him for £5 and a contingent £15 more, of which £13 was paid. [Masson, *Life of Milton*, Vol. vi. 509 *et seq.*]

SIMMONS (THOMAS), bookseller in London; Bull and Mouth near Aldersgate, 1656–62. Publisher of Quaker books.

SIMMONS (THOMAS), bookseller at Birmingham at the sign of the Bible, 1652. His name is found on the imprint to the Rev. Thomas Hall's discourse on baptism, entitled, *The Font Guarded with XX Arguments*, published on March 26th, 1652. The author addressed it especially to his "friends in the town of Birmingham," and it was on sale in London at the shop of George Calvert. This bookseller may be identical with the Thomas Simmons afterwards found in London as a publisher of Quaker literature.

SIMPSON (EDWARD), bookseller (?) in London, 1647. His name occurs on the imprint to Thomas Smith's *Armies last Propositions to the Commons of England* .... *London. Printed for Edward Simpson, 1647.* [Hazlitt, iv. 168.]

SIMS (JOHN), bookseller in London, (1) Cross Keyes in St. Pauls Church-yard, 1656–64; (2) Cross Keyes, Cornhill, near the Royal Exchange. 1661–6. Married Mary Banckes, of St. Botolph, Aldgate, October 8th, 1661. [Chester's *Marriage Licenses*, 1229.] In T. Brook's *Crown and Glory of Christianity*, 1662, are lists of books sold by J. Sims, H. Crips, and H. Mortlock, the joint publishers.

SKELTON (RICHARD), bookseller in London; Hand and Bible in Duck Lane, 1659. His name is found on the imprint to an edition of Aristophanes .... translated by H. H. B. [B.M. 643, b. 47.]

SLATER (F   ), bookseller (?) in London; Swanne in Duck Lane, 1641. According to Hazlitt his name occurs on the imprint to the pamphlet entitled *Gunpowder Plot* .... *by A. B. C. D. E.* [Hazlitt, i. 194.]

SLATER (THOMAS), bookseller in London; Angel in Duck Lane, 1629-53. Took up his freedom May 6th, 1629. [Arber, iii. 686.] Paid £3 as his proportion of the poll money in 1641. [*Domestic State Papers*, Charles I, vol. 483 (11).] He died before March 7th, 165⅔, on which date his widow, Anne Slater, assigned her rights in his copies to James Fletcher or Flesher. [Stationers' Registers, Liber E.]

SMART (TIMOTHY), bookseller (?) in London; Hand and Bible in the Great Old Bailey, near the Sessions House, 1656. His name is found on the imprint to J. Cotton's *Exposition upon the 13th Rev.* 1656. [E. 893 (2).]

SMELT (MATTHEW), bookseller in London; The Ship [next door to the Castle] in Moorfields, 1667-71. His name occurs on the imprint to G. Thorne's *Cheiragogia Heliana*, 1667.

SMETHWICK (FRANCIS), bookseller (?) in London; Saint Dunstans Churchyard in Fleet Street, under the Dyall, 1642. Son of John Smethwick, one of the publishers of Shakespeare's plays, who died before July 15th, 1641. His father bequeathed him his shop and all the books in it, and the copyrights, including *Hamblett, a play, The tameing of a shrew, Romeo & Juliett,* and *Love's Labour Lost,* were assigned over to him on August 24th, 1642. In the same year he published an edition of T. Lodge's *Euphues golden legacy,* but a few days after receiving the copyrights he re-assigned them to Miles Fletcher or Flesher. [Stationers' Registers, Liber D.]

SMITH (EDWARD), bookseller (?) in London, (?) 1643. His name occurs on the imprint to a pamphlet entitled *Joyfull Newes from Plymouth ....: London, Printed for Edward Smith, 1643.* [Hazlitt, ii. 481.]

SMITH (ELEANOR), bookseller (?) in London, 1650. Executrix of Francis Smith. She is mentioned in connection with Vavasour Powell's *Concordance of the Holy Bible,* 1650. [Rowland's *Cambrian Bibliography,* p. 153.]

SMITH (FRANCIS), bookseller in London, (1) Flying Horse Court in Fleet Street; (2) Elephant and Castle, without Temple Bar. 1642-67. There appears to have been several booksellers of this name between 1630 and 1667. Mr. Arber records a Francis Smith as publishing between 1633-6.

[*Transcript*, vol. v.] There was also a Francis Smith who was dead before 1650, leaving a widow Eleanor. He may have been identical with the earlier man. Lastly there was Francis Smith, who in 1659 published, among other things, Capt. W. Bray's *Plea for the people's good cause* [E. 763 (7)], and who was perhaps identical with the Francis Smith better known as "Elephant" Smith of a later period. [Arber, *Term Catalogues*, vol. 1, Index.]

SMITH (G.), bookseller (?) in London, 1642. His name is found on the imprint to the following pamphlet: *Two strange prophesies .... London, Printed for G. Smith*, 1642. [Hazlitt, i. 344.]

SMITH (JOHN), bookseller in London; Paul's Alley, 1641-7. Mentioned as one of the "better sort of freemen" in a list of stationers who in 1641 paid 20 shillings as his proportion of the poll tax. [*Domestic State Papers*, Chas. I, vol. 483 (11).] Several stationers of this name took up their freedom before 1640. [Arber, v. 265.]

SMITH (JOHN G.), (?) bookseller in London, 1642. His name occurs on the imprint to a pamphlet entitled *Newes from New England*, 1642. [E. 144 (22.)]

SMITH (NATHANIEL), (?) bookseller in Cambridge, 1647. Several political pamphlets issued in August, 1647, bear the imprint, *Printed for Nathaniel Smith: Cambridge*. No bookseller of this name is known to have been in Cambridge at that time, and it is probably the name of the author of the pamphlet, if it is not altogether fictitious.

SMITH (RALPH), bookseller in London; [Blue].Bible in Cornhil [near the Royal Exchange], 1642-60. Took up his freedom May 6th, 1639. [Arber, iii. 688.] One of the publishers of the Directory for Publick Worship, 1644. A list of books published by him in 1655, all of them theological, is printed at the end of W. Spurstowe's *Wel's of Salvation*, 1655. Another list of twenty books occurs at the end of David Dickson's *Brief Explication of the first Fifty Psalms*, 1653.

SMITH (THOMAS), bookseller in Manchester, 1643-9. Associated with Luke Fawne, *q.v.*, the London bookseller, in the publication of the following books: R. Hollingsworth's *Examination of sundry scriptures*, 1645. [E. 24

(6)]; R. Heyrick's *Queen Esthers Resolve*, 1646; *Deliberate resolution of the ministers of the gospel within the county of Lancaster*, 1647; *Solemn exhortation made to the .... churches .... within the province of Lancaster*, 1649; R. Hollingsworth's *Main points of church government*, 1649.

SMITH (WILLIAM), printer in Kilkenny and Cork, 1649–67. In 1649 William Smith printed a Proclamation for the Duke of Ormonde at Kilkenny. In 1657 his imprint appears on *The Agreement .... of Associated Ministers at Cork*, and in 1660 to James Davies' *History of Charles II*. As his name is found on Cork imprints as late as 1690, there may have been more than one printer of this name, perhaps father and son. [Information kindly supplied by Mr. E. R. McC. Dix.]

SMITHERS (RICHARD), (?) bookseller in London, 1641. His name occurs on the imprint to a pamphlet entitled *An honourable and learned speech made by Mr. Waller*, 1641. [E. 199 (42).] It may be a misprint for Smithurst, *q.v.*

SMITHURST (RICHARD), (?) bookseller in London; Hosier Lane neer Pye Corner [Smithfield], 1641–48. Publisher of political pamphlets. [Hazlitt, ii. 103, 714.] He may be identical with Richard Smithers.

SOWLE (ANDREW), printer in London, (1) Pye Corner Smithfield; (2) Crooked Billet, Holloway Lane, Shoreditch, 1653–67. Son of Francis Sowle, of the parish of St. Sepulchres, yeoman. Born in 1628. Apprenticed on July 6th, 1646, to Ruth Raworth, *q.v.*, for seven years. [Apprenticeship Register, Stationers' Hall.] Although his name is not found in an imprint before 1683, there is no doubt that he was the printer of most, if not all, of the early Quaker literature. In the obituary notice of him that appeared in *Piety Promoted*, Part I, p. 192, it was stated that he engaged himself freely in printing Friends books, and that his printing materials were several times seized and broken to pieces, and on one occasion a thousand reams of printed books were taken from him. On another occasion he was taken before Sir Richard Browne, who threatened to send him "after his brother Twyn," who had been executed in 1664 for printing a seditious book. Andrew Sowle's daughter, Elizabeth, married in 1685 her father's apprentice, William Bradford, who emigrated to America and set up his press in Pennsylvania, and afterwards in New York. Another daughter, Tace Sowle, succeeded her father in his business, and ultimately married Thomas Raylton. Andrew Sowle died in 1695, aged 67.

SPARKE (MICHAEL), senior, bookseller in London. Blue Bible in Green Arbour Court, Old Bailey, 1616–53. Born at Eynsham, Oxfordshire, son of Richard Sparke, husbandman. Apprenticed for seven years to Simon Pauley, a citizen and stationer of London. Took up his freedom June 10th, 1610. Michael Sparke was William Prynne's publisher, and was condemned to stand in the pillory and pay a fine of £500 for publishing *Histrio-mastix*. Michael Sparke was also a vigorous opponent of the monopolies, and was the author of a pamphlet entitled *Scintilla, or a Light broken into Dark Warehouses*, in which he drew attention to what he considered the excessive prices charged for books, particularly Bibles. Sparke at the same time imported Bibles from Holland, which he sold at cheaper rates than those printed in London. This pamphlet has been reprinted by Mr. Arber in the fourth volume of the *Transcript* (pp. 35 *et. seq.*). He was also the author of a pamphlet entitled *A Second Beacon fired by Scintilla* .... 1652, in which he gave many autobiographical details. Amongst the books he published were John Smith's *History of Virginia*, 1624; Captain Luke Foxe's *North West Foxe*, 1635; Mercator's *Atlas*, 1635, and a devotional work with the quaint title *Crums of Comfort*. Michael Sparke lived at Hampstead, and died there on December 29th, 1653. By his will he left a bequest of a seal ring to William Prynne, Esq. He also left bequests to Constance Jones, Elizabeth Macock and Ellen Cotes, the widows of three printers who worked for him. His son Michael was for a time in partnership with him, but was killed in 1645. [P.C.C. 158, Alchin; *Bibliographer*, New York, December, 1902.]

SPARKE (MICHAEL), junior, bookseller in London; Blue Bible in Green Arbour Court, Old Bailey, 1638–45. Son of Michael Sparke, senior, *q.v.* In partnership with his father, but some books, such as Christopher Love's *England's Distemper*, 1645 [E. 274, 15], have his name only as publisher. He died in December, 1645, having been mortally wounded by his brother. His will was proved March 22nd, 1646. [P.C.C. 52, Fines; *Bibliographer*, New York, December, 1902.]

SPEED (SAMUEL), bookseller in London, (1) Printing Press, St. Paul's Churchyard; (2) Rainbow, between the two Temple Gates. 1658–67. Probably the son of Daniel Speed, stationer, who was publishing from 1603 to 1620. [Arber, v. 266.] In 1658 he was associated with Joseph

Barber. In 1664 he issued a catalogue of books entered in the Register of the Company of Stationers between December 25th, 1662, and December 25th, 1663. [*Bibliographica*, vol. iii. p. 183.] In 1666 he was informed against for selling law books that had been printed during the Commonwealth, and was imprisoned and bound over in three hundred pounds not to sell any more of them. [*Domestic State Papers*, Charles II, 156, 105, 106.]

STAFFORD (JOHN), bookseller in London, (1) Blackhorse Alley, near Fleet Bridge; (2) In St. Bride's Church-yard; (3) Over against St. Bride's Church in Fleet Street; (4) ad insigne Georgii, in vico vulgo vocato, Fleet Street propre pontem; (5) In Chancery Lane. 1637–64. In the year 1634 R. Allot entered several books in the registers of the Company to which a marginal note was added to the effect that they were entered in trust for John Stafford. This may mean that he was Allot's apprentice. He took up his freedom September 28th, 1637. [Arber, iii. 688.] Dealt chiefly in theological literature. The fourth address given above is from an imprint only, preserved by Bagford. [Harl, 5919, 261.]

STAMPE (MRS.), bookseller in London; Queens Head, Westminster Hall, 1663. Mentioned as a bookseller in an advertisement of patent medicines in *The Newes*, December 17th, 1663.

STANTON (ISAAC), bookseller in London; White Hart and Bear, Bread Street, 1662. Mentioned in an advertisment in *Mercurius Publicus*, February 6th, 166$\frac{1}{2}$, relating to the Welsh bible in octavo.

STARKEY (JOHN), bookseller in London, (1) The Mitre at the North Door of the Middle Exchange, in St. Paul's Churchyard, 1658; (2) The Mitre near the Middle Temple Gate; (3) The Mitre, between the Middle Temple Gate and Temple Bar, 1667 [1658–67.] Son of George Starkey, of Isley Walton, in the County of Leicester. Put himself apprentice to John Saywell, *q.v.*, for eight years from November 6th, 1655. Took up his freedom April 20th, 1664. Published several notable books of travel, amongst which may be mentioned Sir P. Ricaut's *Present State of the Ottoman Empire*, 1667. Hazlitt, ii. 527, gives an interesting account of Samuel Pepys' copy of this work, which contains a list of books published by Starkey in 1667. He was one of the founders of the periodical bibliography called *Mercurius Librarius*, which began in Michaelmas Term, 1668, and was afterwards succeeded by the *Term Catalogues*. [Arber, *Term Catalogues*, vol. 1, pp. viii-x.]

STATIONERS, COMPANY OF, Edinburgh, 1650. Mr. H. G. Aldis, in his *List of Books printed in Scotland before 1700*, gives one, *A golden chaine of Time*, No. 1415, with the imprint, "Printed at Edinburgh by the Heires of George Anderson, for the Company of Stationers," which he thinks was distinct from the Society of Stationers. [H. G. Aldis, *List of Books*, p. 120.] Amongst the *State Papers, Domestic*, for 1651, vol. 15 (18), is an undated and unsigned paper headed *The true ground and reason why the Company of Stationers bought their printing house in Scotland*. In this it is stated that four years before (? 1647) upon an overture from the King's Printer there to sell the Company his patent and printing house, the Company made an agreement with him, which cost them a large sum of money, and that owing to the troubles in both kingdoms they had lost heavily over the transaction. The Company further state that they are "now" [*i.e.*, 1651] withdrawing their stock and materials, in regard that by the late Act full provision is made against importation from that kingdom.

STATIONERS, SOCIETY OF, Edinburgh, 1660-90. This press appears to fall into two periods: First period, 1660-71. Succeeding Higgins, *q.v.* This seems to be the Stationers' Company of London. Watson, p. 10, states that, "Tyler made over his part of the forfeited gift to some Stationers at London, who sent down upon us Christopher Higgins and some English servants with him . . . . After he died, these London Stationers appoint Patrick Ramsay, *q.v.*, a Scotsman to be overseer of that House . . . . but the masters living at a distance, and the work coming to no account, they sold this printing house to several booksellers [probably Swintoun, Glen and Brown, *q.v.*] at Edinburgh, who, in a little time after did divide and set up distinct houses." Arber [*Stationers' Registers*, v. xlvii] says that the Company "held for some years a patent for printing in Scotland, granted by the Scotch Parliament. This Scotch Patent . . . . appears to have been abandoned in 1669 upon the death of Christopher Higgins, the Company's agent at Edinburgh, and the stock and plant sold there for £300." [H. G. Aldis, *List of Books*, p. 121.]

STEDMAN (FABIAN), bookseller (?) in London ; In St. Dunstan's Church-yard in Fleet Street, 1665. *An Essay upon the Victory obtained by His Royal Highness the Duke of York, against the Dutch, upon June 3, 1665.* [a broadside.] [Lutt Coll., iii. 90.]

STENT (PETER), printer and engraver in London ; Whitehorse in gilt-spur-street, 1643–67. Printer of maps, pictures and copy books. A list of some of his publications will be found at the end of Richard Fage's *Description of the Whole World*, 1658.

STEPHENS (PHILEMON), bookseller in London, (1) Gilded Lyon in Paul's Churchyard, 1647 ; (2) White Lyon, St. Pauls Churchyard, 1654 [Probably the same house as No. 1] ; (3) Chancery Lane, 1669 (1622–70). Took up his freedom May 3rd, 1620. [Arber, iii. 685.] Partner with Christopher Meredith, *q.v.* Master of the Company of Stationers, 1660. Smyth in his *Obituary*, p. 87, thus records his death, " 15 July 1670, Philemon Stephens, bookseller in Chancery Lane died at Chelsey ; buried at St. Dunstans in ye West." He made a nuncupative will in favour of his wife Dorothy. [P.C.C. 103 Penn.] The house known as the White or Gilded Lion belonged to John Bellamy, and was mentioned in his will. Stephens dealt almost entirely in theological literature. The following works contain lists of his publications : Rev. R. Abbott's *Christian Family builded by God*, 1653 ; John Trapp's *Commentary upon the twelve minor prophets*, 1654. [See also *Bibliographica*, vol. 3, p. 182.]

STEPHENSON (JOHN), bookseller in London ; Sun on Ludgate Hill, 1649–52. Summoned before the Council of State, March 29th, 1649, for selling the Koran, printed by or at the expense of Thos. Ross. [*Calendar of State Papers*, 1649, pp. 59–63.] His name occurs on the imprint to the following book : Raleigh, Sir W., *Marrow of Historie*, 1650. [B.M., 463, h. 4 (2165).]

STORY (EDWARD), bookseller in Cambridge, 1653–74. Nothing of a biographical character appears to be known about this bookseller. Books sold by him in the years 1653, 1668, 1670, 1671, 1674, are noted by Bowes in his *Catalogue of Cambridge books* (pp. 46 *et seq.*).

STRANGHAN (DAVID), (?) *Pseud.* Printer at Aberdeen, 1659. This name is found on the imprint to *Message sent from the King of Scots*. Mr. Aldis thinks it was probably printed by James Brown, *q.v.*, under a feigned name. [H. G. Aldis, *List of Books*, p. 121.]

STREATER or STREATOR (JOHN), (?) bookseller and printer in London; Bible in Budge Row [? Watling Street], 1646–87. Amongst the Bagford fragments [Harl. 5927 (494)] is the following : *Aurefodina Linguæ Gallica, or the Gold Mine of the French language opened* .... *By Edmund Gostlin, Gent., London. Printed for John Streater at the signe of the Bible in Budge-Row, 1646.* No copy of this book can be traced, but if there is no mistake in the date, it would seem to prove that John Streater was a bookseller at the time of the outbreak of the Revolution. His subsequent history is obtained partly from his own petition to Parliament. [Harl. 5928, 13], and from other sources. He served throughout the Civil Wars, and was present at the battles of Edgehill and Newbury, and subsequently went to Ireland as Quarter Master General and Engineer. But in 1653 his views upon public matters changed, and he became a violent opponent of Cromwell, and in August, 1653, was expelled the army and thrown into prison for writing and printing a pamphlet entitled the *Grand Politique Informer.* After a confinement of some months and several appearances before the Judges, he was set at liberty by Judge Rolls. General Desborough urged him to make his peace with Cromwell, and he at length agreed not to print or write anything else against the Government. After Cromwell's death he appears to have been appointed one of the official printers, for on April 11th, 1660, in company with J. Macocke, *q.v.*, he received a warrant for the payment of £528 13s. 3d. for printing Acts, Orders, etc. [*Domestic State Papers,* 1659–60, p. 596.] In the Act of 1662 was a special proviso exempting Streater from its provisions. He held a patent for printing law-books as one of the assigns of Richard and Edward Atkyns, but in 1664 he was imprisoned with other stationers at the instigation of the Stationers' Company for infringing their privileges [Chan. Proc. Rey. Bundle 31, Stationers' Co. *v.* Flesher.] In 1666 he gave information against Samuel Speed for selling law books printed during the Commonwealth, with the result that Speed was apprehended and fined. Streater was also the author of a pamphlet entitled *The King's Grant of Privilege for sole printing Common Law Books defended and the legality thereof asserted,* 1669.

SUMPTNER (CHARLES), printer in London, 1650. His name is found on the imprint to Daniel King's *A Way to Sion* .... London, Printed by Charles Sumptner, for Hanna Allen, at the Crowne in Pope's Head Alley, 1650. [E. 596 (7).]

SWAINE (ROBERT), bookseller in London; Britains Burse, 1629–41. Took up his freedom December 20th, 1628. [Arber, iii. 686.] Mentioned in a list of stationers, dated August 5th, 1641, as one of the better sort of freemen, who paid five shillings to the poll tax. [*Domestic State Papers*, Charles I, vol. 483, 11.]

SWAYLE, or SWALLE (ABEL), bookseller in London; Unicorn, at the West-end of St. Paul's Church-yard, 1665–98. At the end of John Shaw's *Discourse concerning the object of Religious Worship*, 1665, is a catalogue of books sold by Swayle.

SWEETING (JOHN), bookseller in London, (1) Crown in Cornhill, 1639; (2) Angell in Pope's Head Alley, 1639–61. Took up his freedom June 27th, 1639. [Arber, iii. 688.] The following advertisement which appeared in the *Perfect Account* for the week ending Wednesday, January 4th, 1654, will best show the nature of his business: "There is published five new plays in one vollum, viz., The mad couple well matcht; The Novella; The Court Beggar; The City Wit; and the Damoisella; all written by Richard Brown (*sic*) A Collection of those excellent letters to several persons of honour; written by John Donne sometime Dean of St. Paul's London. Likewise a poem called the Shepheards Oracles, delivered in certain Eglogues by Francis Quarls. And the Poems of John Donne . . . . with elegies on the authors death, to which is added divers copies under his own hand never before printed. All which are to be sold by John Sweeting at the Angell in Pope's Head Alley." Sweeting died in 1661, and by his will left a sum of money to the Company of Stationers to be spent on two dinners for all the bachelors that were booksellers and free of the Company. [Timperley, p. 527.]

SWINTOUN (GEORGE), printer and bookseller at Edinburgh, (1) at the Kirk style, at the sign of the Angel, 1649; (2) In the Parliament Yard, 1667. Named among the debtors in Lithgow's Inventory, 1662. Probably one of the booksellers who, in 1671, acquired the business of the Society of Stationers, in which he is believed to have been associated with Robert Brown, Thomas Brown, and J. Glen. [H. G. Aldis, *List of Books*, p. 121.]

SYMMES, *see* Sims.

TAYLOR (JOHN), printer (?) in London, 1660. His name occurs on the imprint to a pamphlet entitled *Rumps last will and testament*. *London, Printed by John Taylor*, 1660. [Hazlitt, ii. 524.]

TAYLOR (RANDAL), bookseller in London; St. Martin's le Grand neer St. Leonards Church-yard, 1664-7. His name occurs on the imprint to Thos. Philipot's *Original and growth of the Spanish Monarchy*, 1664. [Ames Collection, 3165.]

TAYLOR, or TAYLOUR (WILLIAM), bookseller in Winchester: near the 9 Chequer Gate, 1663. Edward Lane's *Look unto Jesus*, 1663, was to be sold at the above booksellers. [B.M. 696, f. 13.]

TEAGE (   ), bookseller at Bristol; The Dolphin; and at Totnes, Devon, 1662-3. In an undated list of printers and booksellers found selling seditious literature in the reign of Charles II, it is stated that Thomas Bruister was to be found " at Teags house ye signe of ye Dolphin at Bristol." [*Domestic State Papers*, Charles II, vol. 67, 161.] He is also mentioned as a bookseller at Totnes, in Devon, in an advertisement of patent medicines in the *Intelligencer* for the year 1663.

TEW (NICHOLAS) bookseller in London; Coleman Street, 1643-60. (?) Son of William Tew, of London, gent. Apprentice to Henry Bird for nine years from September 6th, 1629. [Register of Apprentices, Stationers' Hall.] Took up his freedom October 1st, 1638. [Arber, iii. 688.] In January, 164⅖, he was arrested for printing a "scandalous libel" against Lord Essex and the Duke of Manchester, and confessed that a printing press was brought to his house and used there by Robert Overton and other Independents. In addition to the libel against the generals two other pamphlets have been traced to this secret press. [*Library*, October, 1904, pp. 374 *et seq.*] Edward Dobson, another bookseller, was imprisoned amongst other things for beating Nicholas Tew.

TEY (CHARLES), bookseller (?) in London, (?) 1662. His name is found on the imprint to a pamphlet entitled, *Sad and lamentable newes from several parts of England* .... *Printed for Charles Tey*, 1662. [Hazlitt H. 677.]

TEY (JOHN), bookseller in London ; White Lion in the Strand neer the New
Exchange, 1650–2. Dealer in plays. T. (J.) *Distracted state a Tragedy*,
1650. [E. 618 (5).]

THACKERAY (WILLIAM), bookseller in London, (1) Black Spread Eagle
and Sun, in the Old Bailey, 1666; (2) Sugar Loaf, Duck Lane, 1666–7.
Dealt largely in ballads and theological literature. Was mentioned in the
will of Thomas Passinger.

THOMAS (EDWARD), bookseller in London, (1) Green Arbour Court, Old
Bailey, 1657; (2) Adam and Eve, Little Britain, 1657–82. Succeeded to
the business of Michael Sparke, senr. Mentioned in the Hearth Tax
Roll for the half-year ending Lady Day, 1666, as a bookseller in Little
Britain. [P.R.O. Lay Subsidy, $\frac{252}{32}$.]

THOMAS (JOHN), bookseller in London, 1637–44. Took up his freedom
September 28th, 1633. [Arber, iii. 687.] *The Lord Lowden his learned and
wise speech*, 1641. [E. 199 (13).] His address has not been found.

THOMAS (MARY), bookseller in London, (?) 1642. Her imprint occurs on
a pamphlet entitled *Three proclamations*, 1642. [E. 154 (18).]

THOMAS (MICHAEL), bookseller in Bristol at his shop in the Polzey, 1664–7.
Advertisement for recovery of a watch, in the *Newes*, July 14th, 1664. He
is also mentioned in an information laid by the Mayor of Bristol in 1667,
as having received certain treasonable books concerning the Fire of
London from Elizabeth Calvert. [*Domestic State Papers*, Charles II,
vol. 209 (75).]

THOMAS (WILLIAM), bookseller (?) in London, 1659. His name occurs
on the imprint to a pamphlet entitled *Five strange Wonders*, 1659.
[Hazlitt, ii. 1659.]

THOMASON (GEORGE), bookseller in London ; Rose, or Rose and Crown,
St. Paul's Churchyard, 1627–66. Thomason will always be remembered
as the collector of the literature of the Civil War and Commonwealth
periods. Nothing is known as to his antecedents before the record of his

freedom as a member of the Company of Stationers on June 5th, 1626. [Arber, iii. 686.] His first book entry is recorded in the Registers on November 1st, 1627, and shows him as sharing the copyright with James Boler and Robert Young [*ibid.*, iv. 31, 188, 419]. He is next found in partnership with Octavian Pulleyn, a connection which was apparently dissolved about 1643, when Thomason moved to the Rose and Crown in St. Paul's Churchyard. At the time of the opening of the Long Parliament on November 3rd, 1640, Thomason conceived the idea of collecting and preserving, as far as he could, all the pamphlets printed during the next few years. Not only did he steadfastly carry out the task he had set himself, but he also arranged the collection in the best possible way, that is, chronologically, and made the chronology as precise as possible, by writing on almost every tract the day on which he received it. Thomason failed to get everything, thus many Royalist pamphlets and sheets printed at Oxford are only represented in his collection by a London reprint, and the same remark applies to other provincial or secret presses. It is matter for wonder that he should have collected so much rather than that he should have lost so little. Mr. G. K. Fortescue, Keeper of the Printed Books at the British Museum, gives the figures of the Thomason collection as follows: Pamphlets, 14,942; Manuscripts, 97; Newspapers, 7,216; total, 22,255 pieces, bound in 2,008 volumes. During the Civil War, Thomason sent his collection first into Surrey, afterwards into Essex, and at one time contemplated sending it into Holland, but was fortunately persuaded to give up that idea, and concealed it in his own warehouses, arranging the volumes as tables, and covering them over with canvas. At the Restoration the King commanded his stationer, Samuel Mearne, to purchase the collection, but apparently afterwards went back on his bargain, and not only did not take it into the royal library, but did not repay Mearne for its purchase. Mearne's widow, in 1684, was permitted by the Privy Council to sell it, and the volumes passed into the possession of a relative, Mr. Henry Sisson, a druggist on Ludgate Hill. They were eventually bought for King George III for the paltry sum of £300 and presented by him to the nation in 1762. In 1645-6 Thomason bought up the whole impression of a pamphlet called *Truth's Manifest*, which the Committee of both Houses considered libellous. In 1648 the House of Commons agreed to pay him £500 for a collection of Eastern books, but he had great difficulty in getting the money. In 1651 he was imprisoned for seven weeks in consequence of his complicity in the Love conspiracy, but was released on giving bail for £1,000. George Thomason died on April 10th, 1666, and Smyth in his *Obituary*, p. 71, adds "buried out of Stationers Hall (a poore man)." His will was proved on the 27th April. By this it appears that he had four sons, George, Edward, Henry, and Thomas, living at the time of his death. Negotiations were then on foot for the sale of his collection of pamphlets, which he bequeathed to Dr. Thomas Barlowe, Provost of Queen's College, Oxford, Thomas Lockey, principal librarian of the "public library," at Oxford, and John Rushworth, of Lincoln's Inn, in trust for the benefit of his three children, Edward, Henry and Thomas, but by a codicil he directed that the sum obtained for them, which he anticipated would be Twelve Hundred Pounds or more, was to be divided equally between his daughter Grace and his son Thomas. [D.N.B.; *Bibliographica*, vol. 3, pp. 291–308; Information kindly supplied by Mr. G. K. Fortescue; P.C.C. 64 Mico.]

THOMASON (HENRY), bookseller in London; Rose and Crown St. Pauls Church yard, 1663–7. Son of the preceding. Sometimes used as a device a copperplate showing a rose crowned.

THOMPSON (GEORGE), bookseller in London; White Horse in Chancery Lane, over against Lincolns Inn [Gate], 1642–60. Dealt in political pamphlets, broadsides and law books.

THOMPSON (JAMES), bookseller in London, 1642–50. Published the following: *Treason discovered from Holland* .... *London, Printed for J. Thompson*, 1642. [Hazlitt, ii. 692]; *Manual of Godly Prayers*, 1650. [Hazlitt, ii. 494.] His address has not been found.

THOMPSON (JOHN), the elder, bookseller in London, 1641. Mentioned in a list of stationers who had paid their proportion of the poll tax in 1641. [*Domestic State Papers*, Charles I, vol. 483 (11).]

THOMPSON or THOMASON (JOHN), (?) the younger, bookseller (?) in London, 1660. *Proceedings, Votes, Resolves and Acts of the late half quarter Parliament, called the Rump*, 1660. [Hazlitt, ii. 525.] His address has not been found.

THOMPSON (NATHANIEL), printer in Dublin, 1666. Printed an edition of T. Bladen's *Praxis Francisci Clarke*, 1666. [Ames Collection, 3272.] Some interesting notes about him at a later period will be found in the Hist. MSS. Comm. Report 9, app., pp. 69–79.

THOMPSON (THOMAS), bookseller (?) in London, 1642. Took up his freedom July 6th, 1635. [Arber, iii. 687.] His name is found on the imprint to several political pamphlets in 1642. [Hazlitt, 207, 525.]

THOMPSON (SAMUEL), bookseller in London, (1) White Horse, St. Paul's Churchyard; (2) Bishop's Head in Duck Lane, 1664–8. Shared with Humphrey Robinson, *q.v.*, Richard Thrale, *q.v.*, and Joshua Kirton, *q.v.*, the copyrights of Thomas Whitaker, numbering 109 works. His death is thus recorded by Smyth in his *Obituary*, p. 79, "Octr. 26th, 1668. *Die Lunæ hora 12 sub nocte*, Sam Thompson, bookseller in Duck Lane obit, a good husband and industrious man in his profession." In his will, which was proved on November 9th, 1668, he refers to his late losses in the fireing of London, and to the doubtful value of his stock. His son John was a student at Oxford, and Samuel Gellibrand, *q.v.*, was appointed sole executor. [P.C.C. 146, Hene.]

THORN (EDMUND), bookseller in Oxford, 1652–63. Publisher of Clement Barksdale's *Noctes Hibernæ*, 1652.

THORNICROFT, or THORNYCROFT (THOMAS), bookseller in London, (1) Eagle and Child, St. Paul's Churchyard; (2) Eagle and Child, near Worcester House in the Strand. 1663–7. His second address is found in Paul Festeau's *New and easie French Grammar*, 1667. [Eman. Coll. Camb.]

THORPE (WILLIAM), bookseller in Chester, (1) Hand and Bible near the High Crosse; (2) Stationer's Arms in Watergate Street, 1664. A fragment in the Ames Collection (473 h 1, 121) is a portion of an engraved sheet. At the top are three shields, one of them bearing the arms of the Stationers' Company. Between the two uppermost is the date 1664. Below them is a Bible and Hand and the letters W. T., and beneath this the imprint:—
" Printed for William Thorpp Bookseller in the City of Chester, and are to be sould by him there, at his shop at the hand and Bible neere the high Crosse, and at the Stationers Armes in the Watergate Street, where alsoe Books both new and old are to bee bound and sold."

THRALE (JAMES), bookseller in London, (1) Cross Keys, Pauls Gate; (2) Under St. Martin's Outwich Church in Bishopsgate Street, 1661-7. In partnership with Richard Thrale, *q.v.*

THRALE (RICHARD), bookseller in London, (1) Cross Keys at Paul's Gate, 1650; (2) Cross-Keyes and Dolphin in Aldersgate Street, over against the Half Moon tavern, 1667. Took up his freedom August 6th, 1623 [Arber, iii. 685.] Master of the Stationers' Company in 1664. On March 7th, 1652, in company with Humphrey Robinson, Joshua Kirton, and Samuel Thompson, he took over the copyrights of Thomas Whitaker. This assignment fills four pages of the register, and numbers 109 books. After the fire he moved into Aldersgate Street, where he published an account of the calamity.

THREIPLAND (JOHN), bookseller in Edinburgh, 1639-45. Probably the John Threipland, servant to Jonet Mayne, to whom she owed a "zieres fie" of forty pounds at her death in April, 1639. A debtor to Widow Hart, 1642; R. Bryson, 1645; T. Lawson, 1645. [H. G. Aldis, *List of Books*, p. 122.]

TOMKINS (NATHANIEL), bookseller (?) in London, 1660. His name occurs on the imprint to a pamphlet entitled *Declaration of Maj. Gen. Harrison, Prisoner in the Tower of London* .... London, Printed for Nathaniel Tomkins, 1660. [Hazlitt, ii. 269.]

TOMLINS (RICHARD), bookseller in London, (1) At his house in Green Arbour, in the Old Bailey, 1644; (2) Sun and Bible near Pye Corner [Smithfield], 1644-56. Took up his freedom March 27th, 1637. [Arber, iii. 688.] His first address is found in a pamphlet entitled *England's troubles anatomized*, 1644. [E. 12 (15).] A list of twenty-eight publications sold by him in 1654 is given at the end of a series of sermons by the Rev. C. Sidenham, entitled *Hypocrisie discovered*. [E. 1504 (3).] The following are among the items: *Pleasant notes upon Don Quixot*, folio; *History of the Seven Champions*, quarto; *The False Jew*, quarto; *Erasmus' Colloquies*, octavo.

TOMLINSON (GEORGE), bookseller (?) in London, 1642. Publisher of political pamphlets. Address not found. [B.M., E. 108 (11, 12).]

TOMPSON (RICH. ?), bookseller in London; Bedford Street against the New Exchange. His name occurs on an engraved sheet called the "Fruits of Faith." [B.M., 669, f. 20 (38).]

TOMSON (WILL.), bookseller at [Market] Harborough in Leicestershire, 1655. His name occurs in an advertisement in *Mercurius Politicus*, February 28th, 1655.

TONGE (JOHN), bookseller (?) in Warrington, Lancashire [c. 1653]. In the Registers of the Parish Church of Warrington is the following entry among the burials:—"1653. May 7 John Tounge, 'the stationer.'" Mr. W. H. Rylands when preparing his notes on *Warrington Booksellers and Stationers* had no information about him. [*Transactions of the Historic Society of Lancashire and Cheshire*, vol. 37, pp. 67-115.]

TOPPYN (LANCELOT), bookseller and haberdasher of London; Little Britain, 1641-6. Smyth in his *Obituary* (p. 23), records his death on November 17th, 1646. By his will, proved on November 27th, 1646, it appears that his wife Anne was sister to Dixy Page, *q.v.*, and his sister Elizabeth married Cornelius Bee, *q.v.* [P.C.C. 150, Twisse.]

TOWERS (JOHN), bookseller (?) in London, 1660. His name occurs on the imprint to a broadside entitled *Speech spoken to the Lord General Monk at Goldsmiths' Hall, April 10th, 1660*. [Lutt. i. 86.]

TREAGLE (GEORGE), bookseller at Taunton, 1646-53. Was possibly a relative of John Treagle, who took up his freedom May 7th, 1627. [Arber, iii. 686.] His name is found on the imprints to the following works: G. Newton's *Mans wrath and God's praise*, 1646 [E. 344 (6)]; Francis Fullwood's *Churches and Ministery of England*, 1652 [B.M. 463, h. 4, 2267]; W. Slater's *Civil Magistracy by Divine Authority*, 1653, an assize sermon preached at Winchester.

TRENCH (DAVID), bookseller in Edinburgh, 1662-71. Named among the debtors in G. Lithgow's inventory, 1662. One of A. Anderson's partners in the privilege and appointment as king's printer, 1671. Died 1671. His widow, Janet Mitchell, married Robert Malloch. [H. G. Aldis, *List of Books*, p. 122.]

TROT (ROBERT), printer (?) and bookseller in London; Under the church of Edmond the King in Lombard Street, over against St. Clement's Lane, 1645-9. His name has been met with on the imprints to the following: E. Pagitt, *Heresiography*, 1645; Eikanah Wales, *Mount Ebal levell'd*, 1659. [Ames Collection, 2825.]

TUCKEY (HUMPHREY), bookseller in London; Black Spread Eagle in Fleet Street (between Temple Bar and Chancery Lane, on the north side), 1642-53. Publisher of political tracts and miscellaneous literature.

TURKEY (HENRY), bookseller (?) in London, 1643. Only known from the imprint to the following pamphlet: *Humble petition of the Maior . . . . of the Citie of London to His Majestie . . . . London, Printed for Henry Turkey, 1643.* [Hazlitt, ii. 359.]

TURNER (I.), bookseller in London, 1643. Only known from the imprint to a pamphlet entitled, *Elegies on the death of . . . . John Hampden, Esq. . . . . by J. S. . . . . London, Printed by Luke Norton for I. Turner, 1643.* [E. 7i (4).]

TURNER (WILLIAM), printer to the University in Oxford. 1624-43. Took up his freedom on May 24th, 1622 [Arber, iii. 685], and his first book entry is recorded July 18th, 1623. [Arber, iv. 102.] In 1624 he was appointed printer to the University in succession to James Short. In 1631, in company with Michael Sparks, senr., and other London booksellers, he was tried before the Court of Ecclesiastical Commissioners on the charges of printing unlicensed literature and books that were other men's copies. [*Domestic State Papers*, Charles I, vol. 188 (13); 190 (40).] Much dissatisfaction was expressed by Dr. Richard Baylie, the Vice-Chancellor, in a letter to Archbishop Laud, dated January 16th, 1636-7, at the wretched character of the literature that came from Turner's press. Dr. Baylie writes, "He has been urged to print *Joannes Antiochenes*, and adopt some course for advancing the learned press of Oxford, but without any satisfaction . . . . he prints nothing but almanacks and school-books." [*Domestic State Papers*, Charles I, vol. 344 (20).] This letter may perhaps furnish a clue to the statement made in Wharton's *Remains of Laud* [ii. 174], that Turner had in 1634 abstracted the Savile Greek type. He returned it in February, 16$\frac{43}{40}$. He died about October, 1644, and was succeeded as University Printer by Henry Hall, *q.v.*, who had been one of his apprentices, and who had purchased Turner's presses, letters and utensils. [Madan, *Early Oxford Press*, p. 276; *Chart*, p. 29.

TUTCHEIN (ROBERT), bookseller(?) in London; Phœnix, in the New Rents in S. Paul's Church Yard, 1651. Only known from an imprint preserved amongst the Bagford fragments. [Harl., 5963 (10).]

TUTHILL (JOHN), bookseller in Yarmouth, 1661. His name is found on the imprint to the following pamphlet: Brinsley (John) ΑΓΩΝΟΤΡΟΧΙΑ, *Running of the Christian Race*, 1661. [Ames Collection, 3026.]

TWYFORD (HENRY), bookseller in London, (1) Vine Court in the Middle Temple; (2) Three Daggers in Fleet Street, 1641–75. Took up his freedom January 20th, 1640. [Arber, iii. 688.] Mentioned as one of the "better sort of freemen" in a list of stationers dated August 5th, 1641, as paying ten shillings as his proportion of the Poll Tax. [*Domestic State Papers*, Charles I, vol. 483 (11).] Dealt chiefly in law books, and in 1664 was arrested for illegally selling works of this class, which the Company of Stationers considered as their copyright. [Chan. Proc. Reynardson, Bundle 31, Stationers' Co. *v.* Flesher.]

TWYFORD (TIMOTHY), bookseller in London; At his shop, within the Inner-Temple-Gate, 1660. Possibly a son of the preceding. His name is found on the imprint to the following book: Herne (John), *Law of Charitable uses*, 1660. [Ames Collection, 2933.]

TWYN (JOHN), printer in London; Cloth Fair, 1640–64. Took up his freedom September 4th, 1640. [Arber, iii. 688.] This unfortunate printer, being in a small way of business, apparently did not look too closely at the manuscript supplied to him. At the beginning of the year 1664 he was arrested at the instigation of Sir Roger L'Estrange, for printing, or rather attempting to print, a pamphlet entitled *A Treatise of the Execution of Justice*. He was put on his trial at the Old Bailey on February 20th as a traitor against the King, and the indictment against him was that the book was intended to foment a rebellion. The chief witnesses against him were Joseph Walker, his apprentice, Sir Roger L'Estrange and

Thomas Mabb, a printer, and amongst the jury were Richard Royston,
Samuel Thomson, and Thomas Roycroft. Twyn was found guilty,
condemned to death, and executed at Tyburn. [*An exact Narrative of
the Tryal and condemnation of John Twyn* .... *London*, 1664; Cobbett's
State Trials, vol. 6.]

TYLER (EVAN), printer in Edinburgh, 1633–50; Leith, 1651–2; London:
Ducket Court, Aldersgate Street, 1656 (?)–67. Took up his freedom
July 1st, 1639. [Arber, iii. 688.] The first entry in the Registers under
his name occurs on September 11th, 1644. [Liber D, p. 683.] The
history of this printer is involved in much obscurity. He apparently had
presses in London and Edinburgh simultaneously. Mr. Aldis, in his *List
of Books printed in Scotland* (p. 122), says, "Appears to have been in
charge of R. Young's Edinburgh business in 1637 .... and in 1641
returned to Edinburgh in partnership with Young. In the following year
Young's name dropped out of the imprints and Tyler continued the style
of king's printer. In 1651 he moved to Leith, but seems to have returned
to London in 1652–3, being succeeded in Leith by C. Higgins .... At the
Restoration, Tyler once more returned to Edinburgh, resumed the style of
king's printer, and printed there from 1660 to 1672." Amongst the State Papers
for the year 1651 is an undated and unsigned paper headed *The true reason
why the Company of Stationers bought their printing house in Scotland*, in which
occurs the following passage: "About four years before [*i.e.*, 1647] upon an
overture from the .... Kings Printer there, to sell the company his Patent
and Printing howse, the company made an agreement with him which cost
them a large some of money. Since which time, what with the troubles
there and in this Commonwealth the Company have extremely suffered
there .... The Company are now [*i.e.*, 1651] withdrawing their stock and
materials." This at all events would account for Evan Tyler's return to
London in 1652. He is mentioned in the Hearth Tax Roll for the half-
year ending Lady Day, 1666, as a printer in Ducket Court, St. Botolph's,
Aldersgate. [P.R.O. Lay Subsidy, $\frac{252}{32}$.] Tyler was the printer of the
unfinished Lithuanian Bible in 1662, which Mr. Steele considers was
printed in London. [*Library*, January, 1907.] In contemporary news-
sheets Barnard Alsop was stated to be the printer of many things having
Tyler's name in the imprint.

TYTON (FRANCIS), bookseller in London; Three Daggers in Fleet Street, neer the Inner Temple Gate, 1649–67. Joint publisher with Thomas Underhill, of Richard Baxter's early works. In 1651 he appears to have held some official position under Government, as on March 31st of that year a payment of £54 14s. 7d. was made to him for supplying books and papers to the Commissioners for Ireland. [Calendar of State Papers, 1651, p. 555.] In 1660 he was appointed "printer" to the House of Lords with J. Macock.

TYUS (CHARLES), bookseller in London; Three Bibles on London Bridge, 1656–64. Dealt in ballads, chap books, and miscellaneous literature. Succeeded by his widow, Sarah Tyus.

TYUS (SARAH), bookseller in London; Three Bibles on London Bridge, 1665. Widow of Charles Tyus. This house was afterwards in the possession of Thomas Passinger.

UNDERHILL (JANE), bookseller in London; Bible and Anchor St. Pauls Churchyard, 1660. Probably widow of Thomas Underhill.

UNDERHILL (THOMAS), bookseller in London, (1) Bible in Wood Street, 1644; (2) Anchor and Bible in St. Paul's Churchyard, 1641–59. Associated with Francis Tyton as publisher of Richard Baxter's early writings. Also associated with Giles Calvert in some publications. His earlier address is found in W. Lilly's Prophecy of the White King, 1644.

UNDERWOOD (JAMES), bookseller in London; Near the New Exchange, 1642–3. Took up his freedom June 18th, 1627. [Arber, iii. 686.] Published some political tracts. [Hazlitt, ii. 627, 635.]

UNDERWOOD (THOMAS), bookseller in London, 1643. Took up his freedom September 3rd, 1638. [Arber, iii. 688.] His name appears on the imprint to the following pamphlets: True Copy of a Welsh sermon, 1643; The Welsh ambassadour, 1643. His address has not been found.

UPHILL (ANTHONY), bookseller (?) in London, 1641. Took up his freedom October 2nd, 1620. [Arber, iii. 685.] Mentioned in a list of stationers dated August 5th, 1641, as one of the "better sort of freemen," who paid twenty shillings as his proportion of the poll tax. [Domestic State Papers, Chas. I, vol. 483 (11).]

VALL (THOMAS), bookseller (?) in London, 1657. His name occurs on the imprint to T. Woolsey's *Reasonable Treatise of this age*, 1657. [Hazlitt, ii. 659.]

VAUGHAN (R   ), printer in London, (1) St. Martin's le Grand; (2) King's College, near Puddledock [Thames Street], 1660-1. In partnership with H. Lloyd. His addresses are found in the following books: (1) *Speech and plea of Archibald, Marquis of Argyle*, 1660; (2) *Last words and actions of John James*, 1661.

VAVASOUR (NICHOLAS), bookseller in London; Little South door of Pauls; (2) Inner Temple, 1623-43. Took up his freedom March 22nd, 1622. [Arber, iii. 685.] Amongst his publications was Sir Henry Colthrop's *Liberties, Usages and Customes of the City of London*, 1642.

VEERE, or VERE (THOMAS), bookseller in London, (1) Upper end of the Old Bayley, near Newgate; (2) Angel in the Old Bailey; (3) Angel without Newgate; (4) Cock in St. John Street, 1667. [1646-80.] Dealt chiefly in ballads and broadsides, in which he was associated with F. Coles, Jo. Wright, and W. Gilbertson.

VERE, *see* Veere, T.

VERIDICUS (TH.), Edinburgh, 1650. [*See* H. G. Aldis, *List of Books*, No. 1412.]

VINCENT or VINSON (ANTHONY), bookseller in London; Old Bailey, 1627-48. Took up his freedom June 21st, 1627. [Arber, iii. 686. Hazlitt, iv. 154, records a speech by Rich. Martin as sold by Ant. Vinson.]

WALBANCKE (MATTHEW), bookseller in London; Gray's Inn Gate, 1618-67. Took up his freedom March 22nd, 1617. [Arber, iii. 684.] Mentioned in a list of dealers in "old libraries," who in 1628 were required to send catalogues of their books to the Archbishop of Canterbury. A publisher of and dealer in law books. He was also the publisher of the news-sheet called the *Exact Diary*. Had a son, Matthew, apprenticed to him on March 1st, 164$\frac{9}{0}$.

WALKER (HENRY), bookseller in London, 1641-2. Better known as Walker the Ironmonger. John Taylor, the water poet, wrote a biography of him in 1642, in which he declared that Walker was apprenticed to an ironmonger, and for some years followed that trade, but eventually gave it up to become a bookseller and writer of pamphlets, of which he published as many as four or five hundred thousand copies. Amongst these was one entitled *To your tents, O Israel!* a copy of which he flung into the King's carriage. For this he and the printer were sent to the King's Bench Prison in Southwark, but were subsequently rescued by the mob when on their way to Newgate. After a long hue and cry Walker was recaptured and sent to the Tower. He then made submission. [*The Whole Life and Progress of Henry Walker the Ironmonger . . . . Collected and written by John Taylor,* 1642. 12th July. [E. 154 (29).]

WALKER (JOHN), bookseller in London; Starre in Pope's Head Alley, 1648-50. A stationer of this name took up his freedom October 4th, 1619, but this is probably a different man. His name is found on the imprint to the following pamphlet: *Mercurius Anti-mechanicus, Or, The Simple Cobler's Boy . . . . By Theodore de la Guarden* [*i.e.*, Nath. Ward], London, 1648. [E. 470 (25).]

WALKER (MATHIAS), bookseller in London; (1) 3 Hearts, West End of Pauls, 1664; (2) Under St. Dunstan's Church in Fleet Street, 1667. Chiefly remembered as one of the publishers of the first edition of Milton's *Paradise Lost,* in 1667. His earlier address is found in A. Gordon's *Tyrocynium Linguæ Latinæ,* 1664. [Arber's *Term Catalogue,* vol. i., index.]

WALKLEY (THOMAS), bookseller in London, (1) Eagle and Child, Britain's Burse; (2) Flying Horse, near York House. 1619-58. Took up his freedom January 19th, 1618. On December 1st, 1649, a warrant was issued against him for dispersing scandalous declarations sent from the late King's sons at Jersey. [*Calendar of Domestic State Papers,* 1649-50, p. 557.] He was the publisher of Sir J. Denham's *Coopers Hill,* 1642, Waller's *Poems,* 1647, and much other interesting literature.

WALL (THOMAS), bookseller in Bristol. By the Tolezy in Cornstreet, 1660. Published a sermon entitled, *Plain dealing and Plain meaning . . . . Preacht in the parish church of St. Nicholas, Bristol, April 6th, 1660.* [E. 1026 (5).]

WALLEY, or WALEY (HENRY), bookseller in London; Harts Horn in Foster Lane (?) 1608–55. Grandson of John Walley, or Waley, stationer of London, 1546–86, son of Robert Walley, or Waley, stationer of London, 1578–93. Clerk of the Company of Stationers, 1630–1640. Master of the Company of Stationers in 1655. [Arber, v. 271.]

WALLEY (JOSEPH), bookseller in London, 1666. Stated in a document of that date to be "a great factor for the sectaries." [*Domestic State Papers*, Charles II, 121, 372.] He was possibly a son of the preceding and in business with him.

WALLIS (ELISHA), bookseller in London, (1) Three Black Lyons in the Old Bayley, 1656 ; (2) At the [Golden] Horse-shoe in the [Great] Old Bayley, 1656–61. His name is found on the imprint to an edition of Robert Burton's *Anatomy of Melancholy*, 1660.

WALTON (ROBERT), printer and print seller in London; Globe and Compasses in St. Paul's Churchyard, between the two north doors, 1647-60. Dealer in maps and prints, and the publisher of Edward Cocker's *The Pen's Triumph*, 1660. A catalogue of prints, etc., on sale by him is given at the end of *A compendious view . . . . of the whole world*, 1659. It is called "a catalogue of some pleasant and useful maps and pictures that are cut in copper, being very neat ornaments for houses, gentlemen's studies and closets, and useful for divers callings, as Painters, Embroyderers, &c." His name is variously given as Walters, Waltor, and Walton.

WARD (FRANCIS), bookseller in Leicester, 1661-3. Gave information against the London bookseller Nathan Brooks for dispersing a book entitled *The Year of Prodigies and Wonders*. October, 1661. [*Domestic State Papers*, Charles II, vol. 43, 7, 8, 9.] Mentioned in an advertisement of patent medicines in the *Intelligencer* of 1663.

WARREN (ALICE), printer in London ; Foster Lane (?), 1661-2. Widow of Thomas Warren, printer. Her name is found on the imprint to the second volume of Sir William Dugdale's *Monasticon Anglicanum*, 1661, and the same author's *History of imbanking*, 1662.

WARREN (FRANCIS and THOMAS), printers in London ; Foster Lane, 1663-6. Possibly the sons of Thomas Warren, senr., and Alice Warren. They are mentioned in the Hearth Tax Roll for the half-year ending Lady

Day, 1666, as printers in Foster Lane. [P.R.O. Lay Subsidy, $\frac{242}{33}$.] In a list of the several printing houses taken on July 24th, 1668, amongst the master printers returned as ruined by the Fire of London was Mr. Warren. [*Domestic State Papers*, Charles II, vol. 243, 126.] This has reference, doubtless, to the above printing house.

WARREN (THOMAS), senr., bookseller and printer in London, (1) White Horse in St. Pauls Churchyard, 1641; (2) Foster Lane, 1638(?)–61(?). Appears to have begun as a bookseller in partnership with Joshua Kirton. Their imprint (No. 1 above) is found on the title-page of James Giffard's *French Schoolmaster*, 1641 [Harl. 5927 (439).] Warren afterwards became a printer and was succeeded by his widow, Alice Warren, in 1661.

WARWICK (WILLIAM), bookseller (?) in Colchester (?), 1663. His name is found on the imprint to a pamphlet entitled : *Some worthy proverbs left behind by Judith Zins-Penninck, To be read in the congregation of the saints . . . . London, Printed for William Warwick*, 1663. [B.M. 4152, C. 34.]

WATERSON (JOHN), bookseller in London; Crown, at Cheap Gate in Pauls Churchyard (?), 1620–56. Son of Simon Waterson, 1585–1634. Took up his freedom June 27th, 1620. [Arber, iii. 688.] A dealer in plays, is believed to have given up business in 1641. Smyth in his *Obituary*, p. 41, under date February 10th, 165⅔, records : "John Waterson, once a bookseller, died." He left a son, Simon, who was apprenticed to John Williams, on September 1st, 1645, for seven years. [Register of Apprentices, Stationers' Hall.]

WATERSON (SIMON), bookseller in London; Globe in St. Paul's Churchyard, 1656–7. Son of John Waterson, apprenticed to John Williams, *q.v.*, on September 1st, 1645, for seven years. He was associated with Richard Clavell in publishing an edition of Camden's *Remains*, 1657. [G. 2925.]

WATKINS (R.), bookseller (?) in London (?) 1642. His name occurs on the imprint to a pamphlet entitled *A True and Joyful Relation of Two famous Battels . . . . Printed for R. Watkins, August 27th, 1642*. [Hazlitt, ii. 516; iii. 290.]

WATKINS (ZACHARIAH), bookseller in London; Near Inner Temple Church, 1663. Advertisement in *The Kingdoms Intelligencer*, April 20th, 1663.

WATKIS (   ), bookseller in Shrewsbury, 1663. Mentioned in an advertisement of patent medicines in the news-sheets of this year.

WATSON (HUMPHREY), bookseller (?) in London (?) 1642. His name occurs on the imprint to a pamphlet entitled *A True Relation of Two Merchants of London . . . . . Printed for Humphrey Watson,* 1642. [Hazlitt, iii. 145.]

WATSON (JOSEPH), (?) bookseller in London, 1642. His name is found on the imprints to the following pamphlets: *Parliaments last order and determination for the safety and security of Hull,* 1642 [B.M. E. 108 (10)]; *Portsmouth. New discovery of a design of the French,* 1642. [Hazlitt, ii. 489.]

WATSON (WILLIAM), bookseller (?) in London (?), 1641. His name is found on the imprint to a pamphlet entitled *Resolution of the Women of London,* 1641. 4°. [Hazlitt, i. 262.] A stationer of this name took up his freedom July 25th, 1624. [Arber, iii. 685.]

WAYTE (THOMAS), bookseller at York; The Pavement, 1653-95. Joined the Quakers about 1651, and acted as local agent for Friends' publications. Several tracts, all dated 1653, written by George Fox, Richard Farnsworth, James Nayler and William Tomlinson, have the imprint: "Printed for Tho. Wayte at his house in the Pavement in York," or "Printed for Thos. and are to be sold at his house, etc." Wayte's name occurs in a list of "dispersers of Quaker books," drawn up in 1664. He married the sister of Richard Smith, a tanner of York, and his house became a noted meeting place for Friends. Thomas Wayte died in 1695, six years after his wife. [*The First Publishers of Truth,* p. 318 n.]

WEBB (CHARLES), bookseller in London; Golden Boar's Head, St. Paul's Churchyard, 1658-60. Publisher of miscellaneous literature, including plays.

WEBB (DANIEL), bookseller (?) in London, 1660. His name occurs on the imprint to a pamphlet entitled *Brethren in Iniquity,* 1660. 4°. [Hazlitt, iii. 23.]

WEBB (NATHANIEL), bookseller in London, (1) King's Head, St. Paul's Churchyard, 1660; (2) Royal Oak, St. Paul's Churchyard, 1663 (1646–65). In partnership for a time with W. Grantham, *q.v.* Died March 26th, 1665. [Smyth's *Obituary*, p. 62.] His second address is found on a pamphlet entitled *A Modest Discourse concerning the Ceremonies . . . . used in the Church*, 1660. [E. 1035 (4).]

WEBB (RICHARD), bookseller (?) in London (?), 1642. His name is found on the imprint to John Taylor's *Cluster of Coxcombs*, 1642. [Hazlitt, i. 419.]

WEBB [WILLIAM], bookseller in Oxford, 1629–52. [Madan, *Oxford Chart*, p. 29.] His name is found on a large number of political pamphlets between 1641 and 1652.

WEEKLY (WILLIAM), bookseller in Ipswich, 1657–9. His name is found on the imprints to the following books: C Beck, *Universal Character*, 1657. [E. 1591 (1)]; A. Pringle, *Stay in Trouble*, 1657 [E. 1592 (1)]; M. Lawrence, *Use and Practice of Faith*, 1657 [E. 924 (1)]; Edm. Warren, *Jews Sabbath antiquated*, 1659. [Ames Collection, 2854.]

WELLS (R.), bookseller (?) in London; Royal Exchange in Cornhill (?), 1648. His name is found on the imprint to a pamphlet entitled *Prince Charles his Declaration . . . . London, Printed for R. Wells, and are to be sold at the Royall Exchange in Cornhill*, 1648. [Hazlitt, ii. 105.]

WELLS (WILLIAM), bookseller in London; Princes Arms, Little Britain, 1641–73. Took up his freedom April 3rd, 1637. [Arber, iii. 688.] Mentioned in a list of stationers who on August 5th, 1641, had paid their proportion of the poll tax. [*Domestic State Papers*, Charles I, vol. 483 (11).] Was in partnership for a time with Robert Scott, *q.v.* Died in January, 167$\frac{2}{3}$. Smyth in his *Obituary* records, " Mr. Wells, bookseller in Little Britain (my old acquaintance) died this Satterday morning. Buried at St. Butolphs extra Aldersgate. No sermon."

WENBORN (WILLIAM), bookseller in London; The Rose at the Bridge Foot, 1646. Only known from the imprint to the following pamphlet: Πανταλογία. *The Saints Abundance opened. By Thomas Sterry.* [E. 355 (28).]

WEST (G.), bookseller in Oxford (*c.* 1650–95). [Madan, *Oxford Chart*, p. 31 ; Ames Collection, 3186.]

WEST (SIMON), bookseller in London ; Blackamore's Head in great Wood-street, neer Cheapside, 1637–46. Took up his freedom February 6th, 1637. [Arber, iii. 688.] Became a teacher of shorthand and wrote and published a book on the subject entitled *Arts Improvement: or Short and swift Writing . . . . London, 1647.* [B.M. 1043, c. 45.]

WHALEY (PETER), bookseller in London ; Gun in Ivy Lane, 1645. Associated with C. Greene, *q.v.* Had a son Samuel apprenticed on March 1st, 16$\frac{3}{0}$.

WHITACRE, or WHITACRES, *see* Whitaker.

WHITAKER (RICHARD), bookseller in London ; Kings Arms in St. Paul's Churchyard, 1619–48. Took up his freedom May 3rd, 1619. [Arber, iii. 685.] In partnership with Thomas Whitaker, *q.v.* They had an extensive business, and published much of the best literature of the period. Richard Whitaker was a warden of the Company of Stationers in the years 1643–5. He died on February 5th, 164$\frac{7}{8}$. [Smyth's *Obituary*, p. 25.]

WHITAKER (THOMAS), bookseller in London ; King's Arms, St. Paul's Churchyard, 1642 (?)–50 (?). In partnership with Richard Whitaker, and carried on the business after Richard's death in 1648. Thomas Whitaker died about 1650, and his widow married Mr. Alexander Brome. On March 7th, 165$\frac{2}{3}$, they assigned over all their right and title to the Whitaker copyrights to Humphrey Robinson, Richard Thrale, Joshua Kirton, and Samuel Thompson. This assignment numbered one hundred and nine items, and fills four pages of the Stationers' Register. [*See* also Introduction.]

WHITE (DANIEL), bookseller in London ; Seven Stars in St. Paul's Church Yard, 1659–60. His name is found in the following works : P. Cornelius' *Way to the Peace*, 1659 ; [S. (G.) Poetical Essay, *As an Arrha of a larger Harvest*, 1660 ; *see* Wharton (G.), *Select and Choice Poems*, 1661.

WHITE (JOHN), bookseller in London ; Threadneedle Street, behind the Old Exchange, 1661. His name is found on the imprint to a pamphlet entitled, *Hermas : The Three Bookes of Hermas the Disciple of Paul the*

Apostle .... *Englished by John Pringle* .... *London, Printed for John White in Threadneedle Street, behinde the Old Exchange,* 1661. [Bodleian; Hazlitt, i. 211.]

WHITE (ROBERT), printer in London; Warwick Court, Warwick Lane, 1639–67. Took up his freedom December 7th, 1639. [Arber, iii. 688.] Partner with Thos. Brudenell, in printing the Bible in 1647. They were also joint printers of Sprigge's *Anglia Rediviva,* although only the initials of Robert White occur in the imprint. White was also associated with George Bishop in printing several news-sheets. At the survey of the press taken in 1668 he is returned as having three presses, three apprentices and seven workmen. [Plomer, *Short History,* p. 225.]

WHITING (G   ), bookseller (?) in London (?), 1652. His name occurs on the imprint to a pamphlet entitled *Black Munday turn'd White,* 1652. [B.M. 718, c. 20 (2).]

WHITTINGTON (GEORGE), bookseller in London; Blew Anchor in Cornhill, neer the Royall Exchange, 1643–9 (?). His name is found on the imprint to the following pamphlet: *Humble petition of many thousands of Young Men,* 1646. [E. 378, 15.] Issued some books in partnership with John Partridge and James Moxon and Hannah Allen.

WHITTLESEY (THOMAS), bookseller (?) in London (?), 1662. His name is found on the imprint to John Heydon's *Holy Guide.* [Hazlitt, iv. 47.]

WHITWOOD (WILLIAM), bookseller in London; Swan, Duck Lane, 1666–7. Dealer in ballads and broadsides.

WILCOX (JOHN), bookseller in London; Crown in St. Pauls Churchyard, 1647. His name is found on the imprint to Thomas Philipot's *Poems,* 1647. [Hazlitt, H. 456.] Probably a misprint for John Williams.

WILDEBERGH (C.), bookseller (?) in London; The Globe in St. Katherines, 1662. His name is found on the following broadside, *An exact and true relation of the landing of Her Majesty at Portsmouth,* 1662. [B.M. C. 20, f. 2 (50).]

P

WILFORD (GEORGE), bookseller in London; Little Britain, near the Hospital Gate, 1652. His name is found on a pamphlet entitled, *Looking Glasse for a Drunkard*, 1652 [Hazlitt, H. 171.]

WILKINS (TIMOTHY), bookseller in London; George in Fleet St., 1641. In partnership with John Maynard in the publication of the writings of John Wilkins, Bishop of Chester.

WILLIAMS (JOHN), bookseller in London, (1) Crown, St. Pauls Church Yard, 1636–66; (2) Blue Anchor in Little Britain, 1667. Took up his freedom September 15th, 1634. [Arber, iii. 687.] Paid ten shillings as his proportion of the poll tax in 1641. [*Domestic State Papers*, Charles I, vol. 483 (11).] Joint publisher with F. Eglesfield, *q.v.*, of Herrick's *Hesperides*, 1648. The John Wilcox, *q.v.*, recorded by Hazlitt is probably intended for John Williams.

WILLIAMS (RICHARD), bookseller at St. Albans in Hertfordshire, 1649–56. Three stationers of this name took up their freedom before 1640. [Arber, iii. 683, 686, 688.] The following pamphlets have his name on the imprint: *The Divels Delusions*, 1649 [E. 565 (15)]; *Bloudy Fight in Hartfordshire*, 1649. The name R. Williams is also found on the imprint to a political tract in 1642, entitled *Parliaments Declaration concerning the Kings Majesty* [E. 108 (44)], but whether he was the same with the St. Albans bookseller is unknown.

WILLIAMS (THOMAS), bookseller in London; Bible in Little Britain, 1662–7. His name is found on the imprint to a pamphlet by John Humfrey, entitled *Second Discourse about re-ordination*, 1662. [Ames Collection, 3080.] He is mentioned in the Hearth Tax Roll for the half-year ending Lady Day, 1666, as a bookseller in Little Britain. [P.R.O. Lay Subsidy, $\frac{252}{32}$]. His death is recorded by Smyth in his *Obituary*, p. 79.

WILLIAMSON (ANTHONY), bookseller (?) in London; Queens Arms neer the West-end of St. Paul's Church Yard, 1651–9. His name occurs on the imprint to the following pamphlet: *The Grand Debate concerning Presbytery*, 1652. [B.M. 463, h. 4 (2273).]

WILLIAMSON (ROBERT), bookseller (?) in London, 1648-9. His name is found on the imprint to the following amongst other political pamphlets: *Great fight at Chepstow Castle*, 1648. [E. 443, 14.]

WILMOT (JOHN), bookseller in Oxford, 1637-65. [Madan, *Chart of Oxford Printing*, pp. 29, 31.] His name is found on the imprint to Adrian Heereboord's *Philosophia naturalis*, 1665. [Ames Collection, 3237.]

WILSON (ANDRO), bookseller in Edinburgh, (1) Near the Ladies Steps, 1641; (2) At the Plain Stones over against the Stone Shop at the signe of the Great Book, 1649; (3) At the sign of the Bible, 1649 (1641-54. [H. G. Aldis, *List of Books*, p. 124.]

WILSON (HENRY), bookseller (?) in London, 1642. His name is found on the imprint to a political pamphlet entitled *The Virgins Complaint* [Jan. 31], 1642. [*See* Hazlitt, i. 440.]

WILSON (PATRICK), bookseller at Edinburgh, 1643. Issued a broadside entitled *A merrie Ballad, called Christio Kirk on the Green* [25 Nov.], 1643. [669, f. 8, 38.]

WILSON (ROBERT), bookseller in London; Black Spread Eagle and Windmill, St. Martins le Grand, near Aldersgate, 1660 (?)-62 (?). A dealer in Quaker literature. In a letter to Richard Snead, mercer, of Bristol, written in 1661, he says: "I am exposed in this day through many and frequent sufferings to severall difficulties: for very often am I plundered by ye rulers of my goods; burning them at home and abroad." [*Domestic State Papers*, Charles II, vol. 56, 83.] The same year he was committed to the Gatehouse for selling "seditious pamphlets against the Government of the Church of England A list of books seized at his shop in that year was published in *Mercurius Publicus* on November 28th.

WILSON (THOMAS), printer in London; Three Foxes in Long Lane [Smithfield], 1653-7. Joint printer with John Crouch, of the news-sheet called *Mercurius Democritus*. Their printing house was situated in one of the lowest parts of the City of London, and they were largely employed in printing ballads, broadsides, chap books, and such ephemeral literature.

WILSON (WILLIAM), printer in London (?) ; Three Foxes in Long Lane, 1640–65. Took up his freedom September 4th, 1626. [Arber, iii. 686. ; *see* also Harl. MSS., 5919 (281).]

WILTS (J.), bookseller (?) in London (?), 1660. His name appears on the imprint to the following pamphlet : *Two Grand Traytor's Lamentation,* 1660. [E. 1040 (15).]

WINGATE (R   ), bookseller (?) in London ; Golden Hind, Chancery Lane, 1655. Associated with Twyford, Brookes, and J. Place in the publication of a work entitled *The Complete Clark and Scriveners Guide,* 1655. It is doubtful whether he was a bookseller, and not rather the compiler of the work.

WINNAIN (G), bookseller (?) in (?) London, 1663. This name occurs on a pamphlet entitled, *Articles and charge against the German lady prisoner in the Gatehouse, to be exhibited according to the records of the City of Canterbury* .... London, Printed for G. Winnain, 1663. [Hazlitt, iii. 30.] It may possibly be that of a Canterbury bookseller.

WITHRINGTON (C   ), bookseller (?) in London (?), 1648. His name is found on several political pamphlets issued in that year. [Hazlitt, ii. 103 ; E. 473 (29).]

WODENOTHE, WOODENOTHE, or WOODNORTH (RICHARD), bookseller and haberdasher in London, (1) Star under St. Peter's Church in Cornhill ; (2) Leadenhall Street, next to the Golden Heart, 1645–56. First entry in the Stationers' Registers under his name July 26th, 1645. Is described in the Parish Registers of St. Peter's, Cornhill, as a stationer and haberdasher.

WOOD (RALPH), printer in London, 1642–65. Printer of ballads and popular literature. He was also the printer of Richard Flecknoe's *Poems,* 1660, and John Bunyan's *Sighs from Hell,* 1658. His largest work was apparently the folio edition of the romance called *Cloria,* which he printed for W. Brooke. His address has not been found, but he may have been in partnership with Robert Wood.

WOOD (ROBERT), printer in London, (1) White Hind, without Cripplegate; (2) Near ye Flying Horse in Grub Street. 1642–67. Took up his freedom September 4th, 1637. [Arber, iii. 688.] Printed numerous political pamphlets in which he was associated with J. Greensmith and Edward Christopher. He was possibly a relative of Ralph Wood, and they may have been in partnership together.

WOODHALL (HUMPHREY), bookseller (?) in London, 1617–41. Took up his freedom May 20th, 1617. [Arber, iii. 684.] Mentioned in a list of stationers who paid their proportion of the poll tax on August 5th, 1641. [*Domestic State Papers*, Charles I, vol. 483 (11).]

WOODNORTH, *see* Wodenothe.

WOODNOTHE, *see* Wodenothe.

WREN (JOSEPH), bookseller (?) in London, 1642. *The Poets Recantation .... by John Bond. London, Printed for T. A. and Joseph Wren, 1942* (*sic*). [E. 142 (13).]

WRIGHT (FRANCIS), bookseller (?) in London (?) 1643. Only known from the imprint to a broadside entitled *Good Newes from Plymouth.* [Hazlitt, iii. 64.]

WRIGHT (J), bookseller in London; Next door to the Globe in Little Britain, 1667. His name is found on the imprint to the following book: *Garden of Spiritual Flowers*, 1667. [Ames Collection, 3332.]

WRIGHT (JOHN), senr., bookseller in London; Kings Head in the Old Bailey, 1605–58. Took up his freedom in 1602 and became the publisher of many notable books, including Shakespeare's *Sonnets* and Marlowe's *Faustus*. On January 2nd, 164$\frac{2}{3}$, he was committed to the Compter in Wood Street for publishing a scandalous book against the Parliament [*Commons Journals*, vol. 2, p. 910], but he quickly made his peace with the Government, and when next heard of, he is found to be one of the official printers to the Parliament. On May 11th, 1643, in company with Thomas Bates, he started a news-sheet called *Mercurius Civicus*, which was distinguished by each issue having on the first page a woodcut, or sometimes two, intended to illustrate some event mentioned in it. This news-sheet ran till the close of the year 1646. Wright and Bates were also the publishers of another news-sheet, *The True Informer*. John Wright married Katherine, the daughter of Christopher Hatfield, citizen and cutler of London, and is mentioned in his will [P.C.C. 83, Soame.] He had a son, John Wright, junior. John Wright, senior, died in May, 1658, being buried on the 11th of that month. [Smyth, *Obituary*, p. 47; *Library*, April, 1905, pp. 184–207.]

WRIGHT (JOHN), junior, bookseller in London; Kings Head, Old Bailey, 1634–67. Son of John Wright, senior, and in partnership with him. On June 13th, 1642, he took over the copyrights, sixty-two in number, which had belonged to Robert Bird and Edward Brewster. In addition to theological literature it included *The History of Gargantua, A Book of Riddles*, and Robinson's *Citharine book*. [*Stationers' Registers.*] Either he or his father was a large holder in the ballad stock of the Company, and with Fr. Coles, T. Vere, and W. Gilbertson was the chief publisher of this class of literature.

WRIGHT (JONAS), bookseller (?) in London (?) 1642. His name is found on the imprint to the following pamphlet, *Blasing Starre seen in the West at Totneis in Devonshire*, 1642. [Hazlitt, i. 424.]

WRIGHT (M.), printer (?) in London; Kings Head in the Old Bailey, 1658–62. This name, in company with that of Robert Ibbotson, *q.v.*, is found on the imprint to Thomas Gouge's *Christian Directions*, 1661. [Ames Collection, 3019.] Hazlitt has several entries under it. [Gray's Index to Hazlitt, p. 835.] It may apply to another son of John Wright, senior, *q.v.*

YORK (SIMON), bookseller (?) in Dover, 1654. Only known from the imprint to a pamphlet entitled *An Antidote against Anabaptisme . . . . By Jo. Reading, B.D. . . . . London, Printed by Tho. Newcombe, for Simon York and Richard Barley, dwelling in Dover*, 1654. [Ames Collection of Title-pages, 2410.]

YOUNG (JAMES), printer in London, 1643–53. Son of Robert Young, printer. On July 22nd, 1644, his father's copyrights, numbering 131 works, were transferred to him. [Stationers' Registers.]

YOUNG (MICHAEL), bookseller (?) in London; Blew Bible in Covent
Garden, 1639–64. Published an edition of Sir Thos. More's *History of
Edward the Fifth*, 1641. [Hazlitt, i. 295, ii. 143.]

YOUNG (ROBERT), printer in London, 1625–43. An important member
of the Company of Stationers. Entered into partnership with Miles
Fletcher, or Flesher, and John Haviland, and bought up several large
and old-established printing houses in London. On April 12th, 1632, he
was appointed King's printer in Scotland in succession to T. Finlason.
He appears to have given up his Edinburgh business in 1638, but on
June 30th, 1641, with Evan Tyler, was again appointed the Royal printer
for Scotland. [Aldis, *List of Books printed in Scotland*, p. 124.] There is
also reason to believe that he had the management of the Irish printing
office established by the Company of Stationers, and Mr. F. Madan, in his
Chart of Oxford Printing (p. 29), gives him as having a press in Oxford in
1640. He was dead before September 16th, 1643, and his copyrights, 131
in number, were transferred to his son James Young. The names of two of
his workmen, William Warner, corrector of the press, and Robert Chapman,
compositor, occur in an order of the House of Lords dated August 16th,
1641, reprinted in Nalson's *Affairs of State*, vol. ii., p. 447. The position
of his printing house in London has not been found.

YOUNG (THOMAS), bookseller (?) in London, 1658. Only known from
the imprint to a pamphlet entitled *Natural Magick . . . . In Twenty Books.
London, Printed for Thomas Young and Samuel Speed*, 1658. [Hazlitt, ii.
488.]

Alien Members of the Book-Trade during the Tudor Period. Being an index to those whose names occur in the returns of aliens, letters of denization, and other documents published by the Huguenot Society. With notes by Ernest James Worman. *London: Printed, etc.*, December, 1906. [3s. 6d.]

Abstracts from the Wills and Testamentary Documents of Binders, Printers and Stationers of Oxford, from 1493 to 1638. By Strickland Gibson. *London: Printed, etc.*, February, 1907. [3s. 6d.]

A Dictionary of the Booksellers and Printers at work in England, Scotland and Ireland, 1641 to 1667. By H. R. Plomer. *London: Printed, etc*, February, 1908. [7s. 6d.]

ILLUSTRATED MONOGRAPHS.

[Large 4to. Brown wrappers. Mostly printed at the Chiswick Press.]

I.—Erhard Ratdolt and his work at Venice. A paper read before the Bibliographical Society, November 20th, 1893, by Gilbert R. Redgrave. *London: Printed for the Bibliographical Society, at the Chiswick Press*, April, 1894.
A four-page Supplement, with an additional illustration, reproducing Ratdolt's Trade-List, on a separate leaf, was issued in 1895.
Reprinted December, 1899. [10s. 6d.]

II.—*Jan van Doesborgh, Printer at Antwerp. An essay in bibliography. By Robert Proctor. *London: Printed ... at the Chiswick Press*, December, 1894. [*£1 4s.] Sold only in sets.

III.—An Iconography of Don Quixote, 1605-1895. By H. S. Ashbee, F.S.A. *London: Printed for the Author, at the University Press, Aberdeen, and issued by the Bibliographical Society*, July, 1895. [*16s.] Sold only in sets.
A four-page list of "Corrections, Additions, Omissions," with a note on the engravings, on a separate leaf, was issued to Members applying for it, in 1898.

IV.—The Early Printers of Spain and Portugal. By Konrad Haebler. *London: Printed ... at the Chiswick Press*, March, 1897, for 1896. [16s.]

V.—The Chevalier Délibéré. By Olivier de la Marche. The illustrations of the edition of Schiedam reproduced with a preface by F. Lippmann, and a reprint of the text. *London: Printed ... at the Chiswick Press*, February, 1898, for 1897. [10s. 6d.]

VI.—The First Paris Press. An account of the books printed for G. Fichet and J. Heynlin in the Sorbonne, 1470-1472. By A. Claudin. *London: Printed ... at the Chiswick Press*, February, 1898, for 1897. [10s. 6d.]

VII.—Antoine Vérard. By John Macfarlane. *London: Printed ... at the Chiswick Press*, September, 1900, for 1899. [16s.]

VIII.—The Printing of Greek in the Fifteenth Century. By Robert Proctor. *Printed ... at the Oxford University Press*, December, 1900. [16s.]

IX.—A Book bound for Mary Queen of Scots, being a description of the binding of a copy of the Geographia of Ptolemy printed at Rome, 1490, with notes of other books bearing Queen Mary's insignia. By George F. Barwick. *London: Printed ... at the Chiswick Press*, June, 1901. [10s. 6d.]

X.—Early Oxford Bindings. By Strickland Gibson. *Printed ... at the Oxford University Press*, January, 1903. [16s.]

XI.—The Earliest English Music Printing: a description and bibliography of English printed music to the close of the sixteenth century. By Robert Steele. *London: Printed ... at the Chiswick Press*, December, 1903. [16s.]

XII.—A Chart of Oxford Printing, '1468'-1900. With notes and illustrations. By Falconer Madan. *Oxford University Press*, February, 1904. [10s. 6d.]

XIII.—The Earlier Cambridge Stationers and Bookbinders, and the first Cambridge Printer. By George J. Gray. *Oxford University Press*, October, 1904. [16s.]

XIV.—The Early Editions of the Roman de la Rose. By F. W. Bourdillon. *London: Printed ... at the Chiswick Press*, December, 1906. [16s.]

LaVergne, TN USA
19 May 2010
183283LV00006B/65/A